Writing by Design

Writing by Design

Walter E. Klarner   James M. Williams   Harold L. Harp

Johnson County Community College

Houghton Mifflin Company · *Boston   Atlanta   Dallas   Geneva, Ill.*
Hopewell, N.J.   Palo Alto   London

JAMES AGEE: from *A Death in the Family* by James Agee. Copyright © 1957 by The James Agee Trust. Used by permission of Grosset & Dunlap, Inc. and Peter Owen Ltd.

CLAY ANDERSON: from "In the Mountains" in *The Craftsman in America,* National Geographic Society, Washington, D.C., 1975. Used by permission.

RUSSELL BAKER: "Juglipidity" by Russell Baker, *The New York Times,* September 2, 1965. © 1965 by The New York Times Company. Reprinted by permission.

BEN LUCIEN BERMAN: from "Antidote for War" in *This I Believe* vol. II, by Edward R. Murrow. Copyright © 1954 by Help, Inc. Reprinted by permission of Simon & Schuster, Inc.

RAY ALLEN BILLINGTON: from *Westward Expansion* by Ray Allen Billington. © 1960 by the Macmillan Company. Reprinted by permission.

NICHOLAS MURRAY BUTLER: from "The Marks of an Educated Man" by Nicholas Murray Butler in the *Columbia Daily Spectator.* Reprinted by permission.

SAMUEL BUTLER: from *Erewhon* by Samuel Butler. An Everyman's Library Edition. Published in the United States by E. P. Dutton & Co., Inc., and reprinted with their permission. Also used with permission of J. M. Dent and Sons, London.

WILLA CATHER: from *My Ántonia* by Willa Cather. Copyright 1918, 1926, and 1946 by Willa Siebert Cather. Copyright 1954 by Edith Lewis. Reprinted by permission of Houghton Mifflin Company.

BRUCE CATTON: from *A Stillness at Appomattox,* copyright 1953 by Bruce Catton. Reprinted by permission of Doubleday & Co., Inc.
from *This Hallowed Ground,* copyright © 1955, 1956 by Bruce Catton. Reprinted by permission of Doubleday & Co., Inc.

STUART CHASE: from "Logic in a Taxi" by Stuart Chase in *Harper Books and Authors,* vol. II, November 1956. Reprinted by permission of Harper & Row, Publishers, Inc.

JACQUES-YVES COUSTEAU: from *The Shark,* copyright © 1970 by Jacques-Yves Cousteau. Reprinted by permission of Doubleday & Co., Inc., and Cassell & Co. Ltd.

GEORGE CUOMO: from "A Man Is Crazy to Want to Go to Philadelphia" by George Cuomo, originally published in *Story* magazine, March/April 1963. Reprinted by permission of Monica McCall, International Creative Management. Copyright © 1968 by George Cuomo.

FRANCIS CHRISTENSEN: from *Notes Toward a New Rhetoric,* Harper & Row, New York, 1967. Reprinted by permission of the publisher.

ISAK DINESEN: from *Out of Africa* by Isak Dinesen © 1937, 1938 by Random House, Inc. Reprinted by permission.

ENCYCLOPEDIA INTERNATIONAL: from s.v. "Shark." Reprinted from the *Encyclopedia International* 1976, by special permission of the publisher, Grolier Incorporated, New York.

PAUL ENGLE: from the book *Prairie Christmas,* copyright © 1960 by Paul Engle, published by Longmans, Green and Company, Inc., a division of David McKay Company, Inc. Reprinted by permission of the publisher. Also reprinted by permission of William Morris Agency, Inc. Copyright © 1958, 1959, 1960 by Paul Engle.

ERIK ERIKSON: reprinted from *Childhood and Society,* second edition, revised, by Erik H. Erikson. By permission of W. W. Norton & Company, Inc. and The Hogarth Press. Copyright 1950, © 1963 by W. W. Norton & Company, Inc.

F. SCOTT FITZGERALD: from *This Side of Paradise* by F. Scott Fitzgerald. Used by permission of Charles Scribner's Sons and The Bodley Head.

E. M. FORSTER: from *Aspects of the Novel* by E. M. Forster. Reprinted by permission of Harcourt Brace Jovanovich, Inc. and Edward Arnold Ltd.

GEOFFREY GORER: reprinted from *The American People* by Geoffrey Gorer, revised edition. By permission of W. W. Norton & Company, Inc. and The Cresset Press, Ltd. Copyright 1948 by Geoffrey Gorer. Revised edition copyright © 1964 by Geoffrey Gorer.

JOHN GUNTHER: from *Inside Russia Today* by John Gunther. Reprinted by permission of Harper & Row, Publishers, Inc.

PART-OPENER ART BY STEVE SNIDER.

Printed in the U.S.A.

Library of Congress Catalog Card Number: 76-14652

ISBN: 0-395-24428-5

Contents

Preface

ALL WRITING begins with the desire to communicate. In a school setting, topics may seem alien and difficult because they are assigned by a teacher. Have you ever stared at a blank sheet of paper waiting for something to happen, for an idea to announce itself? Perhaps this was the case because you did not consider your own contact or involvement with a topic. Or, you may have thought that writing is a random, unpredictable process, often the result of "happy accidents." Fortunately, good writing does not depend on chance. Successful writers approach their task equipped with a wide variety of designs, each capable of creating order out of the seeming chaos and complexity of experience. *Writing by Design* focuses on the interrelationship of ideas and presents strategies for developing those ideas. Much attention is given to form, but only as it helps generate ideas.

The most dominant theory of composition employed in this text is that of generative rhetoric, first articulated by Francis Christensen. Professor Christensen's theory, described in his scholarly *Notes Toward a New Rhetoric*, has been implemented by numerous text writers and teachers. The theory is useful because the concepts are concrete and describe the design of writing as brief as a single sentence or as long as an argumentative essay. Moreover, you will find generative concepts equally useful for descriptive, narrative, and expository writing.

Writing by Design is a self-instructional writing program that synthesizes the content of writing (what you say), the structure of writing (how you say it), and the means for learning both. Because writing is a cumulative skill, the organization of the text follows a natural sentence-paragraph-essay progression. Each chapter presents clearly defined learning objectives, writing models by professionals and students, and frequent practice exercises (with answers) that enable you to determine your understanding of the material and your progress toward mastering the learning objectives. In addition to the numerous practice exercises, we have provided writing assignments that ask you to relate *your* experiences, observations, and opinions. As a result, you can feel a personal involvement in the writing and have sufficient information to deal adequately with the topics. Each assignment lists suggested topics that are concretely stated, appropriate for the writing situation, and designed to encourage you to choose a subject about which you can write effectively.

The selections in this text are models of the writing expected from you. Many student writers find an appropriate model paragraph or essay invaluable to their understanding of the assignment. The writing models are generally short and intended to correspond to the length of papers you will write for the course. The authors of the models represent diverse occupations: scientists, philosophers, journalists, novelists, economists, politicians, lawyers, critics, engineers, sociologists, psychologists, explorers, historians, and *students*. Most chapters include a number of student selections that should further help you define writing assignments. In addition, the student selections should reduce the often experienced discrepancy between writing by published professionals and that which you compose.

We wish to thank our typist, Carla Shade, for her prompt response to the various deadlines, and for her helpful suggestions. The classroom testing of *Writing by Design* involved thousands of students and their instructors. We thank those involved for their contributions to this final version of the text. We are grateful to Patricia Robinson and Susan Snyder for their careful consideration of the manuscript, to James Jackson whose interest and enthusiasm allowed the project to get off the ground, to Barbara and Kay for their understanding and encouragement. Special thanks is extended to those reviewers who read the manuscript and offered valuable criticism during the revision stages. They include Michael Atkinson, University of Cincinnati; Elayne Feldstein, York College, CCNY; William S. Flemming, University of Akron; John Hardaway, Phoenix College; David Harrigan, Santa Rosa Junior College; and Frank Hubbard, University of Wisconsin. And finally, we acknowledge our indebtedness to the trustees and faculty of Johnson County Community College for their continuing support.

Walter Klarner
James Williams
Harold Harp

Introduction

Few activities generate as much confusion, frustration, even fear, as writing. Written communication is the product of a complex process that is only partly understood. Much remains shrouded in controversy. Many reputable methods of writing instruction conflict with, and even contradict, each other. The problem is further complicated by the inability of many experts to agree on a workable definition of "good writing." How, then, if experts do not fully understand the process of writing or agree on a definition of good writing or utilize similar methods of instruction, can they possibly pretend to teach one student to write, let alone an indefinite number of students?

The preceding difficulties are compounded when we consider the endless variety of skills, interests, abilities, and personalities of prospective writers. Fortunately, each writer's individuality is more of an advantage than a liability. Much of the interest and significance of writing rests on the uniqueness of the writer. Furthermore, many excellent writers are unaware of language theories; some have not been exposed to formal writing instruction; and a few write without ever defining that which they do so well.

Although a definition of good writing rests ultimately on the reader's subjective judgment, it can be agreed that good writing speaks honestly, from a writer's experience. It is clear: it may be open to various interpretations, but it seeks not to baffle the reader. It is engaging. If the reader asks "So what?" the writing should provide the answer. It enables readers to see their own experience in a new way and finally to wish that the telling had been their own.

For students, unfortunately, good writing is often the product of pain and frustration. A blank sheet of paper can produce anxiety faster than an overdue bill, and the question "What can I write about?" leaves the throat dry.

One way to reduce frustration or discomfort with writing is to keep a *journal.* Any notebook will do, as long as you use it exclusively for this purpose. Reflections, speculations, questions, events, observations, experiments, investigations, or just plain "seeing what an idea looks like on paper"—all are appropriate kinds of entries for your journal. If the subject is interesting or significant to you, write about it! Make an entry each day. A specific time and place will further help to establish the routine. Much of the enjoyment and freshness of thought and expression are likely to be lost if you get behind and then try to catch up. The importance of daily entries cannot be overemphasized. The goal of the journal is a pleasant writing habit. The audience should be limited to you and your instructor. Without grades, negative criticism, or rigid expectations, the journal is an informal vehicle to record . . . *you.*

Journal writing causes you to be more perceptive about your world. After a few days of writing about "what happened at school today" and "today's weather," you will tire of such topics and begin to examine your life in a more critical manner. Soon, you will begin to investigate consequences and motives, not just the immediate experience. You will notice patterns, moods, and relationships. As you exhaust familiar subjects, you will seek new sources of ideas—news events, school topics, your reading. You may experiment with different ways of expressing your thoughts. You may even find your journal to be an excellent source of ideas for formal, assigned papers.

If you thumb through this volume, you will see that most of the chapters require a writing assignment to be submitted to your instructor. You will have to meet a due date and specific objectives. In this case, unlike the journal, you cannot wait until ideas suggest themselves. You must generate ideas quickly.

Brainstorming can produce ideas. You ask every possible question about the subject. The questions follow no order or direction, and you find yourself limited by your personal interests and knowledge. A brainstorming session with other students can produce striking results, because you are exposed to different interests and knowledge. Still, brainstorming is the least organized and most unpredictable of all prewriting strategies.

Word association and *role playing* are slightly more structured techniques than brainstorming. Word association usually takes place between two or more people. One person contributes a word and another responds with the first word that comes to mind. Some associations are not very productive—hot–cold, writing–paper. However, some surprising results can be had—cold–institution, writing–pain. That institutions can be cold (or impersonal) and writing can be painful are topics worth pursuing. To role play, you assume the roles of people who are involved with your subject. For example, the subject of welfare suggests the recipient who is dependent on the system, the taxpayer who must bear the cost of the benefits, the lawmaker who creates the system, even the ineligible and the welfare cheat. Each role causes a particular set of concerns, problems, and conditions to come to mind, and thus creates a broad spectrum of ideas. More important, the perspective of the subject as a whole and your empathy with specific individuals should enhance the accuracy and application of your ideas.

Because writing requires efficiency and accuracy, you will find the following structured systems of inquiry more productive of ideas and well worth the effort.

Learning is organized by *academic disciplines* or viewpoints. Sociology, history, psychology, philosophy, aesthetics, law, and biology are just a few of the departments listed in your school catalogue. Most topics can be examined through a number of such aspects. The possibilities of a topic such as "welfare" become clearer when seen through the viewpoints of sociology, psychology, economics, law, and political science.

Most topics can be restated to present a *problem*. Its source, effect, and solution can then be researched. The solution may be considered in terms of its feasibility and desirability.

The *type of writing*—the nature of description, narration, and exposition—may suggest a number of topics and approaches. As you read this text, the quantity of hints and suggestions may seem overwhelming. However, the wide variety allows you to choose the idea and approach best for you. If the choice is yours, decide which type will allow you to develop your idea. You may be able to communicate cause and effect more clearly in a narration than in an exposition. On the other hand, an analogy (exposition) may clarify an abstract idea better than a more direct application of the idea, which might only confuse the reader.

An extremely productive strategy is the examination of the object, scene, event, person, or concept in terms of *quality, detail, and comparison*. This generative approach is the subject of Chapter 1.

While *levels of generality* are used in this text as a means of *organizing* ideas and images in writing, the process of arriving at a pattern will cause you to investigate some ideas that need more clarification. The concept of levels of generality is discussed throughout the text.

The underlying concept of *Writing by Design* is seen by reducing the Contents to its basic elements:

Part One Sentence Design (Chapters 1–3)
↓
Part Two Paragraph Design (Chapters 4–8)
↓
Part Three Essay Design (Chapters 9–13)
↓
Part Four Thought Design (Chapter 14 *)

As you can see, the text moves forward; each section is a preparation for the next. That sentences are the raw materials of paragraphs and that paragraphs are used to create essays is an obvious conclusion. Christensen underscores another facet of the relationship:

It was just a hundred years ago, in 1866, that Alexander Bain introduced the paragraph into rhetoric as a unit of discourse. Bain based his definition and his rhetoric of the paragraph on an analogy with the sentence. This analogy, a very loose one, has prevailed for a hundred years. I have continued it—but with a difference. Here there is a precise structural analogy, not with just any sentence, but with the cumulative sentence. The topic sentence of a paragraph is analogous to the base clause of such a sentence, and the supporting sentences of a paragraph are analogous to the added levels of the sentence. The validity of the analogy is proved by the fact that a mere change of punctuation will convert some sentences into paragraphs and some paragraphs into sentences.

FRANCIS CHRISTENSEN

Notes Toward a New Rhetoric

If these ideas hold up, sentences, paragraphs, and essays can be described, even created, by means of a common technique.

Outlining is a common method of organizing ideas and experiences. No doubt, on numerous occasions you have had to outline papers or lecture notes. Outlines, as you probably know, take the following form:

    I general idea
    A support
    B support
        1 support
        2 support
    C support

----

* This chapter deals with logic and may either be read as a unit or be used as reference.

If several ideas are to be examined, the structure repeats itself, beginning with "II. General idea." A minor yet important revision of the above scheme is:

1 general idea
  2 support
  2 support
    3 support
    3 support
  2 support

In the traditional outline, the continual shifting from Roman numerals to capital letters to numbers, and back again, is distracting. The structure of the second outline flows more smoothly. In addition, the number *values* indicate the relationship of the various elements of support. In other words, a "3" supports or modifies a "2" and a "2" supports or modifies a "1." Throughout this text, the number values are referred to as "levels of generality."

It is now possible to examine the similar nature of sentences, paragraphs, and essays through the patterns of their levels of generality. Because writing is the goal of this text, generative rhetoric and levels of generality are used to develop your writing skills, not your powers of analysis.

Sentence Design

·≫[1]≪·
Quality, Detail, and Comparison

In order to communicate successfully, writers usually employ three elements to express their basic or central thoughts—quality, detail, and comparison. Since these are basic to the process of generative writing, they are a logical starting point for this part of the book. By utilizing these elements in the form of free modifiers, the student writer can produce clear and interesting sentences that will sharpen general, abstract, or plural thoughts.

After completing this chapter, you should be able

1. to define quality, detail, and comparison as elements of generative rhetoric
2. to list uses of quality, detail, and comparison
3. to identify examples of quality, detail, and comparison in sentences
4. to write appropriate, original examples of quality, detail, and comparison

Objectives

Without the reality of differences and the vocabulary of quality, detail, and comparison, we would exist in a world of utter perfection and complete boredom. Houses would be of one style; roses could only be roses; events would be reduced to monotonous simplicity; and it would be difficult to express our individuality. Yet we do know that the world is incredibly complex, filled with infinite variety. As children we try to learn about this world with a few words—some nouns and verbs. As we mature we realize that simple nouns and verbs cannot accurately picture the world or our response to it. We realize, furthermore, that simple sentences cannot communicate the intricate relationships of thought and action. Without quality, detail, and comparison we cannot sharpen the images proposed by those simple nouns and verbs we learned as children.

Take any object readily available to you. How would you describe it so that another person could identify it?

- Does it have any peculiarities? Imperfections?
- Is it a variation of some common object?
- Is it similar to something most people know?
- Will an evaluation of its overall condition help someone visualize the object?
- Will a listing of its component parts enhance your communication?

If you answered "yes" to the above questions, you have acknowledged the usefulness of quality, detail, and comparison as elements of perceiving. As the fundamental elements of generative rhetoric (the method of this course), quality, detail, and comparison can be used to communicate your experience with the world.

Let us look at three sentences, each employing one or more of these elements:

The mess hall seemed as usual.

When writing about an experience, we often make judgments that, without further clarification, are meaningless to our readers. What does "usual" mean? The writer adds detail to show what he intends:

The mess hall seemed as usual, with clouds of steam curling in through the door and the men sitting shoulder to shoulder.

We can now see what "usual" means. But the writer does not stop here. He wants to further clarify the picture of the men. So he adds comparison:

The mess hall seemed as usual, with clouds of steam curling in through the doors and the men sitting shoulder to shoulder—like seeds in a sunflower. ALEXANDER SOLZHENITSYN

The comparison is used because it is an image that the reader probably knows and therefore it improves the clarity of communication. Sometimes a detail is further developed by the use of another detail (underlined):

The realms of day and night, <u>two different worlds coming from two opposite poles,</u> mingled during this time.   HERMANN HESSE

In the next sentence, the writer shows the action of a person without the motivation for the behavior:

Her gray eyes picked out the swaying palms.

Why did she respond to the palms, certainly only one of many images in her field of vision? Because they were "swaying"? Now the writer tells us:

Her gray eyes picked out the swaying palms, <u>precise and formal against a turquoise sky.</u>   MARJORIE RAWLINGS

The girl was responding to the quality of the palms—"precise and formal."

The following section demonstrates the uses of quality, detail, and comparison. In the sample sentences, the quality, detail, or comparison is underlined.

Quality communicates a subjective response to an image as a whole. The writer's evaluation of the condition of an object, the style or manner of behavior, or the worth of an experience or idea is often found in modification by means of quality:

1. condition of an object or scene (description):

Harold could see the ranch, <u>still tiny with distance.</u>

2. style or manner of behavior (narration):

One hand came up slowly, <u>almost dreamily,</u> from her side and went to her mouth.

3. worth of an experience or idea (exposition):

The humanities, <u>while only subjective and difficult to define,</u> allow men of different personalities and beliefs to understand each other.

While quality is useful in communicating, you should take care not to overuse adjectives and adverbs. Quality can be vague and meaningless, requiring further modification to make clear your impressions, as in the following sentence:

Reaching the summit, they looked down into the valley, <u>lush and beautiful.</u>

Certainly "lush" gives us a vague impression of vegetation, but "beautiful" is a term that, like the humanities, is subjective and difficult to define. A detail should be added, so that the reader will understand the quality:

Reaching the summit, they looked down into the valley, lush and beautiful, exotic palms and orchids growing in the mist of a waterfall.

PRACTICE   1. Underline the words communicating quality.
    a. muddy
    b. rock
    c. house
    d. pathetic
    e. creative
    f. carefully
    g. walking
    h. shaky
    i. mist
    j. difficult

2. Identify the underlined modifiers that communicate quality.

_____ a. He walked into the corner office, a messy cubicle.
_____ b. It was an unusual course, economics for the nonspecialist.
_____ c. She served a repulsive breakfast, heavy, greasy, and altogether too much for one person to consume.
_____ d. Jake looked at her curiously, wondering what she had been through.
_____ e. Depressed and worried, he scratched his neck absent-mindedly.

PRACTICE ANSWERS   1. a. quality
    b. detail
    c. detail
    d. quality
    e. quality
    f. quality
    g. detail
    h. quality
    i. detail
    j. quality
2. a. detail ("messy" alone would be quality)
    b. detail

c. quality
d. quality
e. quality

Detail communicates some part or facet of an image. Note that the following list is a simplification of the uses of detail—one image may exhibit several of the conditions, and one detail may have a multiple effect on the original image:

Condition of image	Effect of detail on original image
1. vague	makes specific
2. abstract	makes concrete
3. generalization	provides fact
4. whole	presents component
5. many	presents one

Following are some examples of detail:

World War I began like a summer festival—all billowing skirts and golden epaulets.   DALTON TRUMBO

The invention of printing did away with anonymity, fostering ideas of literary fame and the habit of considering intellectual effort as private property.   MARSHALL McLUHAN

The justification for a university is that it preserves the connection between knowledge and the zest of life, by uniting the young and old in the imaginative consideration of learning.   ALFRED NORTH WHITEHEAD

He lay freckled and small in the moonlight, his chest white and naked, and one foot hanging from the edge of the bed.   CARSON McCULLERS

The students were ready for the end of the period, the girls repacking purses, the boys in the back row alert to each sound outside the door, everywhere books shut, stacked, and at the ready.

PRACTICE

1. Indicate which words communicate detail and which communicate quality.

a. manuscript _____

b. hoarse _____

c. backpacking _____

d. beautiful _____

e. crevices _____

f. deep _____

g. guitars _____

h. strolling _____

2. Underline the *most specific* detail in each series.
   a. piano, Steinway, instrument
   b. peak, mountain, pinnacle
   c. amble, move, walk
   d. pond, lagoon, water

PRACTICE ANSWERS
1. a. detail
   b. quality
   c. detail
   d. quality
   e. detail
   f. quality
   g. detail
   h. detail
2. a. Steinway
   b. pinnacle
   c. amble
   d. lagoon

Comparison describes an image by showing a similarity to another image. The tendency to compare things is universal, as you will see if you attempt to avoid doing so for any length of time. The word "comparison" is used throughout this text in the sense of estimating similarities. The writer uses something the reader already knows to describe an image or idea that the reader has not experienced:

The fish used its tail like a sculling oar to get started.

The underlined words compare the action of the tail to that of a sculling oar. The comparison is a *bound modifier* because without the comparison we would know nothing of the action of the tail. (Notice that the bound comparison is *not* set off by punctuation.)

The fish worked the pectoral fins alternately, like a soldier crawling on the ground with his elbows.

In this sentence the writer gives us some idea of the action of the fins—with the words "worked" and "alternately." Next, the image is intensified or clarified by adding the underlined comparison. This comparison is a *free modifier* because without the comparison we would still have a reasonable understanding of the action of the fins. (Notice that the free comparison *is* set off by punctuation.)

Here are three more examples of comparison, all written by the same author, Ayn Rand:

The reception room of the office of Fracon & Heyer, Architects, looked <u>like a cool, intimate ballroom in a Colonial mansion.</u>

She spoke on a single, level tone, <u>as if she were reciting an austere catechism of faith.</u>

She looked impersonal, untouched by the words she pronounced, chaste <u>like a young boy.</u>

The uses of comparison may be summarized as follows:

1. As a bound modifier comparison helps communicate the basic image.
2. As a free modifier comparison further intensifies or clarifies the basic image.

In the following sentences, underline the comparison and identify it as bound or free.

PRACTICE

_____ 1. He climbed the ladder as though he had a fear of heights.

_____ 2. He slowly climbed the ladder, shaking at every step, as though he had a fear of heights.

_____ 3. The music was always in the background, like music at a church service.   JOYCE CAROL OATES

_____ 4. She sang as though the words possessed a deep and throbbing meaning for her. . . .   RALPH ELLISON

_____ 5. Thus, in a middle course between these heights and depths, they drifted through life rather than lived, the prey of aimless days and sterile memories, like wandering shadows that could have acquired substance only by consenting to root themselves in the solid earth of their distress.   ALBERT CAMUS

1. as though he had a fear of heights (bound)
2. as though he had a fear of heights (free)
3. like music at a church service (free)
4. as though the words possessed a deep and throbbing meaning for her (bound)
5. like wandering shadows that could have acquired substance only by consenting to root themselves in the solid earth of their distress (free)

Finally, the following grammatical facts should help you avoid confusing quality, detail, and comparison:

- Quality is usually communicated by adjectives or adverbs.
- Detail is usually communicated by nouns or verbs.
- Comparison is usually introduced by the words "like" or "as."

Self-Evaluation

PART I

1. Define the following terms.

Quality _____

Detail _____

Comparison_____

2. List three uses of quality.

a. _____

b. _____

c. _____

3. List five uses of detail.

a. _____

b. _____

c. _____

d. _____

e. _____

4. List two uses of comparison.

a. _____

b. _____

5. Identify the underlined modifiers as quality, detail, or comparison.

_____ a. The class sat in the room, listening to the teacher, intently, like a group of military officers.

_____ b. The new addition, massive and awkward, looked ridiculous.

_____ c. Jason stood at the edge of the path, watching the three men slowly approach.

_____ d. Courses that require hard work appeal to me.

_____ e. They drove away quickly, the car vibrating violently.

_____ f. Noisy and smoke-filled, the student center attracts those who do not like to study alone.

_____ g. The incomprehensible babble of the little boy went on without pause.

_____ h. He entered Mr. Walters's corner office, a cramped, messy cubicle.

_____ i. He just sat there musing, like Rodin's famous statue.

_____ j. He wrote a little every day, brief entries in his personal journal.

(Check your answers with those on page 18. If you do not understand the material, review or see your instructor. When you are successful with Part I, complete Part II and submit it to your instructor.)

PART II

Look at the following example. On a separate piece of paper, write a short sentence of your own. On the next line write at least one sentence of quality, detail, or comparison that modifies your sentence. On the third line combine the sentences from the first two lines. Write five sets of sentences.

EXAMPLE: 1. He could not work under such conditions.
2. The baby was crying. His wife was complaining. (Two examples of detail.)
3. He could not work under such conditions, the baby crying, his wife complaining.

Answers

1. Quality communicates a subjective response to an image as a whole.
   Detail communicates some part or facet of an image.
   Comparison describes an image by showing a similarity to another image.
2. a. expresses condition of an object or scene
   b. expresses style or manner of behavior
   c. expresses worth of an experience or idea
3. a. makes specific
   b. makes concrete
   c. provides fact
   d. presents component
   e. presents one
4. a. as a bound modifier, helps communicate the basic image
   b. as a free modifier, further intensifies or clarifies the basic image
5. a. comparison
   b. quality
   c. detail
   d. quality
   e. detail
   f. quality
   g. quality
   h. detail
   i. comparison
   j. detail

⋯⊰[2]⊱⋯
Free Modifiers and Levels of Generality

This chapter investigates the various methods by which quality, detail, and comparison can be added to simple sentences. Although often employed as elements of the simple sentence, quality, detail, and comparison can be communicated flexibly and creatively in the form of *free modifiers*—punctuated *additions* to the simple sentence.

Objectives

After completing this chapter, you should be able

1. to define the following terms: modification, generative sentence, base clause, free modifier, initial modifier, medial modifier, final modifier, bound modifier, notation of levels of generality, coordinate sequence, subordinate sequence
2. to identify examples of the terms listed in objective 1
3. to identify examples of quality, detail, and comparison as free modifiers in generative sentences
4. to notate levels of generality in sample sentences

So far, you have seen how quality, detail, and comparison contribute to the thinking process and to writing style. In this chapter, you will see the stylistic effect of quality, detail, and comparison in the form of free modifiers. As you work through the chapter, refer to the following definitions.

Definitions

Modification   Process of restricting words, phrases, or clauses in order to intensify images, clarify meaning, or define condition. It is accomplished through the use of detail, quality, or comparison.

Generative sentence   Sentence that contains a base clause and free modifiers in the form of punctuated additions to the base clause.

Base clause   Basic unit of writing, which is modified. It has all the necessary elements of a complete sentence. Often referred to as the "main clause," it contains the most general information of a generative sentence, existing on the first level of generality.

Free modifier   Phrase or clause set off by punctuation, which modifies either the base clause or another free modifier.

Final modifier   Free modifier that follows the base clause.

Bound modifier   Part of a clause or phrase *not* set off by punctuation. (*Exception:* A chain of adjectives must be punctuated.)

Initial modifier   Free modifier that precedes the base clause.

Medial modifier   Free modifier that interrupts or splits the base clause or another free modifier.

Notation of levels of generality   System of indicating the levels of generality of a sentence through numerical values and indentation.

Coordinate sequence   Type of sentence generation in which each free modifier is of the same level of generality.

Subordinate sequence   Type of sentence generation in which each free modifier is more specific.

Free Modifiers

The free modifier is always punctuated. Although the comma is used most often, the semicolon, colon, and dash are also used to set off a free modifier from the base clause or another free modifier. In the sentence below, our first hint of a free modifier is the comma after "usual":

The mess hall seemed as usual, <u>with clouds of steam curling in through the doors and the men sitting shoulder to shoulder.</u>

Another test for a modifier is the presence of a quality, detail, or comparison that intensifies, clarifies, or defines an image in the base clause or in another free modifier. The underlined phrase in the preceding sentence is a detail of the word "usual." The underlined phrase in the following sentence is *not* a free modifier.

The mess hall seemed as usual, with clouds of steam curling <u>in through the doors</u> and the men sitting shoulder to shoulder.

True, it does modify "curling," but it is not set off by punctuation and does not modify an image in the base clause or in another free modifier. We shall refer to this type as a *bound modifier* —bound because it modifies some image in the same clause or phrase, bound because its position in the sentence cannot be changed, and bound because its removal will obscure the meaning of the sentence.

A free modifier, on the other hand, can be moved or removed from a sentence without confusing the reader. The punctuation of a free modifier sets off or frees it from the rest of the sentence. Although punctuation is an excellent clue to the presence of a free modifier, you must also consider the modifier's contribution to the meaning of the sentence in order to determine whether it is free or bound.

Identify the underlined examples of quality, detail, and comparison as free modifiers or bound modifiers.

_____ 1. Unusually passive for a child of three, she just looked at her book.
_____ 2. The free modifier is always punctuated.
_____ 3. He looked into the small and dirty cupboard.
_____ 4. The artist, tired yet earnest, tried to compose himself for the curator.
_____ 5. He smiled, shaking his lower lip.
_____ 6. The engine looked like a surly, crouching animal.
_____ 7. The officer walked across the intersection and tagged the car making loud clanking noises.

1. free (The modifier is free because it can be removed without confusing the reader.)
2. bound (If "always" is removed, the meaning of the sentence changes. The sentence may then imply "often" or "sometimes" and the emphasis is lost.)
3. bound (The position of "small and dirty" cannot be easily changed in the sentence.)
4. free (The underlined modifier can be moved so as to begin the sentence or can be omitted without confusing the reader.)
5. free (Same reason as for Question 4.)
6. bound (Without the modifier the reader cannot understand the appearance of the engine.)

7. bound (The underlined modifier identifies the car that was tagged. Without the restriction in meaning, the reader cannot know which car was violating the law.)

Notation of Levels of Generality

There are many ways to display the structure of a sentence. In the early grades of school, you may have had some experience with the process called "diagramming." If you did, you know that diagramming deals with the function and the position of every word in a sentence. The analysis of a generative sentence does not require such a detailed system. Instead of dealing with the sentence word by word, you need only show how the base clause and the free modifiers relate to each other.

The following is a *generative sentence;* that is, it has a base clause and free modifiers in the form of punctuated additions to the base clause:

The class sat in the room, listening to the teacher, intently, like a group of military officers.

Let's begin by showing the base clause and the free modifiers as individual elements of the sentence:

The class sat in the room,	(base clause)
listening to the teacher,	(free modifier)
intently,	(free modifier)
like a group of military officers.	(free modifier)

While the above arrangement shows the structure of the sentence, little is communicated about the levels of generality (or specificity) existing within the sentence. We do not know, for example, whether "intently" modifies the base clause or one of the free modifiers. Here is a different method of indicating the levels of generality in the sentence:

1 The class sat in the room,
  2 listening to the teacher,
    3 intently,
      4 like a group of military officers.

The base clause is indicated by the number "1" because it contains the most general information in the sentence. The number "2" is assigned to the free modifier "listening to the teacher" because it is a detail that modifies the base clause. The quality suggested by "intently" modifies the second-level free modifier, so it is numbered with a "3." And finally, the comparison "like a group of military officers" is displayed as a fourth-level modifier because it is a more specific image of the previous modifier. As you can see the number assigned to a free modifier is determined by its level of generality. A second-level modifier always modifies a base clause, a third-level modifier always modifies a second-level modifier, and so on.

The preceding notated sentence is an example of a *subordinate sequence,* that is, one in which each free modifier is more specific than the previous one. Here is an example of three free modifiers in a *coordinate sequence;* each modifies the base clause and therefore all are of the same level of generality:

That part of the world I call the House of Intellect embraces at least three groups of subjects: the persons who consciously and methodically employ the mind; the forms and habits governing the activities in which the mind is so employed; and the conditions under which these people and activities exist.   JACQUES BARZUN

NOTATION: 1 That part of the world I call the House of Intellect embraces at least three groups of subjects:
2 the persons who consciously and methodically employ the mind;
2 the forms and habits governing the activities in which the mind is so employed;
2 and the conditions under which these people and activities exist.

So far, you have seen *final* free modifiers, which follow the base clause. Free modifiers may also be written before the base clause. These are termed *initial* free modifiers. Here is a sentence that contains both an initial and a final free modifier:

In the loose rock under the platform, Curt's horse reared, trying to turn.

WALTER VAN TILBURG CLARK

NOTATION: 2 In the loose rock under the platform,
1 Curt's horse reared,
2 trying to turn.

Notice that the initial and final modifiers are given in the natural word order and are notated with a "2" because they modify a word or group of words in the base clause. Note the treatment of the punctuation, each level *ending* with the appropriate punctuation mark.

You will find this process easier if you locate the base clause first. Remember, the base clause has all the elements of a sentence: it has a subject and a predicate and can stand alone. Free modifiers are only phrases or clauses and must exist as punctuated additions to the sentence.

PRACTICE   Notate the following sentences.

1. Heads bowed, without a sign of pleasure or hope, they were like the human masses of the Middle Ages.   ELIA KAZAN
2. I built the chimney after my hoeing in the fall, before a fire became necessary for warmth, doing my cooking in the meanwhile out of doors on the ground, early in the morning: which mode I still think is in some respects more convenient and agreeable than the usual one.   HENRY DAVID THOREAU
3. The leaves dropping from the trees in the autumn, the interior of an airplane engine, the entrails of a dissected rabbit, the city desk of a newspaper, all appear to be chaos if they are seen without comprehension.   JANE JACOBS
4. When a critic deals with a work of literature, the most natural thing for him to do is to freeze it, to ignore its movement in time and look at it as a completed pattern of words, with all its parts existing simultaneously.   NORTHROP FRYE

PRACTICE ANSWERS

1. 2 Heads bowed,
    2 without a sign of pleasure or hope,
  1 they were like the human masses of the Middle Ages.

2. 1 I built the chimney after my hoeing in the fall,
    2 before a fire became necessary for warmth,
    2 doing my cooking in the meanwhile out of doors on the ground,
      3 early in the morning:
      3 which mode I still think is in some respects more convenient and agreeable than the usual one.

3. 2 The leaves dropping from the trees in the autumn,
    2 the interior of an airplane engine,
    2 the entrails of a dissected rabbit,
    2 the city desk of a newspaper,
  1 all appear to be chaos if they are seen without comprehension.

4. 2 When a critic deals with a work of literature,
  1 the most natural thing for him to do is to freeze it,
    2 to ignore its movement in time and look at it as a completed pattern of words,
      3 with all its parts existing simultaneously.

When a free modifier interrupts or splits the base clause or another free modifier, it is called a *medial* modifier:

The shelf clock, <u>old but valuable,</u> attracted the interest of many buyers.

> Notation: 1 The shelf clock, / , attracted the interest of many buyers.
>   2/ old but valuable

Although the phrase "old but valuable" follows the word "clock," it cannot be included with the first-level base clause because it is an addition to the base clause. "Old but valuable" is a punctuated quality of "clock." Therefore, it is a second-level modifier. In the notation, a slash (/) replaces the medial modifier interrupting the base clause. The punctuation that sets off the medial modifier is positioned so as to set off the slash. The slash is repeated after the "2" to indicate that the second-level modifier is a medial and is actually read in place of the slash on the first level. Medial modifiers should always follow the clause or phrase that they modify.

PRACTICE

PART I
Notate sentences with medial modifiers.

1. The young men, under armed guard, were taken below to the captain's cabin.
2. Students, instructors, and administrators attended the conference.
3. Sam Nelson, the first man to climb White Mountain, organized a wilderness club for inner-city youth.

PART II
Here are five more practice sentences to notate. Initial, medial, and final free modifiers may be present. Remember, locate the base clause first and let punctuation signal *most* free modifiers.

1. While Robin deliberated of whom to inquire respecting his kinsman's dwelling, he was accosted by the innkeeper, a little man in a stained white apron, who had come to pay his professional welcome to the stranger.   NATHANIEL HAWTHORNE
2. The most stirring of his early successes, to judge by contemporary reports, was a series of three plays he wrote on the Wars of the Roses.   MARCHETTE CHUTE
3. The sociable country postman, passing through the garden, had just given him a small parcel, which he took out with him, leaving the hotel to the right and creeping to a convenient bench that he knew of, a safe recess in the cliff.   HENRY JAMES
4. Next to the child's mother was a red-headed youngish woman, reading one of the magazines and working a piece of chewing gum, hell for leather, as Claud would say.   FLANNERY O'CONNER

5. Great individual development, such as human beings are driven by their intellectual insights to see, does of course always threaten to break the bond of direct social involvement, that gives animal life its happy unconscious continuity. SUSANNE K. LANGER

PRACTICE ANSWERS

PART I

1. 1 The young men, / , were taken below to the captain's cabin.
    2/ under armed guard
2. (This sentence does not have a medial modifier.)
3. 1 Sam Nelson, / , organized a wilderness club for inner-city youth.
    2/ the first man to climb White Mountain

PART II

1.   2 While Robin deliberated of whom to inquire respecting his kinsman's dwelling,
  1 he was accosted by the innkeeper,
    2 a little man in a stained white apron,
      3 who had come to pay his professional welcome to the stranger.
2. 1 The most stirring of his early successes, / , was a series of three plays he wrote on the Wars of the Roses.
    2/ to judge by contemporary reports
3. 1 The sociable country postman, / , had just given him a small parcel,
    2/ passing through the garden
  2 which he took out with him,
    3 leaving the hotel to the right and creeping to a convenient bench that he knew of,
      4 a safe recess in the cliff.
4. 1 Next to the child's mother was a red-headed youngish woman,
    2 reading one of the magazines and working a piece of chewing gum,
      3 hell for leather,
        4 as Claud would say.
5. 1 Great individual development, / , does of course always threaten to break the bond of direct social involvement,
    2/ such as human beings are driven by their intellectual insights to see
  2 that gives animal life its happy unconscious continuity.

While the position of free modifiers is often determined by the effect the writer wishes to create, care must be exercised to avoid confusing or embarrassing constructions. Consider the following sentence:

In the form of free modifiers, you will be able to see the effect of quality, detail, and comparison on writing style.

"In the form of free modifiers" does not describe "you." This confusion demands a revision:

You will be able to see the effect of quality, detail, and comparison, in the form of free modifiers, on writing style.

However, the revision is awkward, and the sentence is best written without any free modifiers at all:

You will be able to see the stylistic effect of quality, detail, and comparison in the form of free modifiers.

Another difficulty can arise from having too many medial modifiers in a generative sentence. These may obscure the subject-verb relationship in the sentence and consequently confuse the reader. Consider the following sentence (base clause underlined):

<u>Henry</u>, considering his difficulty with his college courses, worrying about possible family conflicts, petty as they might be, concerned about his mounting financial problem, <u>dropped into his counselor's office.</u>

Usually one medial modifier is all that your sentence content and style will require.

Misplaced Modifiers

The following selections demonstrate a wide diversity of sentence style. Each selection is from the opening page of a novel. You will notice that the first selection exhibits relatively short sentences and few free modifiers. The second paragraph, a sort of middle ground, has a higher frequency of free modifiers, and the base clauses tend to be longer than those in the first selection. The final excerpt shows how far the concept of generative sentences can be taken! Not only is there a high frequency of generative sentences, but also many of these sentences have several free modifiers.

Which is best? Each of the three selections is considered

Three Paragraphs: Three Sentence Styles

excellent writing: each writer chose to write as he did because he wished to create a certain effect. Modern practice suggests the middle ground, illustrated by Fitzgerald, is an appropriate goal for student writers. This is a decision that you will have to make, probably with the help of your instructor.

Aunt Hager Williams stood in her doorway and looked out at the sun. The western sky was a sulphurous yellow and the sun a red ball dropping slowly behind the trees and house-tops. Its setting left the rest of the heavens grey with clouds.

"Huh! A storm's comin'," said Aunt Hager aloud.

A pullet ran across the back yard and into a square-cut hole in an unpainted piano-box which served as the roosting-house. An old hen clucked her brood together and, with the tiny chicks, went into a small box beside the large one. The air was very still. Not a leaf stirred on the green apple-tree. Not a single closed flower of the morning-glories trembled on the back fence. The air was very still and yellow. Something sultry and oppressive made a small boy in the doorway stand closer to his grandmother, clutching her apron with his brown hands.

"Sho is a storm comin'," said Aunt Hager.

LANGSTON HUGHES
Not Without Laughter

The repeated simple sentences suggest stagnation, boring repetitive actions, an oppressive life. The writer does little downshifting to communicate quality, detail, or comparison.

Amory Blaine inherited from his mother every trait, except the stray inexpressible few, that made him worth while. His father, an ineffectual, inarticulate man with a taste for Byron and a habit of drowsing over the *Encyclopaedia Britannica,* grew wealthy at thirty through the death of two elder brothers, successful Chicago brokers, and in the first flush of feeling that the world was his, went to Bar Harbor and met Beatrice O'Hara. In consequence, Stephen Blaine handed down to posterity his height of just under six feet and his tendency to waver at crucial moments, these two abstractions appearing in his son Amory. For many years he hovered in the background of his family's life, an unassertive figure with a face half-obliterated by lifeless, silky hair, continually occupied in "taking care" of his wife, continually harassed by the idea that he didn't and couldn't understand her.

F. SCOTT FITZGERALD
This Side of Paradise

The increased number of generative sentences causes the writing to flow. The downshifting is often required to describe abstract ideas and judgments, personality traits and physical appearance.

It is not of the games children play in the evening that I want to speak now, it is of a contemporaneous atmosphere that has little to do with them: that of the fathers of families, each in his space of lawn, his shirt fishlike pale in the unnatural light and his face nearly anonymous, hosing their lawns. The hoses were attached at spiggots that stood out of the brick foundations of the houses. The nozzles were variously set but usually so there was a long sweet stream of spray, the nozzle wet in the hand, the water trickling the right forearm and the peeled-back cuff, and the water whishing out a long loose and low-curved cone, and so gentle a sound. First an insane noise of violence in the nozzle, then the still irregular sound of adjustment, then the smoothing into steadiness and a pitch as accurately tuned to the size and style of stream as any violin. So many qualities of sound out of one hose: so many choral differences out of those several hoses that were in earshot. Out of any one hose, the almost dead silence of the release, and the short still arch of the separate big drops, silent as a held breath, and the only noise the flattering noise on leaves and the slapped grass at the fall of each big drop.

JAMES AGEE

"Knoxville: Summer, 1915"
Prologue to *A Death in the Family*

This selection verges on poetry. The very long sentences slow the reader so that the emotions can be experienced. The continual downshifting creates a strong sense of impression rather than appearance.

Self-Evaluation

PART I

Match each of the terms with the appropriate definition.

Terms

1. _____ modification

2. _____ generative sentence

Definitions

a. part of a clause or phrase *not* set off by punctuation

b. free modifier that follows the base clause

c. basic unit of writing, which is modified

3. _____ base clause

4. _____ free modifier

5. _____ initial modifier

6. _____ medial modifier

7. _____ final modifier

8. _____ bound modifier

9. _____ notation of levels of generality

10. _____ coordinate sequence

11. _____ subordinate sequence

d. system of indicating the levels of generality of a sentence through numerical values and indentation

e. type of sentence generation in which each free modifier is more specific

f. phrase or clause set off by punctuation, which modifies either the base clause or another free modifier

g. the process of restricting words, phrases, or clauses in order to intensify images, clarify meaning, or define condition

h. free modifier that precedes the base clause

i. free modifier that interrupts or splits the base clause or another free modifier

j. type of sentence generation in which each free modifier is of the same level of generality

k. sentence that contains a base clause and free modifiers in the form of punctuated additions to the base clause

PART II

Identify the following examples of the terms by matching the underlined words to the appropriate term.

Terms

1. _____ base clause

2. _____ initial modifier

3. _____ final modifier

4. _____ bound modifier

5. _____ medial modifier

Examples

a. He looked down the street, a dark and barren alley.

b. The young men, under armed guard, were taken below to the captain's cabin.

c. Like a police dog, he trailed them.

d. After topping the hill, they ran, dropping their books and papers behind them.

e. A dark man sat in front of his half-opened window, staring out.

PART III

From the following notations, write the sentences as they would normally read.

1. 1 A scented lily, / , stretched its tender petals and blinked in wonder at the morning sun.
   2/ like an infant opening its eyes for the first time

_____

_____

2. 1 My mother at this time seemed to be always working—
    2 cooking,
    2 washing,
    2 ironing,
    2 cleaning,
    2 and fussing over us eight children.

_____

_____

3. 1 It was wide and massive,
    2 with two glassed porches at the left side,
      3 one stacked on top of the other,
    2 and at the right,
      3 a driveway disappearing around to the rear.

_____

_____

4. 1 The layman, / , imagines the relationship between the various "wild beasts of the jungle"
    to be a bloodthirsty struggle,
      2/ misguided by sensationalism in press and film
    2 all against all.

_____

_____

PART IV

Notate the levels of generality in the following sentences.

1. When the roof leaked, the Lesters moved from one corner of the room to another, their
   movements finally outlasting the duration of the rain.   ERSKINE CALDWELL
2. Astern of the boat the repeated call of some bird, a cry discordant and feeble, skipped
   along over the smooth water and lost itself, before it could reach the other shore, in the
   breathless silence of the world.   JOSEPH CONRAD
3. Half a mile from home, at the farther edge of the woods, where the land was highest, a
   great pine-tree stood, the last of its generation.   SARAH ORNE JEWETT
4. In the summer of 1954, Venice, celebrating the seven hundredth anniversary of the adventurous journeys of one of its most famous citizens, Messer Marco Polo, staged an exhibit of maps used in his times.   VERA MICHELES DEAN
5. Later, we were in the funhouse, prancing around in front of the crazy mirrors, making
   our heads disappear and our sides widen.   THOMAS TRYON

6. Vast flats of green grass, dull-hued spaces of mesquit and cactus, little groups of frame houses, woods of light and tender trees, all were sweeping into the east, sweeping over a horizon, a precipice.   STEPHEN CRANE

7. When the public protests, confronted with some obvious evidence of damaging results of pesticide applications, it is fed little tranquilizing pills of half truth.   RACHEL CARSON

(Check your answers with those that follow. If you do not understand the material, review or see your instructor.)

Answers

PART I

1. g
2. k
3. c
4. f
5. h
6. i
7. b
8. a
9. d
10. j
11. e

PART II

1. d
2. c
3. e
4. a
5. b

PART III

1. A scented lily, like an infant opening its eyes for the first time, stretched its tender petals and blinked in wonder at the morning sun.   MARILYN COLLINS

2. My mother at this time seemed to be always working—cooking, washing, ironing, cleaning, and fussing over us eight children.   MALCOLM X

3. It was wide and massive, with two glassed porches at the left side, one stacked on top of the other, and at the right, a driveway disappearing around to the rear.   C. B. GILFORD

4. The layman, misguided by sensationalism in press and film, imagines the relationship between the various "wild beasts of the jungle" to be a bloodthirsty struggle, all against all.
KONRAD LORENZ

1.   2 When the roof leaked,
       1 the Lesters moved from one corner of the room to another,
         2 their movements finally outlasting the duration of the rain.

2. 1 Astern of the boat the repeated call of some bird, / , skipped along over the smooth water and lost itself,
       2/ a cry discordant and feeble
       2 before it could reach the other shore,
         3 in the breathless silence of the world.

3.   2 Half a mile from home,
         3 at the farther edge of the woods,
           4 where the land was highest,
     1 a great pine-tree stood,
       2 the last of its generation.

4.   2 In the summer of 1954,
     1 Venice, / , staged an exhibit of maps used in his times.
     2/ celebrating the seven hundredth anniversary of the adventurous journeys of one of its most famous citizens,
       3 Messer Marco Polo

5.   2 Later,
     1 we were in the funhouse,
       2 prancing around in front of the crazy mirrors,
         3 making our heads disappear and our sides widen.

6.   2 Vast flats of green grass,
       2 dull-hued spaces of mesquit and cactus,
       2 little groups of frame houses,
       2 woods of light and tender trees,
     1 all were sweeping into the east,
       2 sweeping over a horizon,
         3 a precipice.

7.   2 When the public protests,
       3 confronted with some obvious evidence of damaging results of pesticide applications,
     1 it is fed little tranquilizing pills of half truth.

·◄[3]►·
Types of Free Modifiers

This chapter examines the various types of free modifiers: how they are constructed and how they can be used to create efficient, smooth-flowing sentences.

Objectives   After completing this chapter, you should be able

1. to identify the different types of free modifiers: the noun phrase, the adjective phrase and series, the prepositional phrase, the verb phrase, and the absolute phrase
2. to revise paragraphs by employing free modifiers
3. to write original sentences employing free modifiers
4. to write original paragraphs employing generative sentences that contain appropriate types of free modifiers

———— ❧ ————

Noun Phrase   A noun phrase is usually found in the following pattern:

Noun pointer	+	*Adjective*	+	*Noun*
an		old		bedspread
a		dusty		register
the		moss-covered		stone
his		useless		theory

Noun pointers signal the presence of a noun:

articles: a, an, the
possessive pronouns: my, your, his, her, our, their

Sometimes a plural noun has no pointer:

strange sentinels

Sometimes the noun phrase contains more than one modifier:

a wooden, rickety fence

Notice the comma separating "wooden" and "rickety," both of which modify "fence." If an adverb modifies the adjective, then no comma is required:

an unusually creative student

Now, let's take a base clause and add a noun phrase as a free modifier.

base clause: The big, muscular horse jumped over the obstacle.

The writer wishes to say more about the "obstacle," and so adds a detail:

a fence

Next, the writer wishes to specify certain qualities of the "fence":

a wooden, rickety fence

Finally, the writer adds the noun phrase to the base clause, punctuating with a comma:

The big, muscular horse jumped over the obstacle, <u>a wooden, rickety fence</u>.

NOTATION: 1 The big, muscular horse jumped over the obstacle,
2 a wooden, rickety fence.

In the next sentence, the noun in the noun phrase is not more specific than the image in the base clause:

The man, <u>a humped-over, elderly fellow</u>, smiled at the little children as he inched down the street.

NOTATION: 1 The man, / , smiled at the little children as he inched
down the street.
2/ a humped-over, elderly fellow

Since "fellow" is a synonym for "man," you might wonder how the
noun phrase can be a more specific image of "man":

a <u>humped-over, elderly</u> fellow

The underlined words, bound modifiers of "fellow," communicate
what the man looked like and therefore provide a more specific
image of "the man."

So far, we have discussed the noun phrase as a modifier of a
noun in the base clause. In the next sentence, the noun phrase
modifies a verb in the base clause:

He reached for the frosty glass and drank, <u>a quick gulp.</u>

NOTATION: 1 He reached for the frosty glass and drank,
2 a quick gulp.

Here is an example of a noun synonym modifying a verb in the
base clause:

She turned and gazed at the new boy, <u>a long, observing look.</u>

NOTATION: 1 She turned and gazed at the new boy,
2 a long, observing look.

The bound modifiers, "long" and "observing," characterize
"gazed."

PRACTICE   1. In the following sentences, first identify the noun of the noun
phrase, then identify the image in the base clause that the
noun phrase modifies.

    _____ a. He walked into the corner office, a messy
cubicle.
    _____ b. It had been a worthless meeting, a real car-
toon.
    _____ c. After thinking about the day's events, he
wrote in his journal, a curious and rambling entry.
    _____ d. A hardy boy, he was fond of all sports.

    _____ e. The old man saved and endured, a ques-
tionable sacrifice.

2. Underline the noun phrases written as free modifiers.

    a. The islanders built a fire in an umu, a rock-lined oven in the ground.

    b. He spoke for two hours, a confusing, pointless harangue.

    c. The finished product, a woven coverlet, lies on the rocky ground.

    d. The schooner sailed into the harbor, a deep, calm cove.

    e. The manager, a nervous little guy, tried his best to answer the woman.

3. Combine the following sentences in each group, creating a noun phrase as a free modifier of some image in the base clause.

    a. Re-entering his living room, he activated a full-wall viewer and tuned in a scene he especially liked. It was Mount Rainier.

    ———————————————————

    ———————————————————

    b. Leith is the third port of Scotland. Leith is the port of Edinburgh.

    ———————————————————

    ———————————————————

    c. At midday he went to Dan Burke's and took his lunch. He had a bottle of lager beer and a small trayful of arrowroot biscuits.

    ———————————————————

    ———————————————————

1. (The noun of the noun phrase is given first, then the image modified.)
   a. cubicle, office
   b. cartoon, meeting
   c. entry, wrote
   d. boy, he
   e. sacrifice, saved and endured
2. a. a rock-lined oven in the ground.
   b. a confusing, pointless harangue.

c. a woven coverlet,

d. a deep, calm cove.

e. a nervous little guy,

3. a. Re-entering his living room, he activated a full-wall viewer and tuned in a scene he especially liked—Mount Rainier. POUL ANDERSON

b. Leith, the port of Edinburgh, is the third port of Scotland. G. H. DURY

c. At midday he went to Dan Burke's and took his lunch—a bottle of lager beer and a small trayful of arrowroot biscuits. JAMES JOYCE

(A comma to set off the noun phrases in the first and third sentences is an acceptable answer.)

Adjective Phrase and Series

Adjectives communicate the qualities of the noun they modify. Adjective phrases and series do the same:

The <u>shady</u> grove of <u>tall</u> oaks was a <u>nice</u> spot to take a breather.

Notice that the bound adjectives "shady," "tall," and "nice" do not dominate the sentence. However, adjectives written as free modifiers tend to emphasize qualities of a noun in a sentence. In the following sentence, the adjective phrase is a bound modifier:

The <u>strangely pathetic</u> man slipped away through the night.

In this next sentence, it is a free modifier:

<u>Strangely pathetic,</u> the man slipped away through the night.

The adjective phrase is usually found in the following patterns:

adjective	happy
adverb + adjective	strangely pathetic
adjective + prepositional phrase	grateful for any favor
(or adverb + adjective + prepositional phrase)	

If it is punctuated as a free modifier, the adjective phrase should be placed next to the noun that it modifies. In the previous sentence, "strangely pathetic" cannot be placed after "night" without changing the meaning of the sentence. Sometimes confusion can result if the noun that the adjective phrase modifies is missing:

<u>Grateful for any favor,</u> a wave showed his appreciation.

This sentence should be rewritten because the underlined adjective phrase is a dangling modifier. Certainly the wave was was not grateful!

Some of the most overworked clichés in the English language are adjective phrases (especially the third pattern in the preceding list). You should avoid these, if at all possible. Here are some of the most common offenders:

hard as nails	green as grass
cold as ice	snug as a bug in a rug
dead as a doornail	sharp as a tack
quiet as a mouse	sly as a fox
flat as a pancake	clear as mud

You might try to build a list of your own. There are several hundred in common use.

The adjective series is nothing more than two or more adjectives, punctuated as a free modifier:

The night, cold and rainy, drove us indoors.

The chair, old but valuable, commanded a high price.

These examples represent the usual pattern: two adjectives joined by a conjunction ("and," "but," "yet"), positioned as a medial modifier.

PRACTICE

Underline the free modifiers in the following sentences. Identify the type by using the key: AP = adjective phrase; AS = adjective series; X = no adjective phrase or series present.

_____ 1. Unusually quiet, the crowd waited for the headliners.

_____ 2. Very nimble for a woman of her years, she scampered around the edge of the house.

_____ 3. The night, cold as bare steel, drove us indoors.

_____ 4. Nervous and afraid, the children ran from him.

_____ 5. The house, a split-level with a peaked roof, was for sale.

_____ 6. The children watched, motionless and happy.

_____ 7. Her look, long and pensive, reminded him of a day ten years before.

_____ 8. Cautious, Manny moved to the edge of the grass.

_____ 9. Their faces were ones of joy—smiling eyes and grinning mouths.

_____ 10. Frantic, she called her husband.

PRACTICE ANSWERS

1. Unusually quiet, (AP)
2. Very nimble for a woman of her years, (AP)
3. cold as bare steel, (AP)
4. Nervous and afraid, (AS)
5. a split-level with a peaked roof, (X—noun phrase)
6. motionless and happy. (AS)
7. long and pensive, (AS)
8. Cautious, (AP)
9. smiling eyes and grinning mouths. (X—noun phrase)
10. Frantic, (AP)

Prepositional Phrase

The preposition establishes a relationship, a connection between its object and some other element of the sentence in which it occurs. A preposition plus the words it introduces is called a prepositional phrase. As numerous as any modifier in the language, prepositional phrases are used as both bound and free modifiers.

Common prepositions: about, above, across, after, against, along, among, around, as, at, before, behind, below, beneath, beside, besides, between, beyond, but (except), by, concerning, down, during, except, for, from, in, into, like, near, of, off, on, out, outside, over, past, round, since, through, till, to, toward, under, underneath, until, up, upon, with, within, without.

The prepositional phrase has four common functions:

1. to make a comparison:

From the turn, you hear a high-pitched, angry whine, like a brigade of enraged, giant hornets.   JEFF GREENFIELD

2. to indicate direction or location:

The bed, against the wall, occupied two-thirds of the total space of the room.   JACK LONDON

3. to provide detail:

The obvious leader of the party, Loren Pierce, a rich quarryman, was an old man of medium size and mean attire, with a square, beardless face as hard and impassive as one of his blocks of limestone.   HAROLD FREDERIC

4. to establish time relationships:

On a thyme-scented, bird-hatching morning in May, between two and
three years after the return from Trantridge—silent reconstructive years for
Tess Durbeyfield—she left home for the second time.   THOMAS HARDY

Prepositional phrases may be bound or free:

I saw an unusual sight on my way to school.

On my way to school, I saw an unusual sight.

One sentence has a comma; the other does not. In this case the
comma is necessary only when the sentence begins with a prepositional phrase. However, if the introductory prepositional phrase is
short, the comma may be omitted:

During the argument between two drivers, a crowd had gathered.

During the argument a crowd had gathered.

If the prepositional phrase follows the base clause and modifies
the base clause as a whole, use a comma:

She gathered her children about her, like a mother hen.

The people stood straight and still, in spite of the impending danger they
anticipated.

If the prepositional phrase follows the base clause and modifies
the last word in the base clause, do not punctuate:

Aunt Bert slid way down in the seat.

The houses were dark against the night.

1. Underline the prepositional phrases in the following sentences.   PRACTICE
   Identify each one as a bound or free modifier and indicate
   which function it fulfills (comparison, direction or location, detail, or time relationship).

   _____ a. Since lunch, only three students
                                  left the cafeteria.
   _____ b. With a great surge, the wave
                                  broke over the dike.
   _____ c. Men were gathering in the great
                                  halls to plan their crusade.
   _____ d. He paced back and forth along
                                  the fence, like a caged animal.

2. Create prepositional phrases by combining each pair of sentences. Punctuate where appropriate.

   a. He went through deep canyons and vast mud flats. He followed the river to its source.

   _____

   _____

   b. He moved. His motion was like an eel.

   _____

   _____

   c. He wrote a long, detailed letter of appeal. The letter was to the Director of Taxation.

   _____

   _____

   d. It was a strange little house. It had chimneys poking out of the roof at odd angles and intricate iron grates in front of each window.

   _____

   _____

PRACTICE ANSWERS 1. a. Since lunch (free modifier; time relationship)
b. With a great surge (free modifier; detail)
   over the dike (bound modifier; direction or location)
c. in the great halls (bound modifier; direction or location)
d. along the fence (bound modifier; direction or location)
   like a caged animal (free modifier; comparison)
2. a. Through deep canyons and vast mud flats, he followed the river to its source.
b. He moved like an eel. (Since this is a bound comparison, no punctuation is needed.)
c. He wrote a long, detailed letter of appeal to the Director of Taxation.
d. It was a strange little house, with chimneys poking out of the roof at odd angles and intricate iron grates in front of each window.

Verb phrases use three forms of the verb: present participle, past participle, and infinitive. These are easy to identify in their most common forms as follows:

verb + "ing"   = present participle
verb + "ed," "en" = past participle
"to" + verb   = infinitive

(Some verbs are irregular and form their present and past participles differently.) Verb phrases begin with the verb:

present participle: <u>opening</u> the book to the third chapter
past participle: <u>selected</u> from eighty applicants
infinitive: <u>to understand</u> the roots of conflict

In the following verb phrases, underline the verb and identify its form as present participle, past participle, or infinitive.

_____ 1. running all the way

_____ 2. to prove a point

_____ 3. jerked forward by the sudden stop

_____ 4. stirring beneath the surface.

_____ 5. painted with stylized flowers inside

1. running (present participle)
2. to prove (infinitive)
3. jerked (past participle)
4. stirring (present participle)
5. painted (past participle)

Verb phrases may be used as the subject of a sentence:

<u>Working forty hours</u> leaves me little time for class work.

They may also be used as the object of a sentence:

I can remember <u>walking three miles to school.</u>

However, the emphasis in this text is on the use of the verb phrase as a free modifier, easily added to the base clause in any of the three positions (initial, medial, and final):

Continuing my survey, I perceived a domineering nose shadowing a sprouting moustache.

The trooper, waving his arms wildly, tried to signal the cars off the highway.

We continued our tour through the gallery, stopping at every Rembrandt, listening to an explanation of his style.

Writers often employ several verb phrases in a coordinate sequence. In the following example, we sense the step-by-step process of catching the fish—first comes the "hauling," then the "pulling," and finally the "stunning":

> 1 We caught two bass,
>   2 hauling them in briskly as if they were mackerel,
>   2 pulling them over the side of the boat in a businesslike manner without any landing net,
>   2 and stunning them with a blow on the back of the head.
>
> E. B. WHITE

If there is a chronological sequence apparent in what you write, make sure the verb phrases are in the correct order.

Sometimes, a coordinate sequence indicates nothing more than a number of actions happening simultaneously. If this is the case, try building to the most significant or striking image, as the writer does in the next example:

> 1 She sat quite still for a long time,
>   2 remembering the smell of Francis' cologne on Celia's body,
>   2 recalling the ambiguities of Celia's speech ever since and Francis' oblique contradictory replies when she talked to him about what was in her heart,
>   2 remembering with bitter shock his face and his words,
>   3 "Forty is old to have children."
>
> RICHARD CONDON*

To avoid dangling modifiers, make sure that the verb phrase modifies an image in the base clause (or another modifier). Look at this sentence:

The house was dark, coming home late at night.

---

* Cited in Virginia Tufte, *Grammar as Style*, Holt, Rinehart & Winston, New York, 1971. This text is one of the most comprehensive and useful treatments of sentence style in print.

Who was coming home? Not the house!

Walking down the aisle, the wedding march began to play.

Because the wedding march was not walking, this sentence must be revised:

While the bride and groom were walking down the aisle, the organist started to play the wedding march.

PART I

Underline the verb phrase free modifiers in the following sentences. Identify the type as present participle, past participle, or infinitive.

_____ 1. To avoid the traffic jam at Ninety-fifth Street, take the frontage road.

_____ 2. Cornered by the students, he explained the grading system.

_____ 3. The sea breeze, blowing heavily, whipped our coats around us.

_____ 4. Perceiving detail is important.

_____ 5. The children came toward the porch, screaming as they reached the door, pushing and shoving to be the first one in.

_____ 6. The pitcher tossed the ball to the catcher.

_____ 7. The animal ran for the underbrush, frightened by the gunfire, changing its course at each shot.

_____ 8. He had achieved his goal, to be recognized as the best worker without offending anyone.

PART II

Combine the following sentences by creating verb phrase free modifiers. You may have to change verb tenses.

1. It seemed quite natural to continue not just to the South Pacific but on around the globe. I would stop in rarely visited harbors. I would hole up among other peoples for months at a time. I would eat their bread. I would dance to their pipers.

_____

_____

_____

_____

_____

2. I arrived at Government House. I had a moment of nostalgia.

_____

_____

3. Berenice dealt slowly. She licked her thumb when the sweaty cards stuck together.

_____

_____

4. She was sitting beside his desk now in an aroma of perfumes. She was smoothing the handle of her umbrella and nodding the great black feather in her hat.

_____

_____

_____

PRACTICE ANSWERS

PART I
1. To avoid the traffic jam at Ninety-fifth Street, (infinitive)
2. Cornered by the students, (past participle)
3. blowing heavily, (present participle)
4. There is no free modifier in the sentence. "Perceiving detail" is a verb phrase used as the subject of the sentence.
5. screaming as they reached the door, (present participle) pushing and shoving to be the first one in. (present participle)
6. There is no free modifier in this sentence.
7. frightened by the gunfire, (past participle) changing its course at each shot. (present participle)
8. to be recognized as the best worker without offending anyone. (infinitive)

PART II
1. It seemed quite natural to continue not just to the South Pacific but on around the globe, stopping in rarely visited

harbors, holing up among other peoples for months at a time, eating their bread, dancing to their pipers.   ROBIN LEE GRAHAM

2. Arriving at Government House, I had a moment of nostalgia.
   CARLETON MITCHELL

3. Berenice dealt slowly, licking her thumb when the sweaty cards stuck together.   CARSON McCULLERS

4. She was sitting beside his desk now in an aroma of perfumes, smoothing the handle of her umbrella and nodding the great black feather in her hat.   JAMES JOYCE

Absolute Phrase

The absolute phrase consists of a noun immediately followed by any type of free modifier. Usually the noun of the absolute represents a portion of an image in the base clause. As such, it allows the writer to downshift to a more specific level of generality without starting a new sentence. Wordiness and dangling modifiers can be eliminated by using an absolute phrase. You will find it the most useful of the free modifiers. Many times, just thinking of the effect of an absolute will suggest new ideas or images for your writing.

You can create an absolute phrase in two ways:

1. by eliminating the auxiliary verbs (is, are, was, were) from a complete sentence:

sentence: His eyes were following a pattern of concrete blocks in the school building.

absolute: his eyes following a pattern of concrete blocks in the school building

sentence: A bracelet is around her wrist.

absolute: a bracelet around her wrist

2. by combining a noun with any free modifier studied in this chapter:

noun +	present participle verb phrase
the soldiers	wounding the men
noun +	noun phrase
our crimes	our common cause

noun +	adjective phrase
her manner	pleasant
noun +	adjective series
their colors	bright and cheerful
noun +	past participle verb phrase
their leaves	scattered through the yard
noun +	infinitive verb phrase
the students	to write three essays
noun +	prepositional phrase
the books	on the table
noun +	prepositional phrase (comparison)
the garden	like a feebly landscaped jungle

PRACTICE

1. Create absolute phrases by eliminating the auxiliary verbs in the following sentences.
   a. Confusion is the rule.

   _____

   b. Jones was a most helpful guide.

   _____

   c. The brass was echoing the melody.

   _____

   d. Four jars of tomatoes were on the counter.

   _____

2. Create absolute phrases by combining a noun from the first column with an appropriate free modifier from the second column.

   Nouns   *Free modifiers*

   a. the horse_____   on the kitchen table
   b. the rocks _____   flowing gently
   c. the boy_____   tired

d. the water_____   thirsty
e. Nancy_____   covered with moss

1. a. confusion the rule
   b. Jones a most helpful guide
   c. the brass echoing the melody
   d. four jars of tomatoes on the counter
2. a. the horse tired
   b. the rocks covered with moss
   c. the boy thirsty
   d. the water flowing gently
   e. Nancy on the kitchen table

(These are not the only answers. Other combinations are possible.)

Here are four examples of sentences with absolute phrases written as free modifiers. Each has been notated:

1 The students were ready for the end of the period,
　2 the girls repacking purses,
　2 the boys in the back row alert to each sound outside the door.

1 The officers, / , turned around and walked away.
　2/ their faces red but unemotional

1 A halt to the promising start of this new settlement was brought about by two forces,
　2 one from within,
　2 one from without.

1 The car was resting in a far corner of the junkyard,
　2 hinges rusting,
　2 the windowglass shattered,
　2 and the tires mere representations of their former selves.

In the above sentences, the leading noun of the absolute represents a portion of a noun in the base clause:

students—the girls	two forces—one
the boys	one
officers—their faces	car—hinges
	windowglass
	tires

1. Underline the absolute phrases in the following sentences.
   (Note that two sentences do not contain absolutes.)
   a. They drove away quickly, the car vibrating violently.

b. An art remote from common life, intolerably pursuing ideals opposite to those of society, may seem evasive.
WILLIAM YORK TINDALL

c. Gail danced at the party with great polish, her body moving in time with the music.

d. He drove west on Highway 50, the sun blinding his already fatigued eyes.

e. Will Easton grew his own vegetables, corn, tomatoes, and a strange variety of green pepper.

f. She walked slowly toward town, her brother almost trotting to keep up.

g. Marcel ran with all his might, his muscles straining from his determination.

2. Combine the following groups of sentences so that you create a base clause and an absolute phrase as a final free modifier.

a. The neighbors, including children, came out and watched. Everybody was afraid but nobody was moving to do anything.

_____

_____

_____

b. The man's hands were behind his back. The wrists were bound with a cord.

_____

_____

_____

c. Most of the men sat against the wall smoking. Empty coffee cups and liqueur glasses were before them on the tables.

_____

_____

_____

d. He lay freckled and small in the moonlight. His chest was white and naked. One foot was hanging from the edge of the bed.

1. a. the car vibrating violently.
   b. (Sentence does not contain absolute.)
   c. her body moving in time with the music.
   d. the sun blinding his already fatigued eyes.
   e. (Sentence does not contain absolute.)
   f. her brother almost trotting to keep up.
   g. his muscles straining from his determination.
2. a. The neighbors, including children, came out and watched, everybody afraid but nobody moving to do anything.
      BERNARD MALAMUD
   b. The man's hands were behind his back, the wrists bound with a cord.   AMBROSE BIERCE
   c. Most of the men sat against the wall smoking, empty coffee cups and liqueur glasses before them on the tables.   ERNEST HEMINGWAY
   d. He lay freckled and small in the moonlight, his chest white and naked, and one foot hanging from the edge of the bed.
      CARSON McCULLERS

Self-Evaluation

PART I

On a separate piece of paper, revise the following two paragraphs by creating generative sentences where appropriate. To eliminate as many short, choppy sentences as possible, you will combine sentences as you did in the practice exercises in this chapter. Both selections were written as three sentences. Do not be too disturbed if your answers differ from the actual versions.

1. La Salle was already turning into a drawbridge. It was opening wider. The ends were finally pointing at 45° angles to the skyscrapers lining the river. The traffic was on either side of the gates. The traffic was building. It was backing up for blocks. It was visibly straining and steaming at the delay. Below, the barge was loaded with paper and heading for the dock at the Tribune. It slipped through regally.

(You may wish to check your answer on this paragraph before you try the next.)

2. To-day the large side doors were thrown open towards the sun to admit a bountiful light to the immediate spot of the shearers' operations. This spot was the wood threshing-floor in the centre. It was

formed of thick oak. The oak was black with age and polished by the beating of flails for many generations. This went on till it had grown as slippery and as rich in hue as the state-room floors of an Elizabethan mansion. Here the shearers knelt. The sun was slanting in upon their bleached shirts, tanned arms, and the polished shears they flourished. This was causing these to bristle with a thousand rays strong enough to blind a weak-eyed man. Beneath them a captive sheep lay panting. It was quickening its pants as misgiving merged in terror, till it quivered like the hot landscape outside.

PART II

In the following sentences, underline the base clause and identify each free modifier, using the key: NP = noun phrase; AP = adjective phrase; AS = adjective series; VP = verb phrase; A = absolute phrase; PP = prepositional phrase.

1. I was born in the big city, Chicago, Illinois, and lived there for fourteen years.
2. Mr. Adler, the egg-man, had parked his old jalopy there, the wheels half on the Doherty lawn.
3. In my spare time I work on my car, with the skill of a mechanic.
4. Most times the answer concerns my future, to get an education and make my life worthwhile.
5. The tree, an imposing, forty-foot oak, was about to be cut down.
6. I am an actor, using my emotions as tools, performing a hodgepodge person, in front of my audience.
7. To my surprise, I actually had assignments for the first night.
8. The second day, the bad one, was about to begin.
9. After handing in the exam, I left the room.
10. I take sixteen hours a week, a full schedule.
11. After classes, I come home, lazy yet restless.
12. The students were ready for the end of the period, the girls repacking purses, the boys in the back row alert to each sound outside the door.
13. From here, I plan to go to Kansas University, working my way through.
14. The fire crackled, the sparks flying upward.
15. She turned away from the conversation, estranged beyond hope.
16. Unusually passive for a child of three, she just looked at her book.
17. Built of canes, it was thatched with long, mildewed grass.
18. You are all invited to take a look, long and pensive, at the best and most progressive zoo, the human race.
19. Among our endangered population, I am lucky to be free, not encaged in a zoo.
20. I was carried along with the crowd, inching my way, trying not to lose my suitcase.

(Check your answers with those that follow. If you do not understand the answers, review or see your instructor. When you are successful, complete the writing assignment.

Answers

PART I

(This passage was written by a student.)

1. La Salle was already turning into a drawbridge, opening up wider, ends finally pointing at 45° angles to the skyscrapers lining the river. On either side of the gates, the traffic was building, backing up for blocks, visibly straining and steaming at the delay. Below, the barge, loaded with paper and heading for the dock at the Tribune, slipped through regally.

2. To-day the large side doors were thrown open towards the sun to admit a bountiful light to the immediate spot of the shearers' operations, which was the wood threshing-floor in the centre, formed of thick oak, black with age and polished by the beating of flails for many generations, till it had grown as slippery and as rich in hue as the state-room floors of an Elizabethan mansion. Here the shearers knelt, the sun slanting in upon their bleached shirts, tanned arms, and the polished shears they flourished, causing these to bristle with a thousand rays strong enough to blind a weak-eyed man. Beneath them a captive sheep lay panting, quickening its pants as misgiving merged in terror, till it quivered like the hot landscape outside.

THOMAS HARDY

Far from the Madding Crowd

PART II

1. I was born in the big city, Chicago, Illinois, and lived there for fourteen years. [NP]
2. Mr. Adler, the egg-man, had parked his old jalopy there, the wheels half on the Doherty lawn. [NP] [A]
3. In my spare time I work on my car, with the skill of a mechanic. [PP]
4. Most times the answer concerns my future, to get an education and make my life worthwhile. [VP]
5. The tree, an imposing, forty-foot oak, was about to be cut down. [NP]
6. I am an actor, using my emotions as tools, performing a hodgepodge person, in front of my audience. [VP] [VP] [PP]
7. To my surprise, I actually had assignments for the first night. [PP]
8. The second day, the bad one, was about to begin. [NP]
9. After handing in the exam, I left the room. [PP]
10. I take sixteen hours a week, a full schedule. [NP]

11. After classes, I come home, lazy yet restless. *[PP] [AS]*

12. The students were ready for the end of the period, the girls repacking purses, the boys in the back row alert to each sound outside the door. *[A] [A]*

13. From here, I plan to go to Kansas University, working my way through. *[PP] [VP]*

14. The fire crackled, the sparks flying upward. *[A]*

15. She turned away from the conversation, estranged beyond hope. *[VP]*

16. Unusually passive for a child of three, she just looked at her book. *[AP]*

17. Built of canes, it was thatched with long, mildewed grass. *[VP]*

18. You are all invited to take a look, long and pensive, at the best and most progressive zoo, the human race. *[AS] [NP]*

19. Among our endangered population, I am lucky to be free, not encaged in a zoo. *[PP] [VP]*

20. I was carried along with the crowd, inching my way, trying not to lose my suitcase. *[VP] [VP]*

WRITING ASSIGNMENT

1. For each of the following types of free modifier, write three original sentences containing appropriate phrases as free modifiers.

   noun phrase
   adjective phrase
   adjective series
   prepositional phrase (comparison)
   prepositional phrase (direction or location)
   prepositional phrase (detail)
   prepositional phrase (time)
   present participle verb phrase
   past participle verb phrase
   infinitive verb phrase
   absolute phrase

   Underline the free modifier in each sentence.

2. Write a paragraph on one of the following topics. Write generative sentences, using at least five different free modifiers (see list above). No more than half of the sentences should be generative. Underline the free modifiers.

   a. Explain the value of your favorite free-time activity.
   b. Tell about a moment when you felt strong emotion.
   c. Describe an unusual object that you own.
   d. Describe a person who influenced your life in some way.
   e. Tell about an experience that expanded your awareness.

·⟨ II ⟩·
Paragraph Design

·:[4]:·
The Generative Paragraph

The following pages are not intended to be a comprehensive study of the paragraph, but rather to teach you one form of paragraph basic to English prose—the paragraph developing a topic sentence.

Objectives

After completing this chapter, you should be able

1. to explain the relationship between the generative sentence and the paragraph
2. to define and give an example of a topic sentence
3. to organize sentences into meaningful sequences developing a point

———— ·:❦:· ————

Topic Sentence

The topic sentence is usually a declarative statement. To create one, the writer predicates a judgment about a given topic. A *topic* is simply a name or a noun, for example, "women." Therefore, a topic sentence may be defined as "topic + judgment":

Topic sentence = Women + are psychologically and physically by far
the superior of men.

What we have here is a paraphrase of Ashley Montagu's topic sentence from the following paragraph. This is a statement of the main idea in general terms, a statement that is controversial and demands support. The rest of the paragraph supplies that support in sentences that give examples of the alleged psychic and physical superiority of women.

Physically and psychically women are by far the superior of men. The old chestnut about women being more emotional than men has been forever destroyed by the facts of two great wars. Women under blockade, heavy bombardment, concentration camp confinement, and similar rigors withstand them vastly more successfully than men. The psychiatric casualties of civilian populations under such conditions are mostly masculine, and there are far more men in our mental hospitals than there are women. The steady hand at the helm is the hand that has had the practice at rocking the cradle. Because of their greater size and weight, men are physically more powerful than women—which is not the same thing as saying that they are stronger. A man of the same size and weight as a woman of comparable background and occupational status would probably not be any more powerful than a woman. As far as constitutional strength is concerned, women are stronger than men. Many diseases from which men suffer can be shown to be largely influenced by their relation to the male Y-chromosome. More males die than females. Deaths from almost all causes are more frequent in males of all ages. Though women are more frequently ill than men, they recover from illnesses more easily and more frequently than men.

ASHLEY MONTAGU
The Natural Superiority of Women

Structure of the Paragraph

By a sequence of structurally related sentences I mean a group of sentences related to one another by coordination and subordination. If the first sentence of a paragraph is the topic sentence, the second is quite likely to be a comment on it, a development of it, and therefore subordinate to it. The third sentence may be coordinate with the second sentence (as in this paragraph) or subordinate to it. The fourth sentence may be coordinate with either the second or third (or with both if they themselves are coordinate, as in this paragraph) or subordinate to the third. And so on. A sentence that is not coordinate with any sentence above it or subordinate to the next above it, breaks the sequence. The paragraph has begun to drift from its moorings, or the writer has unwittingly begun a new paragraph.

FRANCIS CHRISTENSEN
Notes Toward a New Rhetoric

As you can see from this quotation, one of the benefits of learning about the generative sentence is that, if you understand its structure, you understand the structure of the paragraph. In short, the structure of the generative sentence corresponds to the structure of the paragraph.

The paragraph can be notated in the same way as the sentence. Specifically, the topic sentence of the paragraph corresponds to the base clause of the sentence, and the supporting sentences of the paragraph correspond to the free modifiers of the sentence. The following array illustrates this correspondence:

Sentence	*Paragraph*
base clause	topic sentence
free modifiers	supporting sentences

Now look at the array in more detail:

Sentence		*Paragraph*
base clause	Both are statements of the main idea in general, abstract, or plural terms.	topic sentence (or base sentence)
Example of base clause of generative sentence: 1 He smiled a little to himself as he ran,		Example of topic sentence of paragraph: 1 He smiled a little to himself as he ran.
free modifiers	With the base clause or topic sentence stated, the forward movement stops; the writer shifts down to a lower level of generality or abstraction or to singular terms and goes back over the same ground at this lower level, using free modifiers for the sentence and supporting	supporting sentences

sentences for
the paragraph.

Example of free
  modifiers (FM)
  of generative
  sentence:

2
holding the ball
  lightly in front
  of him with his
  two hands, (FM)

2
his knees pumping
  high, (FM)

2
his hips twisting in
  the almost girlish
  run of a back in
  a broken field.
  (FM)

Example of sup-
  porting sen-
  tences (SS) of
  paragraph:

2
He was holding
  the ball lightly
  in front of him
  with his two
  hands. (SS)

2
His knees were
  pumping high.
  (SS)

2
His hips were
  twisting in the
  almost girlish
  run of a back in
  a broken field.
  (SS)

IRWIN SHAW

"Eighty Yard Run"

The difference between the preceding sentence and paragraph is the form, not the content, and the difference is the effect achieved by the author because he chose to write it as a sentence. Undoubtedly the sentence is more rhetorically effective; simply, this little narrative sequence is better written as a sentence. Furthermore, if the writer had chosen to write the sequence in paragraph form, he certainly would have given much more detail than he did in a sentence. This example does serve to illustrate, however, the correspondence of the structure of the sentence to that of the paragraph. And this is, of course, the point to be learned.

Here is another example illustrating the correspondence:

Sentence

1
For the three months of the summer Max was idle, (base
  clause)

Paragraph

1
He was exotic for these parts, with
  his new, creased Levis, skin-
  tight, blue silk shirt and scarlet
  trim, and new, black sombrero.
  (topic sentence)

2

basking in the sun by the pool daily, (FM)

2

His belt and hat band were made of linked silver conchas, and he wore on one wrist an old silver bracelet as wide as my hand, and on a finger of the other hand a silver ring with a large matrix turquoise. (SS)

2

playing golf three times a week, (FM)

2

His long hair was tied in a club on his neck and bound with a scarlet band. (SS)

2

reading mystery novels, (FM)

2

He was thin, and exceedingly straight, and had a long, narrow face and aristocratic hands. (SS)

2

and sitting in cabarets at night. (FM)

2

His eyes were rather intentionally direct as he smiled at my examination, a faint, even uncertain smile, but with that same quality of light ridicule. (SS)

WALTER VAN TILBURG CLARK

"The Anonymous"

Again, the same principle operates in both constructions: with the idea stated in general, abstract, or plural terms, the writer shifts down to a lower level of generality or abstraction, or to singular terms, and goes back over the same ground at this lower level, using free modifiers for the sentence and using supporting sentences for the paragraph. In the sentence the base clause tells us that Max was idle and the free modifiers tell us specific things about that idleness—"basking in the sun by the pool," "playing golf three times a week," "reading mystery novels," and "sitting in cabarets at night." In the paragraph the topic sentence (or base sentence) tells us that the Indian was "exotic." The supporting sentences supply the details that led to Clark's conclusion that the Indian was exotic. (Also notice that in Clark's paragraph three out of the five sentences are generative sentences.)

This similarity of construction is again apparent in the following sentence and paragraph:

It was an exciting game, quarterbacks passing for long gains, backs running around ends, and coaches throwing tantrums.

It was magnificent. There were thousands of them marching, hundreds of thousands at the curbs, lined up three, four, ten deep along Broad Street, stamping their feet and clapping their hands in time with the string bands strutting and dancing and two-stepping past. *O Dem Golden Slippers! O Dem Golden Slippers!* They wore satins and gilt, they wore spangles, they had plumes fluttering like banshees in the breeze, trailing ribbons, winding and twisting and snapping, cracking like whips. They were the Liberty Clowns, the Purul Clowns, the Landi Clowns. They went arm in arm; they sang; they danced; they tumbled in the snow. There were ballerinas and cowboys, knights and witch doctors, kings and queens and paperhangers. Everybody applauded and cheered and the mummers hurried down the street, skipping and bowing, trotting alongside the string bands, the fancy bands, keeping time to the music. O Dem Golden Slippers! *O Dem Golden Slippers!*

GEORGE CUOMO

"A Man Is Crazy to Want to Go to Philadelphia"

In the paragraph by Cuomo, the topic sentence, "It was magnificent," states the main idea in an abstract term. The supporting sentences contain details that explain the abstract concept of "magnificent." In the sentence, the base clause, "It was an exciting game," states the main idea in an abstract term. The free modifiers contain details that support the abstract idea of "exciting."

To repeat, the structure of the paragraph corresponds to the structure of the generative sentence. Specifically, the topic sentence corresponds to the base clause and the supporting sentences correspond to the free modifiers. As a further example of this correspondence, the following paragraph has been notated to show levels of generality:

¹The geographical position, and the height of the land combined to create a landscape that had not its like in all the world. ²There was no fat on it and no luxuriance anywhere; it was Africa distilled up through six thousand feet, like the strong and refined essence of a continent. ²The colours were dry and burnt, like the colours in pottery. ²The trees had a light delicate foliage, the structure of which was different from that of the trees in Europe; it did not grow in bows or cupolas, but in horizontal layers, and the formation gave to the tall solitary trees a likeness to the palms, or a heroic and romantic air like fullrigged ships with their sails furled, and to the edge of a wood a strange appearance as if the whole wood were faintly vibrating. ²Upon the grass of the great plains the

crooked bare old thorn-trees were scattered, and the grass was spiced like thyme and bog-myrtle; in some places the scent was so strong, that it smarted in the nostrils. [2]All the flowers that you found on the plains, or upon the creepers and liana in the native forest, were diminutive like flowers of the downs,—only just in the beginning of the long rains a number of big, massive heavy-scented lilies sprang out on the plains.

ISAK DINESEN
Out of Africa

PART I

Notate the levels of generality in the following paragraph:

But his shell—it is simple; it is bare, it is beautiful. Small, only the size of my thumb, its architecture is perfect, down to the finest detail. Its shape, swelling like a pear in the center, winds in a gentle spiral to the pointed apex. Its color, dull gold, is whitened by a wash of salt from the sea. Each whorl, each faint knob, each criss-cross vein in its egg-shell texture, is as clearly defined as on the day of creation.

ANNE MORROW LINDBERGH
Gift from the Sea

PART II

In each of the following paragraphs, underline the topic sentence and study the relationship of the rest of the paragraph with this topic sentence. If you have any questions, feel free to ask your instructor for further explanation.

1. The country was the grandest that can be imagined. How often have I sat on the mountain side and watched the waving downs, with the two white specks of huts in the distance, and the little square of garden behind them; the paddock with a patch of bright green oats above the huts, and the yards and wool-sheds down on the flat below; all seen as through the wrong end of a telescope, so clear and brilliant was the air, or as upon a colossal model or map spread out beneath me. Beyond the downs was a plain, going down to a river of great size, on the farther side of which there were other high mountains, with the winter's snow still not quite melted; up the river, which ran winding in many streams over a bed some two miles broad, I looked upon the second great chain, and could see a narrow gorge where the river retired and was lost.

SAMUEL BUTLER
Erewhon

2. There was Aunt Minnie, in whom everything was narrow save her heart. A harsher age would have called her "skinny." Her skin was paper-thin, so that the veins seemed to be on the outside; her body was so slender it looked as if light would pass through it. Her fingers gripping the back of a chair seemed not like hands holding but like wild grape tendrils growing around it. She moved in a tenuous way, abruptly, by jerks, as if not sure that whatever direction she had taken was the right one. Yet she crossed a room faster than any of us, her feet always a little above the floor.

PAUL ENGLE

Prairie Christmas

3. The river was swollen with the long rains. From Vandencourt all the way to Origny it ran with ever-quickening speed, taking fresh heart at each mile, and racing as though it already smelt the sea. The water, yellow and turbulent, swung with an angry eddy among half-sub-merged willows, and made an angry clatter along stony shores. The course kept turning and turning in a narrow and well-timbered valley. Now the river would approach the side, and run gliding along the chalky base of the hill, and show us a few open colza fields among the trees. Now it would skirt the garden walls of the houses, where we might catch a glimpse through a doorway, and see a priest pacing in the chequered sunlight. Again, the foliage closed so thickly in front that there seemed to be no issue; only a thicket of willows, overtopped by elms and poplars, under which the river ran flush and fleet, and where a kingfisher flew past like a piece of the blue sky. On these different manifestations the sun poured its clear and catholic looks.

ROBERT LOUIS STEVENSON

An Inland Voyage

4. The first lap of a stock car race is a horrendous, a wildly horrendous spectacle such as no other sport approaches. Twenty, thirty, forty automobiles, each of them weighing almost two tons, 3700 pounds, with 427-cubic-inch engines, 600 horsepower, are practically locked together, side to side and tail to nose, on a narrow band of asphalt at 130, 160, 180 miles an hour, hitting the curves so hard the rubber burns off the tires in front of your eyes. To the driver, it is like being inside a car going down the West Side Highway in New York City at rush hour, only with everybody going literally three to four times as fast, at speeds a man who has gone eighty-five miles an hour down a highway cannot conceive of, and with every other driver an enemy who is willing to cut inside of you, around you or in front of you, or ricochet off your side in the battle to get into a curve first.

TOM WOLFE

The Kandy-Kolored Tangerine-Flake Streamline Baby

5. The human being is trapped in the dark confines of his own mind and makes contact with the outside world in five specific ways: by sight, by hearing, by touching, by smelling, and by tasting. It is possible to get through life fairly successfully by seeing and hearing only what is necessary, feeling nothing but pain, smelling only that which is unpleasant, and tasting nothing whatever. If there is any meaning to terms like "poetic sensitivity" or "poetic inclination," it is rooted in the ability—perhaps the compulsion—to see, hear, feel, smell, and taste more in this world than the average human. Usually this is coupled with a desire to share this awareness—poetry as communication. Occasionally there is no such desire—poetry as pure expression. For most poets there is a balance.

STEPHEN MINOT

Three Genres

PART I

Notation of Lindbergh selection:

[1]But his shell—it is simple; it is bare, it is beautiful. [2]Small, only the size of my thumb, its architecture is perfect, down to the finest detail. [2]Its shape, swelling like a pear in the center, winds in a gentle spiral to the pointed apex. [2]Its color, dull gold, is whitened by a wash of salt from the sea. [2]Each whorl, each faint knob, each criss-cross vein in its egg-shell texture, is as clearly defined as on the day of creation.

PART II

1. The country was the grandest that can be imagined.
2. There was Aunt Minnie, in whom everything was narrow save her heart.
3. The river was swollen with the long rains.
4. The first lap of a stock car race is a horrendous, a wildly horrendous spectacle such as no other sport approaches.
5. The human being is trapped in the dark confines of his own mind and makes contact with the outside world in five specific ways.

It is a useful practice to continue this study with any paragraph you read. You will become increasingly aware that good writers, professionals *and* students, use the techniques of writing with which we have been dealing. Do you think you are studying some contrived system of writing, for you are not. Any time you wish to be reassured of this, study the work of a professional writer.

Writing Paragraphs

The only purpose, of course, for what has preceded in this chapter is to prepare you to write paragraphs that are as well organized as possible. Next comes the study of three types of paragraph—descriptive, narrative, and expository. In the following chapters, you will receive writing assignments asking you to demonstrate the specific skills treated in each.

·≼[5]≻·
Description

Although seldom used by itself, description is an essential part of all writing. It provides the sensory basis for exposition, argumentation, and narration. In this chapter, however, description will be isolated from these other types of writing. For the police officer, the scientist, the technical writer, the ability to write objective description is necessary to communicate fact accurately. Yet, as human beings we usually respond to our environment by incorporating our feelings, our attitudes, and our impressions into the scene. This new dimension creates subjective description, which, if it is to communicate, must exhibit a continuity of detail, order, and mood.

Objectives

After completing this chapter, you should be able

1. to distinguish between objective and subjective description
2. to emphasize the dominant mood or impression in a description
3. to select suitable content
4. to focus on the most striking details
5. to choose and execute a natural pattern of order or arrangement
6. to employ sense imagery
7. to employ quality, detail, and comparison in the writing of descriptive paragraphs

The Nature of Description

The basic objective of descriptive writing is the depiction of the appearance of people, places, and things. In so doing, it helps re-create for the reader the sense impressions (sight, sound, smell, taste, or touch) experienced or observed by the writer. Through the depiction of quality, detail, and comparison of the image, the writer creates a "word picture" or a "word-paragraph" that is communicated to the reader.

Limiting the Subject

Since description is creating a word picture, you should decide how much of the subject you wish to describe. Will it be a panoramic view or an extreme close-up? Since the assignments in this chapter are of paragraph length, you will be more successful if you work with as limited a subject as possible.

Limit the subject of your description much as you use the viewfinder of a camera. Include as much of the scene as possible while keeping all the appropriate details (and qualities) in clear focus. As you "zoom in," the details and qualities tend to become more specific and concrete. At fifty feet, the side of a barn might not appear as weathered and dilapidated as observed (and described) from, say, fifteen feet. Most student writers would experience difficulties in describing a vast area such as Cape Cod or Paris. However, a short stretch of beach or a sidewalk café are suitably limited subjects for a short piece of writing. Of course, what you wish to say *about* the subject (topic sentence) will help determine how narrow (or broad) your subject will be.

Objective and Subjective Description

In *objective description,* the writer is not attempting to influence the reader, but rather re-creating the object or scene so that the reader may draw his or her own conclusions. Any attempt to interpret, to analyze, to color the experience should be avoided. The writer should be personally detached from whatever is being described. Here is a short objective description:

The elongate, streamlined body of a shark is covered with abrasive placoid scales, which resemble small teeth. Unlike most fishes, the entire skeleton of a shark is composed of cartilage, frequently hardened by calcification. Without exception sharks are carnivorous and feed on a wide variety of animal life. Curiously, the largest sharks, such as the whale shark, *Rhincodon,* and the basking shark, *Cetorhinus,* feed on plankton composed of squids and crustaceans and on small bony fishes. The majority of sharks feed on larger marine vertebrates, which they swallow whole or bite or tear into chunks. Although the mouth is on the underside of the head, a shark does not ordinarily roll on its side when attacking prey.

Encyclopedia International, s.v. "Shark"

There is no attempt to evaluate the animal. We have no impression of the writer's attitude, only the physical appearance and behavior of the shark. Now, compare the preceding piece with this description:

His entire form is fluid, weaving from side to side. His skin is creased with a thousand silky furrows, emphasizing each pattern of incredible muscle. His head moves slowly from left to right, right to left, timed to the rhythm of his speed through the water. Only the eye is fixed, focused on me, in order not to lose sight for a second of his prey or, perhaps, of his enemy.

There is something of the miraculous in the suddenness of his appearance as well as in his infinite grace; the surface of the water is far above, and its absence contributes to the magical quality of the moment. His silent circling is a ballet. There is no threat, no movement of aggression— and yet he generates fear. Murder is the real function of this ideal form, of this icy-blue camouflage, and of that enormous, powerful tail.

JACQUES YVES COUSTEAU

Shark: Splendid Savage of the Sea

The difference between the two animal descriptions is striking. What is the mood of the first piece? What is the first writer's attitude to sharks? Now consider these questions in regard to the Cousteau paragraph. The primary purpose of Cousteau is to communicate his awe, his fear, his appreciation of the shark. As readers of this *subjective description,* we are more interested in Cousteau's *impression* of the shark than in what the shark really looks like. There exists (and rightly so) personal involvement in his paragraph.

Which paragraph is better? It depends on the reader. If you were a biologist searching for facts, the first piece would be more appropriate. If you were a person interested in the experience of nature, then Cousteau would appeal to you. All paragraphs written in response to this chapter will be subjective. (For practice, you might write first a brief objective description, then a subjective description of the same subject.)

1. List six words or groups of words that give you an insight into Cousteau's regard for the shark.

PRACTICE

a._____   d._____

b._____   e._____

c._____   f._____

2. What type of description is stressed in this chapter?_____

3. Compare the style and structure of the two shark passages. What differences do you notice? Be sure to consider word choice, sentence style, paragraph structure, and any other devices that contribute to the difference between the two pieces.

Objective description   *Subjective description*

_____   _____

_____   _____

_____   _____

_____   _____

_____   _____

_____   _____

_____   _____

_____   _____

_____   _____

_____   _____

_____   _____

_____   _____

_____   _____

1. a. incredible muscle
   b. something of the miraculous
   c. infinite grace
   d. magical quality
   e. a ballet
   f. ideal form
   g. splendid savage
2. subjective
3.

Objective description	Subjective description
some free modifiers	many free modifiers
noun phrases	verb phrases emphasize the movement
deals with the shark as one of a class	deals with one particular shark
emphasizes appearance and function	emphasizes impression and quality of function
most details are the result of many observations	all details are the result of this one experience
writer's attitude is detached, scientific, formal	writer's attitude is immediate, emotional
paragraph is orderly, but most details are inventory attributes of shark	most details support a dominant impression of the shark

Topic Choice

You must have a reason for selecting a place to describe. To include all the appropriate details, to include these details in an intelligible order, and to employ correct grammar is simply not enough if you wish to have your reader ask for another of your papers. Too often, student papers are read only to be followed by the response, "So what?" Your reader is interested in what you think of the place. A listing of details will only leave the reader cold.

Usually, the writer should propose one of the following ideas in a topic sentence located at either the beginning or the end of the description:

1. The scene represents some aspect of the human condition.
2. The scene causes the writer to sense some dominant atmosphere (or mood), such as peace, excitement, nostalgia, curiosity, fear, despair, delight, or anticipation.
3. The scene represents some abstract quality such as beauty or ugliness, complexity or simplicity, order or chaos, good or evil.

In the following examples the topic sentence is underlined:

1. Some aspect of the human condition:

There were the houses, too—a long, lurching row of discontented in- curables, smirched with the age-long marks of ague, fevers, cancer, and consumption, the soured tears of little children, and the sighs of disappointed newly-married girls. The doors were scarred with time's spit and anger's hasty knocking; the pillars by their sides were shaky, their stuccoed bloom long since peeled away, and they looked like crutches keeping the trembling doors standing on their palsied feet. The gummy-eyed windows blinked dimly out, lacquered by a year's tired dust from the troubled street below. Dirt and disease were the big sacraments here—outward and visible signs of an inward and spiritual disgrace. The people bought the cheapest things in food they could find in order to live, to work, to worship: the cheapest spuds, the cheapest tea, the cheapest meat, the cheapest fat; and waited for unsold bread to grow stale that they might buy that cheaper, too. Here they gathered up the fragments so that nothing would be lost. The streets were long haggard corridors of rot- tenness and ruin. What wonderful mind of memory could link this shrink- ing wretchedness with the flaunting gorgeousness of silk and satin; with bloom of rose and scent of lavender? A thousand years must have passed since the last lavender lady was carried out feet first from the last surviving one of them. Even the sun shudders now when she touches a roof, for she feels some evil has chilled the glow of her garment. The flower that here once bloomed is dead forever. No wallflower here has crept into a favoured cranny; sight and sign of the primrose were far away; no room here for a dance of daffodils; no swallow twittering under a shady eave; and it was sad to see an odd sparrow seeking a yellow grain from the mocking dust; not even a spiky-headed thistle, purple mitred, could find a corner here for a sturdy life. No Wordsworth here wandered about as lonely as a cloud.

SEAN O'CASEY

Inishfallen, Fare Thee Well

2. Dominant atmosphere (mood):

The night had a sinister aspect. A heated breeze from the south slowly fanned the summits of lofty objects, and in the sky dashes of buoyant cloud were sailing in a course at right angles to that of another stratum, neither of them in the direction of the breeze below. The moon, as seen through these films, had a lurid metallic look. The fields were sallow with the impure light, and all were tinged in monochrome, as if beheld through stained glass. The same evening the sheep had trailed homeward head to tail, the behaviour of the rooks had been confused, and the horses had moved with timidity and caution.

THOMAS HARDY

Far from the Madding Crowd

3. Abstract quality:

It was magnificent. There were thousands of them marching, hundreds of thousands at the curbs, lined up three, four, ten deep along Broad Street, stamping their feet and clapping their hands in time with the string bands strutting and dancing and two-stepping past. *O Dem Golden Slippers! O Dem Golden Slippers!* They wore satins and gilt, they wore spangles, they had plumes fluttering like banshees in the breeze, trailing ribbons, winding and twisting and snapping, cracking like whips. There were the Liberty Clowns, the Purul Clowns, the Landi Clowns. They went arm in arm; they sang; they danced; they tumbled in the snow. There were ballerinas and cowboys, knights and witch doctors, kings and queens and paperhangers. Everybody applauded and cheered and the mummers hurried down the street, skipping and bowing, trotting alongside the string bands, the fancy bands, keeping time to the music. O Dem Golden Slippers! *O Dem Golden Slippers!*

GEORGE CUOMO

"A Man Is Crazy to Want to Go to Philadelphia"

PRACTICE

Here are four more topic sentences that begin descriptive paragraphs. Determine which of the ideas listed on page 71 best describes each sentence:

_____ 1. Australia, the *Terra Incognita* of the Old World, the last continent to be discovered, is a study in variety and sameness.   MARJORIE BARNARD

_____ 2. It was one of those extraordinarily bright days that make things look somehow bigger.   DOROTHY PARKER

_____ 3. A sombre, yet beautiful and peaceful gloom here pervaded all things.   EDGAR ALLAN POE

_____ 4. The civilization round Concord to-day is an odd distillation of city, village, farm, and manor.   E. B. WHITE

PRACTICE ANSWERS

1. abstract quality
2. dominant atmosphere
3. dominant atmosphere
4. human condition

Observation

Successful descriptive writing requires good observation. You must perceive (see or sense) a scene or object before re-creating it for a reader. You cannot expect casual or hurried observations to provide the foundation of a penetrating and accurate description that says something. You must take time to observe, to examine, to use every sense possible. Gustave Flaubert's advice to his fellow writer de Maupassant underscores the way a writer should "see":

We must look at everything we want to express long enough and attentively enough to discover an aspect of it that has never been seen and described by anyone else. There is something unexplored in everything, because we are accustomed to using our eyes only with the memory of what has already been thought about what we are seeing. Anything, however slight, contains something that is still unknown. Let us find it. To describe a blazing fire or a tree in a plain, let us remain before that fire or that tree until it no longer looks to us like any other tree or any other fire.
  It is in this way that one becomes original.

GUSTAVE FLAUBERT

Quoted in the Introduction to Pierre and Jean by Guy de Maupassant

If possible, visit the place you wish to describe. The more immediate the experience, the sharper your word picture. Writing "on location" allows you to examine each detail—its condition (quality), its situation, and its contribution to your impression of the place. You should spend your time observing, not trying to remember.

Selection of Details

After observing as much of the subject as possible, you must decide which details contribute to the mood, atmosphere, or idea of your paper. Certainly some details do little, if anything, to support your topic sentence. These should be discarded.

In the following description of a small town, notice how the writer communicates the atmosphere of the whole town in a description of one street and the atmosphere of the street in a description of one building, the Minniemashie House. After Lewis is finished with the hotel, he returns to the street and selects only those images that emphasize the dreariness, the decay, and the drabness of Gopher Prairie:

When Carol had walked for thirty-two minutes she had completely covered the town, east and west, north and south; and she stood at the corner of Main Street and Washington Avenue and despaired.
  Main Street with its two-story brick shops, its story-and-a-half wooden residences, its muddy expanse from concrete walk to walk, its huddle of

Fords and lumber-wagons, was too small to absorb her. The broad, straight, unenticing gashes of the streets let in the grasping prairie on every side. . . .

She glanced through the fly-specked windows of the most pretentious building in sight, the one place which welcomed strangers and determined their opinion of the charm and luxury of Gopher Prairie—the Minniemashie House. It was a tall lean shabby structure, three stories of yellow-streaked wood, the corners covered with sanded pine slabs purporting to symbolize stone. In the hotel office she could see a stretch of bare unclean floor, a line of rickety chairs with brass cuspidors between, a writing-desk with advertisements in mother-of-pearl letters upon the glass-covered back. The dining-room beyond was a jungle of stained tablecloths and catsup bottles.

She looked no more at the Minniemashie House.

A man in cuffless shirt-sleeves with pink arm-garters, wearing a linen collar but no tie, yawned his way from Dyer's Drug Store across to the hotel. He leaned against the wall, scratched a while, sighed, and in a bored way gossiped with a man tilted back in a chair. A lumber-wagon, its long green box filled with large spools of barbed-wire fencing, creaked down the block. A Ford, in reverse, sounded as though it were shaking to pieces, then recovered and rattled away. In the Greek candy-store was the whine of a peanut-roaster, and the oily smell of nuts.

There was no other sound nor sign of life.

SINCLAIR LEWIS
Main Street

Read the following paragraph and then answer the questions.　　　PRACTICE

In many places the coast is rock-bound, or, more properly, clinker-bound; tumbled masses of blackish or greenish stuff like the dross of an iron-furnace, forming dark clefts and caves here and there, into which a ceaseless sea pours a fury of foam; overhanging them with a swirl of grey, haggard mist, amidst which sail screaming flights of unearthly birds heightening the dismal din. However calm the sea without, there is no rest for these swells and those rocks; they lash and are lashed, even when the outer ocean is most at peace with itself. On the oppressive, clouded days, such as are peculiar to this part of the watery Equator, the dark, vitrified masses, many of which raise themselves among white whirlpools and breakers in detached and perilous places off the shore, present a most Plutonian sight. In no world but a fallen one could such lands exist.

HERMAN MELVILLE
The Encantadas

1. Write the topic sentence.

   _____

   _____

2. List the most striking details that support the atmosphere (mood) proposed in the topic sentence.

   a. _____

   b. _____

   c. _____

   d. _____

   e. _____

   f. _____

3. In your own words, describe any similarities exhibited by the six most striking details.

   _____

   _____

   _____

4. List any six "quality" words that intensify the atmosphere suggested by the details, for example, "*haggard* mist."

   a. _____

   b. _____

   c. _____

   d. _____

   e. _____

   f. _____

5. List any comparisons, bound or free.

_____

_____

1. In no world but a fallen one could such lands exist.
2. grey, haggard mist
   dismal din
   dark clefts
   ceaseless sea
   fury of foam
   oppressive, clouded days
   screaming flights of unearthly birds
   a most Plutonian sight (a dead world)
   no rest
   detached and perilous places
   rock-bound, clinker-bound
   a fallen one (suggests hell)
3. The details suggest the punishment, torture, and damnation that fit the traditional image of hell.
4. dismal
   dark
   oppressive
   unearthly
   ceaseless
   fury
   screaming
   grey
5. like the dross of an iron-furnace

Use of Sense Images

When asked to describe a scene, most people think of how it looks. But sight is only one of several senses useful to description. Sound, smell, taste, and touch sensations are also present in any scene. Of course, it is not always possible or practical to use all five senses in creating a word picture of a scene. In the following selection notice how the writer, while portraying visual images, emphasizes sounds and then odors:

After the quietness of the ranch, where a whole day often passed with no other sounds than her own and her father's and mother's voices, and where the chief diversions, perhaps, were those of digging up a trap-door spider, or freeing a butcher-bird's victim, the sights and sounds of a beach town on a Sunday afternoon were almost too exciting to be borne.

First, there was the strange light touch of the penetrating wind off the sea on her warm inland body. Then there was the constant, half-heard beat of the surf, hissing as it ran smoothly up the sand, thundering as it crashed against the rocks of the breakwater. There were all the smells of salt and seaweed, of fish and water and wind. There were all the human smells too of the hundreds of people who filled the boardwalk: ladies in print dresses smelling like passing gardens; swimmers with their scents of sun-tan oils and skin lotions; there were the smells of the eating places: of mustard and onions, of hamburgers frying; and the sudden sharp smell of stacks of dill pickles, as brisk in the nose as a sudden unintended inhalation of sea water. There was the smell of frying fish from the many fish grottos. And outside these places, in the middle of the boardwalk like miniature, land-locked seas, the glass tanks, where passers-by might admire the grace and color of their dinners before eating them. It was hard to say who did the most looking; fish outward from these sidewalk aquariums, at the strange pale gill-less pedestrians, or pedestrians inward at the finny swimmers.

JESSAMYN WEST

Cress Delahanty

The writer of the next sample relies heavily on touch sensations. She had to because she was both blind and deaf:

When I think of hills, I think of the upward strength I tread upon. When water is the object of my thought, I feel the cool shock of the plunge and the quick yielding of the waves that crisp and curl and ripple about my body. The pleasing changes of rough and smooth, pliant and rigid, curved and straight in the bark and branches of a tree give the truth to my hand. The immovable rock, with its juts and warped surfaces, bends beneath my fingers into all manner of grooves and hollows. The bulge of a watermelon and the puffed-up rotundities of squashes that sprout, bud, and ripen in that strange garden planted somewhere behind my finger tips are the ludicrous in my tactual memory and imagination.

HELEN KELLER

The World I Live In

Sense Images: Detail, Quality, and Comparison

You can generate many useful ideas for descriptive writing by examining each of the five senses through quality, detail, and comparison. More than likely, you will be able to propose additional considerations of your own. Many of the examples in the following section are taken from passages quoted earlier in the chapter.

Detail   Does one detail dominate the scene? Are a number of details related by their function, proximity, or shape? Are there interesting juxtapositions of detail? Are the specific details moving or stationary? Does this contribute significantly to the scene? Will a brief mention of its source help explain light pattern? Examples: shadows created by tall buildings; light streaming through a skylight.

Quality   Do any of the details show the effects of use or misuse? Care or neglect? Are the colors important? Does the light intensity affect individual details or the scene as a whole? Examples: brilliance, gloom.

Comparison   Can you compare the shape, function, or condition of the images to more familiar or suggestive images? Examples: "[the glass tanks] like miniature, land-locked seas" (Jessamyn West); "[The buildings] looked like crutches keeping the trembling doors standing on their palsied feet" (Sean O'Casey).

Detail   Are there specific sound details? Example: "where a whole day often passed with no other sounds than her own and her father's and mother's voices" (Jessamyn West). Is onomatopoeia (use of words that imitate sounds) useful? Examples: hiss, whir, rumble, buzz, pop. Does an identification of the source of the sound make clear the detail? Examples: the clank of heavy stamping machines; car doors opening and closing.

Quality   Does sound level and its complexity contribute to the mood or impression of the scene? Are the sounds pleasant or offensive? Do patterns of sounds (rhythms) contribute to the scene? Example: "half-heard beat of the surf" Jessamyn West).

Comparison   Can you clarify a vague sound image through comparison? Example: the clicking . . . like a dog's nails on a tile floor. Is the sound comparable to that of a specific musical instrument? Example: like a muted cello. Can you suggest musical qualities through an indirect or general comparison? Examples: melodious, lyrical, or like a prelude.

Detail   Are any details present that can be tasted or suggest the taste of something? Examples: "onions," "pickles," and "hamburgers" (Jessamyn West).

Quality   Do taste qualities contribute to the scene? Examples: bitter, sour, sweet, salty, tangy. Do certain taste qualities suggest chewing or texture? Examples: crisp, pasty, pulpy, crunchy.

Comparison   Will taste comparisons make the sensory image striking or understandable? Example: bland as the eraser on the end of a six-cent pencil.

Detail   Are specific odors present in the scene? Example: "salt and seaweed, . . . fish and water and wind" (Jessamyn West).

Quality   Are the odors strong or faint, pleasant or repulsive? Will certain adjectives denoting quality help in communicating the nature of the odors? Examples: fragrant, acrid, putrid, aromatic, spicy, rancid, pungent, musty. Will an identification of the source make clear the nature and significance of the odor? Example: "swimmers with their scents of sun-tan oils and skin lotions" (Jessamyn West).

Comparison   Will a comparison clarify the odor or the sensing of the odor? Examples: "ladies in print dresses smelling like passing gardens"; "the sudden sharp smell of stacks of dill pickles, as brisk in the nose as a sudden unintended inhalation of sea water" (Jessamyn West).

TOUCH   *Detail*   Are there specific details present in the scene that suggest a tactile (touch) experience? Examples: "juts . . . grooves and hollows," "bulge . . . and the puffed-up rotundities" (Helen Keller); "the . . . touch of the penetrating wind . . . on her warm inland body" (Jessamyn West).

Quality   Does the texture of the detail suggest a tactile response? Examples: hot or cold, hard or soft, wet or dry, oily or sticky, smooth or rough, scratchy or polished, weathered, silky. Are there interesting juxtapositions of qualities?

Comparison   Will a comparison clarify the tactile image? Examples: coarse like old burlap; almost smooth like worn-out sandpaper.

Order or Arrangement of Descriptive Details

Good descriptive writing, like good narrative and expository writing, *must* have a carefully worked out organizational pattern or order. While a number of organizational options are available, the writer will find the following two most usable:

1. *Importance:* The writer should decide which parts of the subject are most important, which parts are least important, and then arrange them by (a) beginning with the most important and progressing to the least important or (b) beginning with the least important and progressing to the most important. For emphasis as well as reader interest, the writer will find the second option to be more effective. Notice how Mark Twain begins the following description with a few incidental details and builds up to the most outstanding and humorous image of the cruet:

The furniture of the hut was neither gorgeous nor much in the way. The rocking-chairs and sofas were not present, and never had been, but they were represented by two three-legged stools, a pine-board bench four feet long, and two empty candle-boxes. The table was a greasy board on stilts, and the table-cloth and napkins had not come—and they were not looking for them, either. A battered tin platter, a knife and fork, and a tin pint cup, were at each man's place, and the driver had a queensware saucer that had seen better days. Of course this duke sat at the head of the table. There was one isolated piece of table furniture that bore about it a touching air of grandeur in misfortune. This was the caster.* It was German silver, and crippled and rusty, but it was so preposterously out of place there that it was suggestive of a tattered exiled king among barbarians, and the majesty of its native position compelled respect even in its degradation. There was only one cruet left, and that was a stopperless, fly-specked, broken-necked thing, with two inches of vinegar in it, and a dozen preserved flies with their heels up and looking sorry they had invested there.

MARK TWAIN

Roughing It

The following notation of the paragraph shows how Twain narrows and narrows:

```
1
  2
  2
  2
    3
      4
    3
      4
        5
          6
```

2. *Spatial:* When this organizational pattern is used, the various parts of the subject are placed in a "space" or location relationship to one another. In other words, the writer decides on a starting and a finishing point and arranges the details accordingly. For example, in describing your back yard, do not just say that there are two trees, a barbecue, and a concrete patio. The reader needs to know the spatial relationships of these details:

Two mulberry trees border a patio of crushed stone approximately thirty feet square. In the corner, under one of the trees, stands a rusty charcoal barbecue.

---

* A round rack that holds jars containing salt, pepper, oil, vinegar, and mustard.

You will find the following words and phrases helpful in locating details in space:

to the left	in front of	beneath
on the right	beyond	farther on
under	between	behind
over	on the edge	at the center
next to	across	

Spatial order may take various forms, but the following are among the most usable:

near to far *or* far to near
high to low *or* low to high
left to right *or* right to left
inside to outside *or* outside to inside

The nature of the subject to some degree dictates the particular spatial order. Whatever you do, avoid jumbling and confusing your reader. No spatial order will work if you, the observer, continually move about. Establish a fixed or stationary vantage point that permits you to see your subject in its entirety. Imagine trying to read a description that is the product of a moving vantage point. It is something like watching a film of jump cuts, or sudden transitions. If you must move, inform the reader of the change in your location.

In the following passage from *Erewhon*, Samuel Butler expresses his reaction to the landscape in the topic (first) sentence. The underlined portion of the second sentence establishes his vantage point. The remainder of the paragraph presents the descriptive details in a spatial order of near to far:

The country was the grandest that can be imagined. How often have I sat <u>on the mountain side</u> and watched the waving downs, with the two white specks of huts in the distance, and the little square of garden behind them; the paddock with a patch of bright green oats above the huts, and the yards and wool-sheds down on the flat below; all seen as through the wrong end of a telescope, so clear and brilliant was the air, or as upon a colossal model or map spread out beneath me. Beyond the downs was a plain, going down to a river of great size, on the farther side of which there were other high mountains, with the winter's snow still not quite melted; up the river, which ran winding in many streams over a bed some two miles broad, I looked upon the second great chain, and could see a narrow gorge where the river retired and was lost.

SAMUEL BUTLER

Erewhon

Yes, Austria was far from the world, and asleep, and our village was in the middle of that sleep, being in the middle of Austria. It drowsed in peace in the deep privacy of a hilly and woodsy solitude where news from the world hardly ever came to disturb its dreams, and was infinitely content. At its front flowed the tranquil river, its surface painted with cloud-forms and the reflections of drifting arks and stone-boats; behind it rose the woody steps to the base of the lofty precipice; from the top of the precipice frowned a vast castle, its long stretch of towers and bastions mailed in vines; beyond the river, a league to the left, was a tumbled expanse of forest-clothed hills cloven by winding gorges where the sun never penetrated; and to the right a precipice overlooked the river, and between it and the hills just spoken of lay a far-reaching plain dotted with little homesteads nested among orchards and shade trees.

MARK TWAIN

The Mysterious Stranger

1. Write the topic sentence of this paragraph.

   _____

   _____

2. List the images (details and qualities) that support the atmosphere (mood) proposed in the topic sentence.

   _____

   _____

3. List the words or phrases that locate the images in space. (Begin with the third sentence.)

   _____

   _____

   _____

   _____

4. Identify the specific organization of details. _____

1. Yes, Austria was far from the world, and asleep, and our village was in the middle of that sleep, being in the middle of Austria.

2. drowsed in peace
   deep privacy
   infinitely content
   woodsy solitude
   disturb its dreams
   tranquil river
3. at its front
   behind it
   to the base
   beyond the river
   to the right
   among
   from the top
   a league to the left
   between
4. spatial (near to far)

Here are three examples of student writing. In the first selection, notice the atmosphere or mood established in the first sentence (topic sentence) and the arrangement of details (least important to most important). The piece is particularly effective because so many of the images (detail and quality) contribute to the atmosphere of the place:

The large windows and high ceiling cannot alleviate the cheerless gray atmosphere of the bus depot. Because it is very early morning, the windows allow the leaden sky to enter and chill the room. The unnatural bluish fluorescent light cast from suspended fixtures, by contrast, heightens the darkness of upper regions of the ceiling, and radiates a pale unhealthy color to faces below. Beige plastic chairs, too slick and cold to be comfortably sat in, are scattered about the room, offering travelers forlorn seclusion. Occupants of the uninviting chairs slump and wait, many with feet propped up on a travel-scarred suitcase, in the manner of one drooping elderly woman. The rest of her luggage consists of a shopping bag and a shapeless brown satchel of a purse, both marks of the little-old-lady class of bus traveler. Her work-roughened hands, veined and muscular, fingernails blunt and cracked, are folded over a book in her lap, a broken-spined paper-back entitled *One Hundred Clues to Personal Success*.

The writer of the next selection describes the atmosphere of the Peanut Tavern by focusing upon two representative patrons. The man and woman sum up the scene much as the Minniemashie House does in the selection from *Main Street* by Sinclair Lewis.

This passage, however, tends more toward a character sketch; the reader may sense the need for more details if the writing is to adequately describe the tavern as a whole:

A curious pair were the only lunchtime patrons of the old Peanut Tavern. Oblivious to the darkness and unswept surroundings, they were equally unaffected by the acrid smell and chilling damp. An unlikely barfly, the old woman sat at a table, her shiny aluminum walker parked nearby. A young man seemed more at home having draped his long, cat-like body upon an unwashed barstool. His tapered fingers curled around the waist of a pilsner glass of beer. The woman's tiny hands lay unmoving on the gray formica table bearing greasy smears as evidence of the part they played in feeding her from a half eaten bowl of chili. The bar was littered with beer glasses drained by the man, blurred by fingerprints. They defined each other in opposites thereby describing the atmosphere of the tavern. His body suggested economy, while her copious flesh surrounded an assumedly equal number of bones and organs in a more generous fashion. Soiled blue denim hugged his thighs scarcely concealing the firm muscles beneath. Ill-fitting, dotted jersey spanned her belly and ample bosom. Thin hair lay like damp feathers on her creased forehead. A cobweb against the winter cold, she wore a frayed cotton scarf tied under her uncountable chins. It had been set awry by a breeze and remained pointing upward toward the unlit ceiling. Blond hair bloomed like dandelion fuzz on his head standing three inches from his scalp. It appeared impermanent as if the same breeze which had disarranged her scarf could have blown him bald. A wet, yellow mustache porched his unusually full mouth. She had applied orange lipstick to spots beneath her nose where perhaps memory convinced her that lips still existed. But they had long since thinned and disappeared with loss of teeth. Unlikely companions in an unlikely rendezvous, yet as he rose to leave he spoke, "See you tomorrow, Mrs. Murphy."

This final paragraph was written in response to the third topic suggestion in the writing assignment that follows. Notice how the student describes the effect of the storm on the scene:

And suddenly the weather changed. A silence, eerie and oppressive, settled over the land like a shroud, a silence so intense it seemed it would weigh down on the land until it smothered it. Even the birds sensed something in the making, each hushing its noisy chatter and disappearing into the woods. A brisk wind sprang from the southwest, a howling wind, which knifed through the silence, chilling everything to the bone. With the wind came dark billowing clouds, rumbling with pent-up energy, choking out the sun, casting a bleak pall over the landscape. *Then,* as if on cue, everything broke loose at once. The wind ripped across the hill-tops and down through the valleys, bending the slender saplings to the ground, as if they were bowing before some unseen god. Lightning branched across the sky, sporadically sending one of its fiery tentacles to touch some susceptible tree. Thunder rolled like waves across the green hills cast in an almost iridescant hue. The rain fell in torents, moving in horizontal planes, dense and impenetrable. Water flooded down the slopes, drowning or saturating everything in its path. And then, as quickly as it had come, the storm was gone.

WRITING ASSIGNMENT

Choose one of the following places to describe. This place should be familiar, and you should have some definable feeling about it. Establish the location *and* your attitude, emotional state, or impression (or a dominant mood of the place) in the topic sentence. Support your topic sentence in the remainder of the paragraph through careful selection of detail, quality, and comparison. Be sure to limit your description to something that can be dealt with in one paragraph.

1. Describe a room in a friend's home. Focus on the relationship between the physical appearance of the room and the values or tastes of the occupant. Indirectly, you will be commenting on the character of the occupant.
2. Describe a public place such as a bus depot, air terminal, theater lobby, church, large restaurant, barn, or museum foyer. Describe only the interior and stay in one place. As this is a public setting, you will need to describe people and their actions. However, do not attempt to sequence their actions into a narrative.
3. Describe an outside scene in which the season, time of day, or weather sets the mood or atmosphere. Be sure to describe the effect of the mood or atmosphere on the *specific* details of the landscape.
4. Describe an outdoor scene. Focus on your desire as a writer to get close to and understand nature. Stress the details that reveal the mood or atmosphere of the location.
5. Describe a place that is dominated by sounds; a factory, hospital, restaurant, or service station might be a likely candidate. However, your selection really depends on what is accessible to you and on the potential of the sound images of that place. Include other sense images, but focus or concentrate on the sounds.
6. Describe a neighborhood. Emphasize those details that define either the conditions under which the people live or their values. Generally, you are commenting on the quality of their lives as they have created it, or as they have had to accept it.

⋯⊰[6]⊱⋯
Narration

Narratives exist in many forms and for many purposes. Scientific and technical processes are usually expressed in narrative form. History begins with the re-creation of the sequence of events in a period or culture. Insurance, police, and industrial reports are often short narratives, describing the step-by-step unfolding of some incident. News journalism, that daily, even hourly, reporting of events, is essentially narration. And finally, the most sophisticated form of narration is the creating of fiction, short stories and novels.

On a more personal level, narration is one of the most familiar forms of communication. We are continually asked to entertain and instruct our friends and others by relating our experiences. The *entertainment* provided by narratives relies heavily on action and suspense—in other words, "What happens next?" The *instruction,* or point, of narratives is based on the unfolding of a conflict and its resolution. The emphasis of this chapter, therefore, is the writing of autobiographical narratives that entertain and instruct.

After completing this chapter, you should be able

Objectives

1. to select a topic (event) suitable for an interesting and significant narrative
2. to employ appropriate aspects of physical setting and characterizations in the narrative
3. to plot the events into a meaningful and clear sequence that reveals the action of the narrative

4. to identify and emphasize qualities of conflict and suspense present in the story
5. to maintain a consistent point of view in the narrative
6. to write a narrative based on your own experience

———————⚜———————

Storytelling is the oldest and most natural form of communication. Surely cave dwellers, huddled around their campfires, shared tales of exciting hunts and long, arduous migrations. Some stories, repeated for many generations, were refined into sophisticated religious myths. Even before the advent of written languages, tens of thousands of years ago, cave paintings portrayed events that held some significance for people. This was, no doubt, the earliest attempt to "get it down on paper"!

Children, once they learn the names of objects and people, begin to organize their experiences into stories. They have little difficulty explaining "what happened at school today." The organization of their stories is in chronological order, one event after another, just as they happened. Here is a brief narrative written by a third-grader:

One day at this boy's house he came home for lunch from school. And his name was Steve and he was having ravili for lunch. And his dad was home instead of his mother. He lived in New York. And so his dad cooked him ravoli. So when it was done., His dad taught him how to eat it. And his Dad said "here's how: You spear it and blow on it, always remember to blow on it and you eat it, one for me, one for you, two for me, one for you, three for me, one for you." The boy said, "Dad, Dad!" Dad said, "I have a bigger mouth than you!" *

While there are irregularities of spelling, sentence structure, and punctuation, this story exhibits many of the techniques you will use in your own narratives—characters, a natural time sequence, plot, dialogue, and a point worth considering. Let us now examine these elements in detail.

Topic Good narrative, like all writing, requires the selection of a suitable topic. The papers resulting from this chapter will be true narratives of events that you have experienced. While you will not be creating fictions (made-up stories), you will have to approximate some of the details as you try to remember the past. Occasionally

———————

* Quotation marks added.

you may wish to modify, slightly, certain details to emphasize a personality trait, a mood, or some aspect of a conflict. Your first step, however, is to choose an event that you would enjoy writing about and that another person would enjoy reading about. A note of caution about the word "enjoy." Entertainment is only half of the effect of narrative writing; you will also attempt to instruct your reader about life, the world, yourself.

What makes a good story? Usually something that the reader can identify with or that expands the reader's experience. A story with a theme, moral, or lesson can be successful, if handled well. The topic suggestions at the end of this chapter are designed to narrow your choices, that is, to force you to write about something with possibilities.

A second condition of good narration is the selection of an event that can be dealt with in the space available. As your assignments are quite short, you must choose something that can be covered in a page or two. Your life history, your senior year in high school, last year's trip to the Rockies—none of these can be developed in such a short space. Instead, you may cover only a few minutes or part of a day as you relate what happened to you. You will notice that the topic suggestions are quite specific, limiting you to certain types of human situations that can occur during a relatively short time period.

A third condition of good narration is unity. Isolate the point to be made and stick with it. You will find that superfluous or irrelevant details must be quickly dismissed or eliminated. Any details that are minor should be treated as incidental or background. If part of your narration seems to be "another story," you may have to eliminate it. A good test for unity is to determine the effect of removing these details. If you follow this approach, you should have no difficulty with unity.

Be extremely wary of a story that has nothing going for it except violence, strong language, intimate scenes, or outrageous, improbable behavior. Unless any of these contribute *directly* and *logically* to the story as a whole, choose another story. Pure chance, such as an automobile accident, is another circumstance that does little to make an intelligent point.

Generally, choose your topic with the following questions in mind:

- Does the story entertain and instruct?
- Can the story be told within the limits of the writing situation?
- Is there a single story line?

Setting

Place and time provide the backdrop or stage for your story. The greatest difficulty students have with setting is giving too much attention to physical description. The key to narration is *action;* so you do not want to overemphasize what the house or street or garage looked like. A quick mention of its irregularities or other qualities that communicate character or uniqueness is sufficient. Remember, a setting is only important in terms of its contribution to the mood and action of the narrative.

Character

Because the narrative assignments in this chapter are short, you will not have the opportunity to develop several major characters. You will probably develop only one or two personalities. One flaw of student narration is overpopulating the setting. Of course, the actual incident will determine the number of people involved, but consider the importance of each character. If additional characters do not contribute to the thrust of the narrative—the action— remove them. Sometimes you need to include persons who act as a backdrop for the action. If this is the case, treat these "walk-ons" as flat or stock characters. For example, the police officer, a group of students, a crowd of bargain hunters—all that is necessary is to identify them as members of a category.

Your main character may need more personalizing, the development of those traits that contribute to the actions of your story. Your reader may need some physical description to be able to visualize the person. Often, facial expression is enough, and then only when the character is speaking or responding to some action. You may find a quick reading of the next chapter, "The Character Sketch," helpful. But notice that the selections from Twain and Yevtushenko, later in this chapter, give little space to the physical aspects of character. They concentrate on action and dialogue.

Ultimately, your reader will react to inner motivation and corresponding behavior far more than to external physical characteristics. Your reader can learn about the motives of a character only through what the character says and does. The exception to this is a first-person narrator telling about himself or herself. Both Twain and Yevtushenko, first-person narrators, tell us things that no one else could know. They start with their state of mind and throughout the story tell us their thoughts and feelings. The assignments in this chapter generally require you to do at least one of the following:

- expose a character for what he or she is
- show a conflict within a character
- show the effect of a character's behavior on others
- show the effect of environment (setting or other characters) on a central character

As you can see, all of these rely heavily on the motivation and action of a character.

The plot of a narrative is the sequence or order of events that answers the question "What happens next?" You must decide how the story will begin, what conflicts will be introduced by which events, at what point the story will reach its climax, and how the story will end, that is, the resolution or solution to any remaining conflicts. The development of your narrative will probably look something like Figure 1 below.

Figure 1

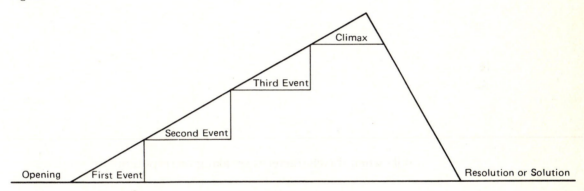

You may have a different number of intermediate events, but your story will start at the beginning and move forward to its finale. In the *opening,* give any background information required by the reader to follow your story. The traditional "when," "who," "what," and "where" should be covered early in the plot. Here are three examples:

One night after our week's theatrical season was over and forgotten, I began to experiment with make-up.

When young Dr. Sargent arrived at the college to assume his duties as a member of the faculty, he reversed a life-long custom.

When I was walking home the other night, I heard a person running toward me. I decided to hide.

Each of these statements gives the reader a general idea of the story, enough to understand the next event in the plot. Another approach is to begin immediately with the first event without providing background:

A few minutes before ten, the phone rang. Mary hurried to quiet it. "Hello?"

JAMES AGEE

A Death in the Family

Even though this example is not as complete as the three background sentences on the previous page, we do know enough to get started with the scene.

Some rhetoricians suggest the use of a purpose statement in the opening of the story. However, this can destroy the natural suspense of the plot. Here is an example:

Little did I know how difficult the enrolling process was to be!

Instead of a purpose statement, you can provide some focus and sustain suspense by foreshadowing the conflict of your narrative:

Everything was going well. I had paid my fees; my program plan was complete, and all my textbooks were sitting in the study, ready to be opened.

Notice how Mark Twain opens the selection from *Life on the Mississippi* with the implication that such a perfect mood is about to be shattered:

Well, one matchless summer's day I was bowling down the bend above Island 66, brimful of self-conceit and carrying my nose as high as a giraffe's, when Mr. Bixby said . . .

Once you have your opening, you will begin to examine the events, selecting some and eliminating others. Each event should do one of the following:

- expose the tastes, thinking, values, or behavior of the main characters
- interrupt or modify the freedom of the major character's desire to act
- introduce some detail or quality of setting that will force the action to move forward or change direction
- present some conflict or clash between opposing forces
- further complicate one of the above
- introduce mood or atmosphere
- create a turning point in the action
- provide necessary preparation or foreshadowing for one of the above

The *climax* is the peak of action. All the crises have occurred; all conflicts are apparent. If the narrative focuses on a problem to be solved by a character, he or she succeeds or fails at the climax of the story. In the selection from *Life on the Mississippi,* the climax occurs when Mark Twain completely loses his confidence, yet knows he was correct from the beginning. In the selection from *A Precocious Autobiography,* the climax occurs when Yevtushenko no longer feels like going to see Stalin's coffin. In both selections, the remaining material is a resolution, a brief statement of what the narrator learned. Notice that neither author belabors his message. There is no prolonged moralizing, no attempt to bore the reader by telling what the narrative means. If your narrative is well told, the reader will know what you had in mind.

E. M. Forster makes a useful distinction between a simple story and a plot:

Let us define a plot. We have defined a story as a narrative of events arranged in their time-sequence. A plot is also a narrative of events, the emphasis falling on causality. "The king died and then the queen died," is a story. "The king died, and then the queen died of grief" is a plot. The time-sequence is preserved, but the sense of causality overshadows it. Or again: "The queen died, no one knew why, until it was discovered that it was through grief at the death of the king." This is a plot with a mystery in it, a form capable of high development. It suspends the time-sequence, it moves as far away from the story as its limitations will allow. Consider the death of the queen. If it is in a story we say "and then?" If it is in a plot we ask "why?" That is the fundamental difference between these two aspects of the novel.

E. M. FORSTER
Aspects of the Novel

This does not mean that you must invent cause and effect, but you should make it clear, when possible.

You will find the plotting of your story much easier if you organize your initial thoughts as a generative paragraph. Even if your story eventually requires the structure of several short paragraphs, the plot (story line) will be similar to the following notation:

(1) topic sentence (may be implicit and not written)
    2 event
    2 event
    2 event
    2 event
(The quantity of events will vary from story to story.)

As you can readily see, this notation is bare bones; the second-level events need developing. The next step is to generate additional levels for each event, if necessary. While an infinite variety of notations are possible, the following example is typical:

(1)
  2
    3
      4
  2
    3
      4
        5
  2
    3
      4
  2
    3

PRACTICE   Read the following paragraph and notate the levels of generality:

When I was living in Jamaica, West Indies, my family was expecting a visitor from the United States to spend a couple of weeks with us. Because the rains fell three times a day, we didn't want to have the floors cleaned until the day of his arrival so a lot of mud wouldn't get tracked in. That morning when we asked the maid to do the floors, she put up her usual fuss. With some grumbling, she started to clean the floors. Jamaicans clean floors with kerosene and a brush made by sawing a coconut in half. After she finished with the floors, the smell of kerosene was almost too much to bear, but we figured that by the time we picked up our friend from the airport, a two hour drive, the fumes would be gone. We pulled into the driveway to see the maid come running off our front porch waving her arms frantically and shouting, "Mistah Belle, Mistah Belle, come quick. Dey is duppies * in dey house." "Mary, what are you talking about?" I asked. "Yes, suh, come quick," she replied, "dey is two large ones an one small one in deh." "Mary, are you crazy?" I asked. "There aren't any duppies in our house." "Not crazy, suh. Dey in deh alright; dey com in an take down all de pictures off de wall an put dem on de floor." "Mary, I don't know what you are talking about," I replied, "you had better come in and show me." "NOOO SUH," she said, "My nah go in dat house any more!" So we went in ourselves, and sure enough when we got inside, every picture in the house was sitting on the floor leaning up against the

* Household ghosts.

wall. After trying to figure it out for about fifteen minutes, we finally came up with the answer. The glue on each picture frame holder was loosened by the kerosene fumes. We knew that had to be the only explanation, but from that day Mary believed that there were two large duppies and one small one living somewhere in our house.

The point of this student narrative is implicit; therefore there is no first-level topic sentence.

2 background
   3 complication
      4 maid's reaction
2 cleaning begins
   3 method of cleaning
      4 unhappy result
2 agitated maid introduces "duppies" to narrator
   3 narrator asks for clarification
      4 maid enumerates and describes "duppies"
         5 narrator disagrees with the maid
            6 maid stands her ground, explaining what happened
               7 narrator suggests a visit to the house
                  8 maid refuses
2 narrator and family enter house and discover the pictures on the floor
   3 they try to solve the mystery
      4 the solution
         5 maid's inability to accept the solution

Point of View

The topic suggestions of this chapter suggest the use of a first-person narrator; that is, you will use the first-person pronoun "I" whenever appropriate. As a first-person narrator your role can be one of the following:

1. The central character and a participant in the major events of the narrative. The purpose of the writing rests on what you learned by experience.
2. A minor character, sometimes a participant in events. The purpose of the narrative rests on what you learned by observation.
3. An outside observer, never a participant in the action. The purpose is, once again, learning by observation.

The first role is probably the easiest and most natural for the assignment choices at hand. (Follow the lead of Twain and Yevtushenko.)

Dialogue

The portions of a narrative in which characters speak for themselves can be among the most interesting. It is a good technique to use conversation whenever it suggests itself. However, dialogue should either contribute to the action, moving the plot along, or it should reveal aspects of character. Try to make the dialogue as realistic as possible. This can be accomplished by reproducing the character's speech patterns, dialect, and variances in grammar usage, so that the reader can make inferences about character or personality. Always place dialogue in quotation marks and make sure the reader knows who the speaker is. This can be accomplished by the occasional use of dialogue tags (such as "Barbara said").

In the following selection the dialogue tags have been removed. Notice how difficult it is to keep track of the speakers:

"Do you like me?"

"Of course I do."

"Why?"

"Well, we have some qualities in common. Things that are spontaneous in each of us—or were originally."

"You're implying that I haven't used myself very well?"

"Well, I can't judge. A man, of course, has to go through a lot more, and I've been sheltered."

"Oh, don't stall, please, Clara, but do talk about me a little, won't you?"

"Surely, I'd adore to."

Imagine the confusion if this continued much longer without tags. The scene is repeated below as actually written by F. Scott Fitzgerald. While only two dialogue tags are used, we have two additional clues to speaker identity: "Clara hesitated" and "She didn't smile."

"Do you like me?"

"Of course I do," said Clara seriously.

"Why?"

"Well, we have some qualities in common. Things that are spontaneous in each of us—or were originally."

"You're implying that I haven't used myself very well?"

Clara hesitated.

"Well, I can't judge. A man, of course, has to go through a lot more, and I've been sheltered."

"Oh, don't stall, please, Clara," Amory interrupted; "but do talk about me a little, won't you?"

"Surely, I'd adore to." She didn't smile.

F. SCOTT FITZGERALD

This Side of Paradise

As you write your dialogue tags, consider using more descriptive words than "said" to show the manner of speaking. Furthermore, an absolute or verb phrase as a free modifier is an efficient way to show gestures or other relevant physical action. Really, the possibilities are endless, but here are a few examples from *All Creatures Great and Small* by James Herriot:

"Morning, Boardman," I said, as I opened the garage door.

"Aye, it is," Mr. Alkinson replied, obviously surprised.

"Efficiency," he said, crinkling his eyes.

"Thank you, thank you very much indeed," Tristan said in a flat voice, still looking straight to his front.

"Look at that!" I quavered.

Begin a new paragraph whenever you change speaker, time, location, or mood. Follow the models at the end of the chapter. Use transition devices whenever a change in time occurs. Remember, narration is the sequence of events in time; therefore, keep the reader aware of any changes. Typical examples of time-transition words and phrases are the following:

Paragraphing and Transitions

presently	in the meantime	beforehand
the next day	thereupon	with that out of the way
when I returned	meanwhile	following this
thereafter	at length	from then on
soon	by that time	at that very moment
soon afterward	at last	afterwards
shortly	earlier	immediately
later	before	within an hour

Read the following examples of narrative writing. Next, attempt to locate and identify the various narrative techniques discussed in this chapter:

Narratives by Two Professionals

Well, one matchless summer's day I was bowling down the bend above Island 66, brimful of self-conceit and carrying my nose as high as a giraffe's, when Mr. Bixby said:

"I am going below awhile. I suppose you know the next crossing?"

This was almost an affront. It was about the plainest and simplest crossing in the whole river. One couldn't come to any harm, whether he ran it right or not; and as for depth, there never had been any bottom there. I knew all this, perfectly well.

"Know how to *run* it? Why, I can run it with my eyes shut."

"How much water is there in it?"

"Well, that is an odd question. I couldn't get bottom there with a church steeple."

"You think so, do you?"

The very tone of the question shook my confidence. That was what Mr. Bixby was expecting. He left, without saying anything more. I began to imagine all sorts of things. Mr. Bixby, unknown to me, of course, sent somebody down to the forecastle with some mysterious instructions to the leadsmen, another messenger was sent to whisper among the officers, and then Mr. Bixby went into hiding behind a smokestack where he could observe results. Presently the captain stepped out on the hurricane-deck; next the chief mate appeared; then a clerk. Every moment or two a straggler was added to my audience; and before I got to the head of the island I had fifteen or twenty people assembled down there under my nose. I began to wonder what the trouble was. As I started across, the captain glanced aloft at me and said, with a sham uneasiness in his voice:

"Where is Mr. Bixby?"

"Gone below, sir."

But that did the business for me. My imagination began to construct dangers out of nothing, and they multiplied faster than I could keep the run of them. All at once I imagined I saw shoal water ahead! The wave of coward agony that surged through me then came near dislocating every joint in me. All my confidence in that crossing vanished. I seized the bell-rope; dropped it, ashamed; seized it again; dropped it once more; clutched it tremblingly once again, and pulled it so feebly that I could hardly hear the stroke myself. Captain and mate sang out instantly, and both together:

"Starboard lead there! and quick about it!"

This was another shock. I began to climb the wheel like a squirrel; but I would hardly get the boat started to port before I would see new dangers on that side, and away I would spin to the other; only to find perils accumulating to starboard, and be crazy to get to port again. Then came the leadsman's sepulchral cry:

"D-e-e-p four!"

Deep four in a bottomless crossing! The terror of it took my breath away.

"M-a-r-k three! M-a-r-k three! Quarter-less-three! Half twain!"

This was frightful! I seized the bell-ropes and stopped the engines.

"Quarter twain! Quarter twain! *Mark* twain!"

I was helpless. I did not know what in the world to do. I was quaking from head to foot, and I could have hung my hat on my eyes, they stuck out so far.

"Quarter-*less*-twain! Nine-and-a-*half!*"

We were *drawing* nine! My hands were in a nerveless flutter. I could not ring a bell intelligibly with them. I flew to the speaking-tube and shouted to the engineer:

"Oh, Ben, if you love me, *back* her! Quick, Ben! Oh, back the immortal *soul* out of her!"

I heard the door close gently. I looked around, and there stood Mr. Bixby, smiling a bland, sweet smile. Then the audience on the hurricane-deck sent up a thundergust of humiliating laughter. I saw it all, now, and I felt meaner than the meanest man in human history. I laid it in the lead, set the boat in her marks, came ahead on the engines, and said:

"It was a fine trick to play on an orphan, *wasn't* it? I suppose I'll never hear the last of how I was ass enough to heave the lead at the head of 66."

"Well, no, you won't, maybe. In fact I hope you won't; for I want you to learn something by that experience. Didn't you *know* there was no bottom in that crossing?"

"Yes, sir, I did."

"Very well, then. You shouldn't have allowed me or anybody else to shake your confidence in that knowledge. Try to remember that. And another thing: when you get into a dangerous place, don't turn coward. That isn't going to help matters any."

It was a good enough lesson, but pretty hardly learned.

MARK TWAIN

Life on the Mississippi

I will never forget going to see Stalin's coffin. I was in the crowd in Trubnaya Square. The breath of the tens of thousands of people jammed against one another rose up in a white cloud so thick that on it could be seen the swaying shadows of the bare March trees. It was a terrifying and a fantastic sight. New streams poured into this human flood from behind, increasing the pressure. The crowd turned into a monstrous whirlpool. I realized that I was being carried straight toward a traffic light. The post was coming relentlessly closer. Suddenly I saw that a young girl was being pushed against the post. Her face was distorted and she was screaming. But her screams were inaudible among all the other cries and groans. A movement of the crowd drove me against the girl; I did not hear but felt with my body the cracking of her brittle bones as they were broken on the traffic light. I closed my eyes in horror, the sight of her insanely bulging, childish blue eyes more than I could bear, and I was swept past. When I looked again the girl was no longer to be seen. The crowd must have sucked her under. Pressed against the traffic light was someone else, his body twisted and his arms outflung as on a cross. At that moment I felt I was treading on something soft. It was a human body. I picked my feet up under me and was carried along by the crowd. For a long time I was afraid to put my feet down again. The crowd closed tighter and tighter. I was saved by my height. Short people were smothered alive, falling and perishing. We were caught between the walls of houses on one side and a row of army trucks on the other.

"Get those trucks out of the way!" people howled. "Get them out of here!"

"I can't do it! I have no instructions," a very young, tow-headed police officer shouted back from one of the trucks, almost crying with helplessness. And people were being hurtled against the trucks by the crowd, and their heads smashed. The sides of the trucks were splashed with blood. All at once I felt a savage hatred for everything that had given birth to that "I have no instructions," shouted at a moment when people were dying because of someone's stupidity. For the first time in my life I thought with hatred of the man we were burying. He could not be innocent of the disaster. It was the "No instructions" that had caused the chaos and bloodshed at his funeral. Now I was certain, once and for all, that you must never wait for instructions if human lives are at stake—you must act. I don't know how I did it, but working energetically with my elbows and fists, I found myself thrusting people aside and shouting: "Form chains! Form chains!"

They didn't understand me. Then I started to join neighboring hands together by force, all the while spitting out the foulest swearwords of my geological days. Some tough young men were now helping me. And now people understood. They joined hands and formed chains. The strong men and I continued to work at it. The whirlpool was slowing down. The crowd was ceasing to be a savage beast. "Women and children into the trucks!" yelled one of the young men. And women and children, passed from hand to hand, sailed over our heads into the trucks. One of the women who were being handed on was struggling hysterically and whimpering. The young police officer who received her at his end stroked her hair, clumsily trying to calm her down. She shivered a few times and suddenly froze into stillness. The officer took the cap off his straw-colored head, covered her face with it, and burst out crying.

There was another violent whirlpool further ahead. We worked our way over, the tough boys and I, and again with the help of the roughest curses and fists, made people form chains in order to save them.

The police too finally began to help us.

Everything quieted down.

"You ought to join the police, Comrade. We could use fellows like you," a police sergeant said to me, wiping his face with his handkerchief after a bout of hard work.

"Right. I'll think it over," I said grimly.

Somehow, I no longer felt like going to see Stalin's remains. Instead, I left with one of the boys who had been organizing chains. We bought a bottle of vodka and walked to our place.

"Did you see Stalin?" my mother asked me.

"Yes," I said coldly, as I clinked glasses with the boy.

I hadn't really lied to my mother. I had seen Stalin. Because everything that had just happened—that was Stalin.

YEVGENY YEVTUSHENKO

A Precocious Autobiography

Self-Evaluation

Read the following student narratives and complete the questions after each story.

PART I

I found it in the old trunk in the attic when I was sorting through things after my mother's funeral. It was not surprising she had kept it all those years, and as I rubbed the scuffed brown leather it was like rubbing a genie lamp, and I could not stem the outpouring of memories brought back by the little shoe. Certainly, my relationship with my father was never the same after the day my brother died.

The day it happened was bright with the promise spring always brings. We were playing outdoors in the new sunshine and the neighborhood rang with the squeaks and squeals of children. My older sister, Eileen, and I were jumping rope across the street with the Wheeler girls. Our five-year-old brother was playing marbles in the Doherty's corner yard. Mr. Adler, the egg-man, had parked his old jalopy there, the wheels half on the cindered road, and half on the Doherty grass.

"Hi, Mr. Adler," we called as he delivered the Wheelers' eggs. He knew us all; he was part of the neighborhood composite. He waved and crossed the street to the old car. Then the nightmare descended with such speed we were helpless to stop it.

We saw Mr. Adler climb into his car from the cindered roadside. We saw Danny, our brother, crawl under the car from the grassy side to retrieve a marble. He heard the car start and tried frantically to wiggle backwards. He was too late. The car moved heavily over him.

"Danny, Danny!" Eileen screamed, running to lift his crumpled little body. The horrified screeches of children brought mothers to their porches, and I remember seeing Eileen hand her limp burden into my mother's arms. I picked up the pathetic, unlaced shoe that had fallen off Danny's foot on his journey home. I don't remember much for a while after that. I don't know how my mother got Danny to the hospital. I don't know how my father was notified at work. I don't recall being taken inside the house.

But I remember that Thelma came. She was the neighborhood girl who "had a way with children," and was studying to be a teacher. That day her games held no appeal and we had no appetite for the supper she put on the table. With our two younger sisters, Eileen and I sat in the terrible silence of a house full of children where one is missing. Sometimes we cried, and then it was quiet again.

"You've got to think of other people," Thelma said at last. "Try to be cheerful for your parents' sake. If they see you crying, it'll be so much harder for them. Be smiling when they come home," she coaxed.

I stared at my brother's shabby, untied shoe, still lying where I had dropped it by the door. Thelma's words began to make sense to me. I pondered the problem, heavy-hearted, and decided to be a brave seven-year-old.

Finally I went outside to watch for my parents' car, and when I saw it turn the corner at the crest of the hill, I began to run up and down the sidewalk, skipping, hopping and jumping.

"Merrily we roll along," I sang as the car pulled into the driveway. Then I saw the anguish in my mother's face and I knew that my brother was dead. I sang louder.

My father angrily called me to him, yelling above my song. "How can you behave this way when your brother is dead?" he bellowed. His fury exploded into the sort of scolding children grow old from.

"But Daddy," I protested, "I was doing it for you!"

I did not understand then, as I do now, that he was lashing out at me from the depths of his own grief. I lost more than my brother that day.

"The Little Shoe"

1. Read the list of suggested topics on page 109. Which topic best describes the story?

   Number _____ How? _____

   _____

   _____

   _____

2. Which point of view best describes the narrator's role in the story?
   a. central character
   b. minor character
   c. outside observer

3. a. Where and when does the story take place?

   _____

   b. How much time passes as the story is told?

   _____

4. How many major characters appear in the story (including the narrator)?

   _____

5. a. To what degree does the narrator employ dialogue?

   _____

   b. What is the effect of the dialogue?

   _____

6. The story begins with
   a. time, place, and first event.

b. time, place, and foreshadowing.

c. flashback.

7. Briefly describe the event that introduces the most significant conflict or complication in the story.

_____

_____

_____

8. How does the story end? Are all conflicts resolved?

_____

_____

_____

PART II

Sunday afternoon and it was Luxembourg. I went up to the ticket desk at the airport.

"I have an open ticket to New York and would like to go back as soon as possible. When does the next plane leave?" I asked a tired-looking man behind the desk.

He wiped his brow as he examined my ticket to see if it was valid. "The last plane for the States left 20 minutes ago," he replied in accented English. "There is a flight for New York leaving at 10:15 tomorrow morning. We'll have to put you on stand-by though. Here, sign this list," he said, thrusting a clip-board towards me. "There, you are number two. Come back here tomorrow morning at 9:00 and we'll put you on the plane if anyone has cancelled their reservations."

I hadn't really planned on spending the night here but it looked as if I had no choice, besides, I was too tired to get upset with the man.

The next morning I was early. There was some commotion in front of the ticket desk. People were crowding and pushing, trying to get up to the front. Loud voices.

"Look, you promised we could leave today."

"I've been waiting here since last Friday."

"Yeah," another one shouted, "don't you remember? I called here Saturday from Dusseldorf and you confirmed my reservations."

"What's the matter?" I asked a man closest to me.

"Oh, it seems like the company has overbooked the plane by forty seats and all these people want to go home today. Of course, they can't. There is nothing we can do but wait. Wait until another plane comes and the first forty can get on. Can you imagine? A plane being overbooked by forty seats!"

The man at the desk had his arms up trying to calm the crowd. "Please, be a little quieter. I know this is very unfortunate and many of you are inconvenienced but there is nothing I can do. I didn't overbook the plane. I'm sorry. Please, be calm. Go back to your hotels. Come back tomorrow."

"Go back to our hotels?" some shouted. "We have no more money! We'll stay here and wait."

"O.K.," the man behind the desk agreed. "Go in the back room and I'll see what I can do."

Most of the people were Americans, and most of them looked to be college students. They took their back-packs and went into the back room, sitting in a large circle on the floor, some playing cards, others eating, some trying to nap. Mothers tended crying babies and restless children.

I remained seated on my trunk by the door somehow remaining calm. I knew I would get out someday. When, I didn't know. There was another plane that left in the afternoon. Maybe there would be a place on that one.

A few minutes later, the man came back to the desk calling to the people, "There is a plane leaving for Chicago at 1:30. If any of you have $67, we can put you on that flight."

The people were interested by this proposition. Although Chicago was not their destination, at least it was in the United States and once there they would have no problems getting home. Several of them approached the desk asking, "Will you take a check, Master Charge?"

"No, we cannot accept those. We must have cash."

The people grew angry again, uneasy. They went back to wait.

The next morning, the crowd was larger, the shouts were louder. The people, red-faced, were pushing and shoving to get to the desk, shouting obscenities and calling the people on the other side liars. Tempers were flying. Nerves were strained. The harried man at the desk could hardly stand up to them and retain the calmness expected of him. He was just a ticket agent he explained, not responsible for what was happening.

One lady shouted, "You just better get me out of here today or I won't be responsible for my actions!"

The crowd agreed. The crowd was uneasy. The crowd was on the verge of a riot.

The agent responded, "There is no room on the plane leaving this morning. By a quarter to one I will know if there is room on the afternoon flight." His voice was hoarse from trying to shout above the crowd, his face was now beaded with sweat, his hair separated into wet strands.

Never had a clock been so closely watched. The people waited tensely. At a quarter to one, the man had good news. The first fifty people on the waiting list could board the three o'clock flight. Relief escaped from the people like steam under pressure as they pushed and shoved their way upstairs to the terminal. I was carried along with the crowd, inching my way, trying not to lose my suitcase or drop the ticket clutched tightly in my hand or the precious piece of paper with the number two written on it. Once past the inspection station, the mood shifted. People smiled. People laughed.

"Airport"

1. Read the list of suggested topics on page 109. Which topic best describes the story?

Number _____ How? _____

_____

_____

_____

2. Which point of view best describes the narrator's role in the story?
   a. central character
   b. minor character
   c. outside observer

3. a. Where does the story take place?

_____

   b. How much time passes as the story is told?

_____

4. How many major characters appear in the story (including the narrator?) _____

5. a. To what degree does the narrator employ dialogue?

_____

   b. What is the effect of the dialogue?

_____

6. The story begins with
   a. time, place, and first event.
   b. time, place, and foreshadowing.
   c. flashback.
7. Briefly describe the event that introduces the most significant conflict or complication in the story.

_____

_____

_____

8. How does the story end? Are all conflicts resolved?

_____

_____

_____

PART III

It was a warm summer afternoon, just welcoming an exciting game of cops and robbers or kick-the-can. The usual neighborhood gang began to gather on our front porch. Just as we started to organize our day's activities, one of the boys happened to glance up the street.

   "Aw heck!" he said with a tone of disappointment. "Here comes Jimmy."

Jimmy was a snot-nosed little brat who never got along with any of the gang. None of us wanted anything to do with him and he was just too naive to realize it.

In quick desperation I said, "Hurry, hide in the garage!" Everyone scattered and I ran inside the house.

Within a few minutes I heard the doorbell ring. After making certain that things were quiet in the garage, I opened the door.

"Hi," said Jimmy. "Are you coming out?"

Groping for some excuse to turn him away, I said, "Not today. I've got to stay in the house and help my mother with some things."

"Where are all the kids?" he asked.

"Don't know," I said hurriedly. "Haven't seen 'em all day. Maybe we'll be out tomorrow."

"O.K.," he said as he sadly turned away.

I shut the door, proud that I had put on such a good show. After Jimmy had gone out of sight, I returned to the garage.

"He's gone," I said.

With a sigh of relief, we again began to organize our plans. It was decided that we play kick ball. Teams were chosen and three bases were set up on the street.

Shortly after the game was under way, we heard the sirens. They seemed to be growing closer, and within a couple of minutes the ambulance appeared on our street. Forgetting about our game, we chashed after the red lights speeding up the road.

"Hurry!" I shouted. "I think it stopped just around the corner!"

When we reached the top of the hill, I noticed that the flashing red lights had stopped in front of Jimmy's house. Jimmy's older sister stood in the front yard, screaming at the top of her lungs.

"My God!" she cried. "My God, it hit him!"

Looking over towards the commotion in the middle of the street I saw an old Ford station wagon, and at the front of the car, under the wheels, lay Jimmy.

"Get that stretcher over here!" yelled one of the ambulance attendants. "Clear these people out of here! Quiet that girl down and see if you can find out what happened!"

They put a mask over Jimmy's face, lifted him onto the stretcher, and put him into the ambulance. Within seconds, its sirens began to howl, and it raced down the street.

By that time, the crowd that had gathered began to filter away. We walked away in silence.

I was helping my mother set the dinner table that evening when we heard on the news that Jimmy had died on the way to the hospital. "What a tragic thing to happen," my mother said as the family gathered to the table. She looked my way and said, "I thought that Jimmy was playing with you kids this afternoon?"

"No," I said hesitantly as I hung my head low. "I hadn't seen 'im all day."

"Haven't Seen 'Em All Day"

1. Read the list of suggested topics on page 109. Which topic best describes the story?

Number _____ How? _____

_____

_____

_____

2. Which point of view best describes the narrator's role in the story?
   a. central character
   b. minor character
   c. outside observer
3. a. Where does the story take place?

   _____

   b. How much time passes as the story is told?

   _____

4. How many major characters appear in the story (including the narrator)?

   _____

5. a. To what degree does the narrator employ dialogue?

   _____

   b. What is the effect of the dialogue?

   _____

6. The story begins with
   a. time, place, and first event.
   b. time, place, and foreshadowing.
   c. flashback.
7. Briefly describe the event that introduces the most significant conflict or complication in the story.

   _____

   _____

   _____

8. How does the story end? Are all conflicts resolved?

   _____

   _____

   _____

Answers

1. Topics 2, 4, or 7. Narrator learns, or at least sees, the workings of the adult world. In the process, the narrator loses the innocence and trust that is typical of most children.
2. a
3. a. at the narrator's home, during early childhood
   b. less than one day
4. Two—narrator and father (Thelma could be considered a third major character because she is characterized, she speaks, and she introduces the complication—the instruction to be cheerful.)
5. Much of the story is *reported* by the narrator. The relatively small amount of dialogue is, however, crucial to portraying the situation.
6. c. (The first paragraph takes place after the rest of the story. From the second paragraph on, the events unfold themselves in strict chronological order.)
7. Thelma's suggestion that the narrator be cheerful introduces the seeds of the conflict with the father. Danny's death is not the point of the story. Indeed, the reader is informed of his death in the first paragraph.
8. The conflict is not resolved. The narrator understands why the father acted as he did, but there is no attempt at a contrived, happy ending. What the narrator learned was a lesson in life.

PART II

1. Topics 3 and 6. The behavior of the passengers and the airline are central to the story. While the airline does not adequately deal with the people, the passengers become a mob.
2. b
3. a. crowded airline terminal in Luxembourg
   b. two full days
4. one, the ticket agent (The narrator, who might be considered a major character, is in the same predicament as the other passengers. Therefore, the storyteller contributes no more than the other stranded passengers.)
5. Approximately half of the writing is dialogue. The dialogue moves the action along and serves to characterize the participants.
6. a
7. No single event causes the conflict. Instead, the problem grows as it is further complicated by the series of delays and excuses. The first delay does not upset the narrator.
8. The immediate difficulty is resolved; the airline accommodates the passengers. Yet we wonder if this won't happen again, and if the people will be just as helpless.

PART III

1. Topics 2, 3, or 8. The story shows the typical behavior of a child and the terrible sense of guilt children can experience. Indirectly, the narrator shows how difficult, even painful, the lessons of life can be.

2. a
3. a. narrator's neighborhood, during early childhood
   b. three or four hours
4. one, the narrator (Jimmy is characterized and appears briefly. But most of the story rides on the actions and reactions of the narrator.)
5. At least half of the writing is dialogue. It moves the action along, characterizes the speakers, and, of course, communicates the ironic denial, "Haven't seen 'em all day."
6. b (There is some suggestion that this marvelous afternoon is about to be disturbed by what one of the boys sees as he glances up the street.)
7. the narrator's lie to Jimmy
8. The lie must be retold, and so there is no resolution. The irony is intensified by the repetition of the same words.

WRITING ASSIGNMENT

Select one of the following topics and write a narrative that comes from your own experience or observations. Consult your instructor about paper length and any alternative topics.

1. an experience in which your moral, social, political, or philosophical views differed from those of your friends
2. an experience that caused you to learn something about life (Example: Life is not always "fair.")
3. an experience that caused you to learn something about human nature (Example: Some people will never learn.)
4. an experience that caused you to radically change your estimation of someone you *thought* you knew.
5. an experience in which you show how the complexity or fast pace of contemporary life deterred from the quality of your life
6. an experience in which you show how some organization or institution failed to deal with people as human beings
7. an experience in which you first had to assume the responsibilities of the adult world
8. an experience that caused you to learn something about yourself
9. an experience in which part of your formal education became relevant, useful, or even understandable
10. the happiest or funniest moment in your life (Be sure that your story entertains *and* instructs.)

·•❧[7]❧•··
The Character Sketch

One of the most valuable assets you can have is the ability to evaluate and portray people. Such judgment of character, whether on first acquaintance or from long friendship, is constantly demanded of you. In college you must choose friends, candidates, instructors, counselors; later you will be called on to select employers and employees, public officials, and a husband or wife.

The character sketch is merely a means of presenting, in written form, your version of what a person is like. A letter home about your roommate, your friends, your instructors; a report on the qualifications of a fellow student for campus office; an answer to an examination question requiring the characterization of a figure in history, current affairs, or literature—all involve the same general mental process.

Objectives   After completing this chapter, you should be able

1. to select details that define or emphasize character through physical appearance
2. to select details that define or emphasize character through behavior
3. to employ appropriate techniques of description and narration in the writing of a character sketch

————————❧————————

The character sketch is a logical sequel to Chapters 5 and 6, "Description" and "Narration," in that the character sketch requires careful selection of both descriptive details and narrative incidents. Successful characterization is primarily analysis, reducing the many facets of personality to the few, very revealing characteristics that make the person an individual.

It is a natural tendency to first survey physical features—facial expression, skin tone, wrinkles, scars, or any sign of the effect of life upon the individual. Dirt under a fingernail, unkempt hair, bloodshot eyes, even body odor can provide insight into a person's self-image. Next, you can inspect the costume of the subject, noting the style, quality, and condition of clothing. Observe watches, rings (especially wedding bands), and any other adornment. Finally, look at posture and the way people walk, sit, and gesture with their hands—in general, a person's body language.

Notice in the following example how the writer selects certain physical details that emphasize the character of the old man:

The very appearance of John Webber, in spite of physical peculiarities which struck one at first sight as strange, even a little startling, suggested qualities in him as solid and substantial as the houses that he built. Although he was slightly above the average height, he gave the impression of being shorter than he was. This came from a variety of causes, chief of which was a somewhat "bowed" formation of his body. There was something almost simian in his short legs, bowed slightly outward, his large, flat-looking feet, the powerful, barrel-like torso, and the tremendous gorilla-like length of his arms, whose huge paws dangled almost even with his knees. He had a thick, short neck that seemed to sink right down into the burly shoulders, and close sandy-reddish hair that grew down almost to the edges of his cheekbones and to just an inch or two above the eyes. He was getting bald even then, and there was a wide and hairless swathe right down the center of his skull. He had extremely thick and bushy eyebrows, and the trick of peering out from under them with the head outthrust in an attitude of intensely still attentiveness.

THOMAS WOLFE

The Web and the Rock

In the next sketch, Robert Penn Warren goes even further, describing both the physical features and the style, quality, and condition of clothing of the individual. You should also sense a stronger picture of the effect of life upon the person:

You have seen him a thousand times. You have seen him standing on the street corner on Saturday afternoon, in the little county-seat towns. He wears blue-jean pants, or overalls washed to a pale pastel blue like the color of sky after a shower in spring, but because it is Saturday he has on a wool coat, an old one, perhaps the coat left from the suit he got married in a long time back. His long wristbones hang out from the sleeves of the coat, the tendons showing along the bone like the dry twist of grapevine still corded on the stove-length of a hickory sapling you would find in his woodbox beside his cookstove among the split chunks of gum and red oak. The big hands, with the knotted, cracked joints and the square, horn-thick nails, hang loose off the wristbone like clumsy, homemade tools hung on the wall of a shed after work. If it is summer, he wears a straw hat with a wide brim, the straw fraying loose around the edge. If it is winter, he wears a felt hat, black once, but now weathered with streaks of dark gray and dull purple in the sunlight. His face is long and bony, the jawbone long under the drawn-in cheeks. The flesh along the jawbone is nicked in a couple of places where the unaccustomed razor has been drawn over the leather-coarse skin. A tiny bit of blood crusts brown where the nick is. The color of the face is red, a dull red like the red clay mud or clay dust which clings to the bottom of his pants and to the cast-iron-looking brogans on his feet, or a red like the color of a piece of hewed cedar which has been left in the weather. The face does not look alive. It seems to be molded from the clay or hewed from the cedar. When the jaw moves once, with its deliberate, massive motion on the quid of tobacco, you are still not convinced. That motion is but the cunning triumph of a mechanism concealed within.

ROBERT PENN WARREN

The Patented Gate and the Mean Hamburger

In this selection, notice how the description of the woman tells something about the character of the man:

She was tall, pronounced of bone, and erect of carriage; it was somehow impossible to speculate upon her appearance undressed. Her long face was innocent, indeed ignorant, of cosmetics, and its color stayed steady. Confusion, heat, or haste caused her neck to flush crimson. Her mild hair was pinned with loops of nicked black wire into a narrow knot, practical to support her little high cap, like a charlotte russe from a bake-shop. She had big, trustworthy hands, scrubbed and dry, with nails cut short and so deeply cleaned with some small sharp instrument that the ends stood away from the spatulate finger-tips. Gerald Cruger, who nightly sat opposite her at his own dinner table, tried not to see her hands. It irritated him to be reminded by their sight that they must feel like straw matting and smell of white soap. For him, women who were not softly lovely were simply not women.

DOROTHY PARKER

Horsie

When using physical appearance to communicate character, take care not to make an unfounded judgment. Just because a person does not measure up to some physical ideal does not mean that he or she lacks other qualities that are admirable. Physical appearance is often used to *emphasize* character traits. As such, it frequently is used in combination with representative behavior of the person.

If it is generally agreed that we should not judge one another on appearance alone, then we must consider behavior. Bravery, honesty, warmth, kindness, sensitivity, generosity, intellect, humility, and self-knowledge are often exposed by the way a person behaves. Indeed, such qualities or the lack of them ultimately cause us to respond positively or negatively, even to the point of acceptance or rejection. For example, if a person tends to boast about accomplishments, willfully hurts another person, and generally seeks to satisfy only his or her own needs, you probably would think negatively of this individual. However, one isolated instance of such behavior is not enough to convince your reader; you must build a case. By selecting specific but representative acts, you can bring the entire person into focus. The more varied the examples, the more comprehensive the profile. A character sketch can become, therefore, a carefully organized collection of anecdotes. The *anecdote* is short and to the point:

Typical of Einstein is the story of the popular lecture he was finally prevailed upon to give, for it shows his incapability of behavior that was not genuine. He had been asked many times to speak to a certain audience, but had always begged off on the basis that he had nothing to say. Finally, however, the pressure became so great that he was forced to accede. Came the evening of the lecture, and amidst applause Dr. Einstein was led to the front of the stage and introduced. For a few moments he looked out at the audience, tongue-tied and silent. Finally he could stand it no longer and, smiling sheepishly, said, "I find that I have nothing to say," and returned to his seat.

GEORGE R. HARRISON

Albert Einstein: Appraisal of an Intellect

In this selection, the writer presents a short anecdote that illustrates a part of Einstein's character. Two things are accomplished—Harrison *tells* us of Einstein's personal integrity and *shows* us an appropriate incident to prove the point. There follows an even shorter anecdote, which reveals the individual's expertise in the weaving room:

Mary recalls, "Daddy could step into the building and listen and know what loom was running, what loom was down, and what was wrong with it."

CLAY ANDERSON
"In the Mountains" in *The Craftsman in America*

In the following example, Willa Cather characterizes Mrs. Harling with a combination of descriptive details and narrative incidents. Notice that the narrative incidents (anecdotes) are not completely developed. In your character sketch you will wish to expand the narrative incidents:

Mrs. Harling was short and square and sturdy-looking, like her house. Every inch of her was charged with an energy that made itself felt the moment she entered a room. Her face was rosy and solid, with bright, twinkling eyes and a stubborn little chin. She was quick to anger, quick to laughter, and jolly from the depths of her soul. How well I remember her laugh; it had in it the same sudden recognition that flashed into her eyes, was a burst of humour, short and intelligent. Her rapid footsteps shook her own floors, and she routed lassitude and indifference wherever she came. She could not be negative or perfunctory about anything. Her enthusiasm, and her violent likes and dislikes, asserted themselves in all the everyday occupations of life. Wash-day was interesting, never dreary, at the Harlings'. Preserving-time was a prolonged festival, and house-cleaning was like a revolution. When Mrs. Harling made garden that spring, we could feel the stir of her undertaking through the willow hedge that separated our place from hers.

WILLA CATHER
My Antonia

So far we have seen how physical appearance, costume, habits, and actions can reveal character. There are additional areas that you can examine:

- What people say often gives a clear indication of their values, especially if their actions are consistent with their statements.
- How a person talks can give an idea of education, culture, and mental abilities.
- The way a person approaches his or her work can give important information concerning dedication, skill, and attention to detail.
- The possessions and condition of a person's home or office can give telling clues to personality.
- The attitude or response to an individual by other people can

communicate much about personality, sometimes without the individual ever appearing in the narrative incident.

In the following short sketch, the author uses several of the aforementioned techniques to characterize Willard Watson:

The day I wandered down the gravel road, Willard had been up at four in the morning working in the weathered building with the sign that announces "Willard Watson's/Woodworks/Within."

Encouraged by folk-toy entrepreneur Jack Guy of Beech Creek, North Carolina, Willard began making wooden toys about ten years ago. He has picked up a pattern here and there, worked out many more on his own, varied them frequently. His toys would do credit to a trained engineer: a quartet of chickens alternately pecking feed from a bucket, a walking mule, a kicking pig, a climbing lizard, and dozens of others for young and old.

Willard won't belong to any organization or guild. "I can stay right at home here and do all I want to do. When I get behind real bad and everybody a-wantin' somethin', I get awful tired of it.

"It's just a matter of what you want to do. A satisfied mind is one of the finest things that's ever been. I work here. When I get tired, I don't have to ax my cap'n when I wanta go . . ."

It grew time for me to go. Ora was bending over the quilting frame. I set off along the winding gravel road, and Willard went up on the side of the mountain "to finish diggin' a row and a half of taters."

CLAY ANDERSON

"In the Mountains" in *The Craftsman in America*

In the next selection Lytton Strachey uses *only* the habit of "saving things" to examine a facet of Queen Victoria's character. Note that the peculiarity of the habit lies in her *manner* of displaying the objects. The extensive listing, the careful arrangements, even the use of a camera to insure the exact position of the objects in the room—all point to an eccentric, if not unbalanced, mind:

She gave orders that nothing should be thrown away—and nothing was. There, in drawer after drawer, in wardrobe after wardrobe, reposed the dresses of seventy years. But not only the dresses—the furs and the mantles and subsidiary frills and the muffs and the parasols and the bonnets—all were ranged in chronological order, dated and complete. A great cupboard was devoted to the dolls; in the china room at Windsor a special table held the mugs of her childhood, and her children's mugs as well. Mementoes of the past surrounded her in serried accumulations. In every room the tables were powdered thick with the photographs of relatives; their portraits, revealing them at all ages, covered the walls; their figures, in solid marble, rose up from pedestals, or gleamed from brackets in the form of gold and silver statuettes. The dead, in every shape—in miniatures, in porcelain, in enormous life-size oil-paintings— were perpetually about her. John Brown stood upon her writing-table in solid gold. Her favorite horses and dogs, endowed with a new durability, crowded round her footsteps. Sharp, in silver gilt, dominated the dinner table; Boy and Boz lay together among unfading flowers, in bronze. And it was not enough that each particle of the past should be given the stability of metal or of marble: the whole collection, in its arrangement, no less than its entity, should be immutably fixed. There might be additions, but there might never be alterations. No chintz might change, no carpet, no curtain, be replaced by another; or, if long use at last made it necessary, the stuffs and the patterns must be so identically reproduced that the keenest eye might not detect the difference. No new picture could be hung upon the walls at Windsor, for those already there had been put in their places by Albert, whose decisions were eternal. So, indeed, were Victoria's. To ensure that they should be the aid of the camera was called in. Every single article in the Queen's possession was photographed from several points of view. These photographs were submitted to Her Majesty, and when, after careful inspection, she had approved of them, they were placed in a series of albums, richly bound. Then, opposite each photograph, an entry was made, indicating the number of the article, the number of the room in which it was kept, its exact position in the room and all its principal characteristics. The fate of every object which had undergone this process was henceforth irrevocably sealed. The whole multitude, once and for all, took up its steadfast station. And Victoria, with a gigantic volume or two of the endless catalogue always beside her, to look through, to ponder upon, to expatiate over, could feel, with a double contentment, that the transitoriness of this world had been arrested by the amplitude of her might.

LYTTON STRACHEY
Queen Victoria

PRACTICE

In the following long paragraph, Yeats creates a well-rounded character sketch, employing most of the techniques discussed in this chapter. Make a list of the techniques employed by the author. Key your list to the numbers of the sentences. In addition, notate the structure of the paragraph. Hint: each anecdote begins on the second level:

[1]Some of my misery was loneliness and some of it fear of old William Pollexfen, my grandfather. [2]He was never unkind, and I cannot remember that he ever spoke harshly to me, but it was the custom to fear and admire

him. [3]He had won the freedom of some Spanish city, for saving life perhaps, but was so silent that his wife never knew it till he was near eighty, and then from the chance visit of an old sailor. [4]She asked him if it was true and he said it was true, but she knew him too well to question and his old shipmate had left the town. [5]She too had the habit of fear. [6]We knew that he had been in many parts of the world, for there was a great scar on his hand made by a whaling-hook, and in the dining-room was a cabinet with bits of coral in it and a jar of water from the Jordan for the baptizing of his children and Chinese pictures upon ricepaper and an ivory walking-stick from India that came to me after his death. [7]He had great physical strength and had the reputation of never ordering a man to do anything he would not do himself. [8]He owned many sailing ships and once, when a captain just come to anchor at Rosses Point reported something wrong with the rudder, had sent a messenger to say "Send a man down to find out what's wrong." [9]"The crew all refuse" was the answer, and to that my grandfather answered, "Go down yourself," and not being obeyed, he dived from the main deck, all the neighborhood lined along the pebbles of the shore. [10]He came up with his skin torn but well informed about the rudder. [11]He had a violent temper and kept a hatchet at his bedside for burglars and would knock a man down instead of going to law, and I once saw him hunt a party of men with a horsewhip. [12]He had no relation for he was an only child and, being solitary and silent, he had few friends. [13]He corresponded with Campbell of Islay who had befriended him and his crew after a shipwreck, and Captain Webb, the first man who had swum the Channel and who was drowned swimming the Niagara Rapids, had been a mate in his employ and a close friend. [14]That is all the friends I can remember and yet he was so looked up to and admired that when he returned from taking the waters at Bath his men would light bonfires along the railway line for miles; while his partner William Middleton whose father after the great famine had attended the sick for weeks, and taken cholera from a man he carried in his arms into his own house and died of it, and was himself civil to everybody and a cleverer man than my grandfather, came and went without notice. [15]I think I confuse my grandfather with God, for I remember in one of my attacks of melancholy praying that he might punish me for my sins, and I was shocked and astonished when a daring little girl—a cousin I think—having waited under a group of trees in the avenue, where she knew he would pass near four o'clock on the way to his dinner, said to him, "If I were you and you were a little girl, I would give you a doll."

WILLIAM BUTLER YEATS
Autobiography

1. Introductory sentence—announces subject.
2. Topic sentence—narrows character traits by stating the typical response of others (fear and admiration).

PRACTICE ANSWERS

3–5. Anecdote demonstrates relationship of husband and wife.

6. Describes Pollexfen's extensive travel through the objects and curios he collected.

7–10. Anecdote pointing out Pollexfen's physical strength and integrity. Notice the dialogue.

11. Again, Pollexfen is shown as independent and rugged.

12. This information suggests a pattern; rarely close to people, little reliance on others.

13. Pollexfen's only friends are other rugged individualists.

14. Comparison of responses of his men further emphasizes the quality and effect of Pollexfen's strong personality.

15. A touch of irony appears in this last anecdote. Yeats, as a child, sees William Pollexfen as a fearful figure capable of punishment while the little girl apparently sees through the grandfather's tough exterior.

NOTATION:
2
  1
    2 (anecdote)
      3
        4
    2
    2 (anecdote)
      3
        4
          5
    2 (anecdote)
    2 (anecdote)
      3
    2 (anecdote)
    2 (anecdote)

Here is a character sketch written by a student. The approach employed is primarily attention to physical appearance. Notice also the topic limitation in the first sentence:

Even in civilian attire, he was unmistakably a military man. His existence was justified by, and would be carried out according to, the standards and traditions of military society. He was inordinately pleased by total strangers who addressed him as "Sarge." His strong-jawed face was topped with sparse receding hair, a condition entirely due, in his opinion, to the continual pressure of his flight engineer's hardhat. Brown eyes with 20–20 vision looked out through the "regular-issue" aviation sunglasses, which had left a groove above his ears that returned to normal only during his two 15-day leaves each year. Perhaps a civilian would consider the waxed, drooping mustache an incongruity, but it was a mark of "flair"—that quality known to other Air Wing personnel as just the bit of ingenious aggressiveness required to be outstanding but never to approach rebellion. His sport coat bore the American Legion lapel pin, identifying him to his peers in the same manner as did the ribbons on his uniform blouse. For more casual wear, he donned a leather flight jacket. His shirt tucked smoothly into plain-colored trousers (no Continental or mod styles here), secured by a belt extending exactly 3⅝" beyond the buckle. The trouser hem above the mirror gloss on his shoes fell to the top of the shoe heel in back and rose ⅝" toward the front, as set forth in Uniform Regulations. In addition, perhaps as an afterthought, he wore a wedding ring—a staff sergeant should be married at this point in his career or he'd be thought a little odd by promotion review boards. Essentially, his mode of dress was not so much body covering as a statement that the Marine Corps occupied a position in his life equivalent to mother, education, hobby and religion. He was conceived of the recruiter, born of the Commandant, suffered under the Drill Instructor, was helicopter-crashed, died and was not buried. On the third day, he did not rise again, and his widow continued to mow the grass in rows, leaving the cuttings in neat ranks across the lawn.

This sketch, also written by a student, emphasizes behavior. Notice the effect of the anecdotes:

Commander John G. Mason looked like a pushover. Somebody we enlisted types could finally deal with.

It seemed that everyone's first impression of him was the same. His short, slightly rotund stature, clipped British mustache, and manner of not presuming on anyone led one to believe he had just walked away from his afternoon tea. I often thought of him as Herman Milquetoast. I first met him when he was introduced to me and my crew as our new Assistant Air Boss, aboard the U.S.S. *Shangri-La*.

From the first encounter we knew he was no "hardnose" officer. And having known mostly only hardnose officers, I assumed this was a man I could manipulate. Such a mistake. In fact, this man magnificently manipulated me.

The new "Boss" immediately gained my favor when he commenced to loosen the military atmosphere on the control tower. Because our function was the life-and-death movement of high-performance jet aircraft, the Boss felt that we should spend less time recognizing military etiquette, and more time concentrating on our job. His was certainly a fresh approach.

Commander Mason would frequently spend hours with us after flight operations relating incidents in his career which, through his wit, intelligence, and love of speaking, were never boring. Rather, they were exciting enough to keep us up long after we had intended to retire. But beyond recounting those incidents personal to him, he would share with us the experience of his years concerning love, hate, education, politics, and any other topic he thought would be beneficial to us in life. He could at once speak like an old philosopher, counsel like a father, listen sympathetically like a priest, and sympathize like a friend.

Though normally quite mild-mannered, he could erupt with the force of a grenade when pushed to his limit. But he infrequently did so because his biting satire was usually all that was necessary to get his way. I recall an incident concerning the submission of a tardy report by one of his junior officers. After playing word games over the telephone with the errant Lieutenant, the Commander abruptly ended the conversation with, "Well, Ed, I don't care how long it takes you to get the report, but have it at my stateroom in five minutes." The Lieutenant was at the stateroom, report in hand, within the allotted time.

Commander Mason was annoyed to think that anyone might put him on some kind of pedestal because of his officer status. One such incident occurred prior to entering Hong Kong. The Boss told us that he would show us around that city and have a few drinks with us. One young man of my crew was so impressed with the idea that he was moved to exclaim, "Golly, you mean we gonna go drinkin' with an officuh?" The Boss fixed the lad with a withering look and snapped, "Officers are no different than you, son. We all put our trousers on one leg at a time."

I have many fond memories of "my old dad" as he frequently referred to himself. I'm a richer person for having known him. And I still find myself comparing others to my memory of him. Perhaps that's what constitutes a pleasant memory.

The following student piece also emphasizes behavior through the use of anecdotes. Several of the incidents are typical rather than specific, one-time events. Notice the effect of the dialogue as it reinforces the military image of Mrs. Elgin:

My grandmother Elgin was a person I will always remember, a short, stocky, white haired lady of some untold years, with the work lines of raising eleven children clearly etched into her face and hands. Not that the years or kids had slowed her down a bit, no sir, she was still the commanding general of the house and everyone around her. She scurried around her kitchen issuing orders crisply, starting the fire in her old wood stove, no gas for her, and kneading the bread for supper. Her strong stubby fingers would poke, squeeze, then slap the dough into the proper shape. All this time she was surveying the area, checking with everyone to make sure all the chores were completed. "Jess, did you get that old sow back in?" "How about the wood box? Is it filled?" "Did you ever get those pickles and tomatoes from the garden like I asked you to, John?"

"We need them for supper." I don't know what would have happened if our tasks hadn't been completed, they always were; she just didn't leave any doubt in your mind about what you were supposed to do. When supper was ready she was the last one to sit down, and the first one to crack the hand of any unfortunate who reached for something to eat before grace had been said. She always seemed to me like a little wrinkled whirlwind, buzzing around continuously, so much in fact I often wondered if she slept. She would be up and have breakfast ready before I was awake every morning, especially on Sunday, which was her day. I don't believe she ever missed church, and I know she had forgotten more about the Bible than the preacher ever knew. If you didn't have religion before you came to visit grandma, you had it when you left.

At nine-o'clock sharp, every Sunday, all available personnel were unceremoniously herded into her old 1940 Chevy and carried to church, there to receive, as she called it, "The bread of life." I never remember her being mean or harsh, she was a kindly old woman, always in control of everything, never leaving any room for speculation.

Write a character sketch. Select an individual whom you know very well. Do not use the real name of the subject or any other person in your sketch. Instead, create fictitious names to insure the privacy of your subject. You should be able to gather enough information from your own observation; an interview is not necessary.

Limit your paper topic by focusing on some estimation of the person's character. However, do not vaguely categorize the individual as either good or bad. *Be specific!*

The assignment may take one of two approaches:

1. You may follow the example by Robert Penn Warren and focus on appearance.
2. You may follow the example by Yeats and focus on behavior.

Be sure to confer with your instructor about which approach to take.

·⋅❧[8]❧·⋅
The Expository Paragraph

A great part of your life is spent in making conclusions about what goes on around you. Still another significant part is spent in communicating those conclusions, trying to convince someone of their validity. The process of stating a conclusion and supporting its validity is called *exposition*. Much of the writing you will do in college or on the job will be of an expository nature. Whether you are writing a history paper or a job report, you will find a knowledge of expository writing valuable. Since you are likely to spend much of your life explaining, you should learn to do it effectively.

The first step in developing the ability to write effective exposition is to master the expository paragraph. If you learn to develop paragraphs with topic sentences plus related support sentences (generative paragraphs), the next step, writing an expository essay, will be an easy one. An essay is, after all, nothing more than a series of related paragraphs.

Objectives   After completing this chapter, you should be able

1. to recognize examples of expository writing
2. to demonstrate an understanding of the following methods of paragraph development: example, illustration, analysis, comparison/contrast, analogy, cause and effect, and definition
3. to write expository paragraphs using these methods of development
4. to demonstrate an understanding of the use of the topic sentence

To attach a single-sentence definition to expository writing is difficult since it can be defined more accurately by listing its characteristics. In fact, exposition seldom exists in pure form, but for the sake of clarification and definition, we will first look at its dominant traits. Although not exhaustive, the following list gives an idea of the typical purposes of exposition:

- setting forth ideas about a subject
- clarifying a subject
- informing about a subject
- explaining a subject

Such an attempt at definition is still vague because all forms of writing may do one or more of the above, so another way of defining exposition is to distinguish from the other classic forms of discourse—narration, description, and argumentation. Narration focuses on actions or events that occur in a time sequence. Description focuses on conveying the sensate appearance (sight, sound, smell, touch, or taste) of a subject. Argumentation focuses on conveying information for the purpose of changing readers' thinking about the subject. The key word in all three definitions is *focus,* which suggests the primary purpose of a given paper.

Now that you have some idea of what exposition is, you may wonder when to write it rather than one of the other classic forms of discourse. The following considerations should help you decide when to write exposition:

1. What *question* are you attempting to answer in the paper? You may find that you want to answer one or more of the following questions:

    a. Why is it (subject) important?
    b. How is it done?
    c. How does it work?
    d. What is it?
    e. What does it mean?
    f. What is its function or purpose?
    g. What causes it? What is the effect?
    h. How is it like or different from a related subject?
    i. What are its parts?
    j. What are the reasons why it happens?

If you answer one or more of these questions, then you want to write exposition.

2. What is the *focus* of your paper? Is it the depiction of action or the depiction of appearance? Are you trying to change the readers' opinion about the subject, convince them of the validity of your point of view? If the answer to one of these questions is

yes, then you do not want to write exposition, but rather narration, description, or argumentation. However, if the answer is no, and if you decide the focus of your paper is to explain, to inform, to clarify, or to set forth your opinion, then you do want to write exposition.

3. Does the *topic* for your paper lend itself to an expository framework? Common sense and careful attention to the assignment will be the best guides in answering this question. For instance, if your instructor asks you to write a paper in which you describe a scene in nature or one in which you relate the events that culminated in a climactic moment, then he or she is not asking you to use an expository framework. Expository assignments usually contain such words as "explain," "analyze," "compare," "discuss," or "evaluate."

If you are still in doubt concerning the nature of exposition, just consider that much of what you read is exposition, including information in newspapers, magazines, encyclopedias, and textbooks. In fact, you are reading expository writing at this very moment.

Probably the easiest way to distinguish exposition from other forms of writing is to examine samples of each. Read the following paragraphs, noting the *focus* of each. The first and third paragraphs were written by students:

I always knew we were nearing grandma's house when I could see the gnarled limbs of the old pin oak tree, stretching out above the dusty road. Of all the familiar landmarks on her farm, the giant tree was the friendliest, the one I knew would never change or die. It was always there, when I was born, when my mother was born, and when my grandmother was born. To me it was a world in itself. Its dense foliage created a green canopy, spreading out against the hot Arkansas sun, rustling above me like a soothing symphony, muting the sounds of the red and white chickens scratching the ground below. And when summer showers fell, I was guarded and kept safe and dry by the umbrella-like leaves. Huge winding roots, twisting out above the red clay soil, became the walls of my imaginary house, its fallen acorns making my cups and bowls, and its twigs serving as my furniture. Cradled in the arms of this magnificent tree, I came to know every minute curve and bump of the massive, intricately patterned trunk. There was nothing that we needed, my tree and I; we were at peace.

Slowly the minutes ticked away toward the zero hour. Officers, their watches synchronized, waited with guns in air, ready to fire the shots that signaled the opening. At last the revolvers barked, and along the line pandemonium broke loose. Men whipped up their horses, wagons careened wildly forward, horses freed from overturned vehicles galloped madly about—all was hurrah and excitement. The Santa Fe trains, steaming slowly forward at a regulated pace which would not give their passengers an undue advantage, disgorged riders along the route as men leaped from roofs or platforms and rushed about in search of a claim. Noise and confusion reigned as the shouts of successful "Boomers," the crash of hammers on stakes, the clatter of wagons, the crash of overturned vehicles, and the curses of disappointed homeseekers mingled to create a bedlam unique in the annals of the nation.

RAY ALLEN BILLINGTON
Westward Expansion

Women can be their own worst enemy, and there is nowhere that such a statement is more evident than in a cocktail lounge. Working as a cocktail waitress is like being in the middle of an eternal territorial struggle. From the very moment a new girl starts to work, she is confronted with a territorial struggle. Seniority has little to do with this struggle. Possession is arrived at by other devious ways, such as how many regular customers you can acquire ownership of, or how well you can get the bartender to cater to you quickly. With the more experienced waitresses, there is no pretense. The newcomer will be assaulted with, "The front station is my territory. John Smith and Bob Jones are my regular customers, so stay clear!" If, by chance, the new waitress is also experienced, an open battle always comes quickly. Getting John Smith to move from the front to the back station is a direct attack which will be countered, and no harmony will exist until one waitress quits or gets fired for "accidentally" spilling a beer on the other one. Since money is the primary, if not the single reason for the territorial struggle, it becomes a constant battle for survival, with only the strong surviving. Behind the scenes in the world of the cocktail waitress, sisterhood is definitely dead.

In the first paragraph, such sensory phrases as "gnarled limbs," "green canopy," "red and white chickens," and "red clay soil" indicate that the focus is on appearance; thus, the focus of the paragraph is on description. The second paragraph also contains descriptive words, but transitional words as "at last" indicate a time sequence; thus, the focus of the paragraph is on action and events, so it is narration. The last paragraph combines elements of description and narration, but for a different purpose—to illustrate and support the topic sentence ("Women can be their own worst enemy, and there is nowhere that such a statement is more evident than in a cocktail lounge.") Since the focus is on explanation, the last paragraph is an example of exposition. Finally, these paragraphs also illustrate an important concept, namely, that description, narration, and exposition often overlap and are used in combinations. To repeat, the classification of writing is based on the primary focus or intention of the writer.

PRACTICE

PART I
List four purposes or traits of exposition that help define and distinguish it from narration, description, and argumentation.

1. _____

2. _____

3. _____

4. _____

PART II
List any five questions an expository paper may answer.

1. _____

2. _____

3. _____

4. _____

5. _____

PART III
Indicate whether each of the following sentences focuses on narration, description, argumentation, or exposition.

_____ 1. She has lusterless blonde hair, not golden blonde, but more the color and texture of wet straw.

_____ 2. I ran for the fence, looking fearfully back over my shoulder at the charging bull, which was gaining on me with every stride.

_____ 3. The purposes of the demonstration were to acquaint the audience with the product and, in the process, sell it.

_____ 4. Politics in America have become so corrupt that honest men no longer want to be involved.

PART I

1. sets forth ideas about a subject
2. clarifies a subject
3. informs about a subject
4. explains a subject

PART II

(Any five)

1. What question are you answering?
2. Why is the subject important?
3. How is it done?
4. How does it work?
5. What is it?
6. What does it mean?
7. How does it function?
8. What are its causes? its result?
9. How is it like or different from a related subject?
10. What are its parts?
11. What are the reasons why it happens?

PART III

1. description (The *focus* is on the *visual appearance* of the hair.)
2. narration (The *focus* is on the *action* of the person running from the bull.)
3. exposition (The *focus* is on *informing* readers of the purposes of the demonstration.)
4. argumentation (The *focus* is on *convincing* readers of the validity of the assertion by appealing to their emotions.)

In the first paragraph of this chapter, exposition was defined as writing intended to support or explain the validity of a conclusion. The stated conclusion is the topic sentence, and the rest of the paragraph is an attempt to support that conclusion. Support may be generated by examples, illustrations, analysis, comparison/contrast, analogy, cause and effect, or definition—or almost any combination of them.

The key to good writing is to make and communicate significant conclusions. The most interesting support is only wasted when used to develop trite conclusions. *Think!!!*

Before reading the rest of this chapter, review the section on the topic sentence in Chapter 4.

Example

A topic sentence or a conclusion is reached as a result of observing a number of examples and then forming a generalization. This is called *induction*. One of the most effective ways to support the validity of a conclusion is to relate a few typical examples that led you to such a conclusion in the first place.

An *example* is a specific detail used to attempt to make an abstract idea concrete or a general idea specific. A good example has three characteristics: it is specific in time, in place, and in action.

For purposes of illustration let's say you are a student at a conservative college, living in the dorm. If you notice that the housemother locked Mary Smith out all night because she returned from a date five minutes after closing, that Sally Edwards was locked in a broom closet for two days because she was not suitably dressed for Wednesday night dinner, and that Betty Liscomb was beaten about the head and shoulders with a fly swatter because she dressed and talked in a manner unbecoming to a lady in the lobby on a Sunday, you would probably reach the generalization that the housemother was overly harsh, overly crazy, or overly something.

If you then felt it necessary to communicate such a conclusion, you would write a paragraph in which you stated the conclusion and supported its validity by relating some of the incidents or examples that led you to that generalization in the first place. Such a paragraph might resemble the following:

The housemother at Titus Hall on the State College campus is unquestionably overly harsh. For example, look what she did to Mary Smith. Mary came back at 8:05, five minutes after closing last Tuesday night, found the doors locked, and had to spend the night sleeping on the park bench because the housemother would not unlock the door. She locked Sally Edwards in a broom closet all of Thursday and Friday because she was attired in body-hugging jeans at the Wednesday night dinner instead of the required dress and hose. But worst of all, she beat Betty Liscomb about the head and shoulders with a fly swatter in front of thirty-three astonished parents because she appeared in the lobby on a Sunday afternoon wearing short shorts and uttering four-letter words.

This is an absurd paragraph, but it does illustrate two things: how examples are specific in time, place, and action; and how good examples need no editorial comment. The examples stand by themselves—the reader does not need to be told they are instances of the housemother's harshness. It is obvious.

The following paragraph was written by a professional writer and is developed by examples:

It is a miracle that New York works at all. The whole thing is implausible. Every time the residents brush their teeth, millions of gallons of water

must be drawn from the Catskills and the hills of Westchester. When a young man in Manhattan writes a letter to his girl in Brooklyn, the love message gets blown to her through a pneumatic tube—*pfft*—just like that. The subterranean system of telephone cables, power lines, steam pipes, gas mains and sewer pipes is reason enough to abandon the island to the gods and the weevils. Every time an incision is made in the pavement, the noisy surgeons expose ganglia that are tangled beyond belief. By rights New York should have destroyed itself long ago, from panic or fire or rioting or failure of some vital supply line in its circulatory system or from some deep labyrinthine short circuit. Long ago the city should have experienced an insoluble traffic snarl at some impossible bottleneck. It should have perished of hunger when food lines failed for a few days. It should have been wiped out by a plague starting in its slums or carried in by ship's rats. It should have been overwhelmed by the sea that licks at it on every side. The workers in its myriad cells should have succumbed to nerves, from the fearful pall of smoke-fog that drifts over every few days from Jersey, blotting out all light at noon and leaving the high offices suspended, men groping and depressed, and the sense of world's end. It should have been touched in the head by the August heat and gone off its rocker.

E. B. WHITE

Here Is New York

For an exercise, go through this paragraph and number the examples. If you have questions, first ask some of your fellow students. If you still have questions, then feel free to ask your instructor.

Here is another example of a paragraph by a professional writer developed by examples:

For six hours every day the Soviet Council of People's Commissars met under Lenin's chairmanship, and a fantastic stream of decrees began to pour out of Smolny. Nothing like it had been seen in the world before; it was a program that uprooted every institution and tradition in Russian life. The abolition of private ownership in land was followed by the nationalization of the banks, of the merchant marine, and of all industrial enterprises. The stock market was swept away, and so were the rights of inheritance. All state debts were annulled, and gold was declared a government monopoly. Wages of the People's Commissars were pegged at 500 rubles a month for single people with additional payments for families. The old criminal courts were supplemented or replaced by "revolutionary tribunals" made up of a president and six peasants, workers and soldiers, and any citizen could appear as a lawyer. Men and women were declared equal in law, and the strict Czarist code governing marriage

and divorce was abolished; a civil marriage now took the place of the church ceremony, and divorce could be obtained by either party of the marriage merely asking for it. All titles were submerged into the universal "Citizen" or "Comrade." The church was permitted to continue but in a drastically truncated form; its lands—and they were enormous—were confiscated and religious teaching was forbidden in the schools. The state religion was now Leninism. The Western calendar, which was now thirteen days ahead of the old Russian calendar, was declared law, and even the alphabet was pruned of various letters and signs. Later on, strikes were declared to be treason.

ALAN MOOREHEAD

The Russian Revolution

Try the same exercise of numbering the examples to test your ability to recognize them.

Two paragraphs developed by example by professional writers follow. Each reads as a list supporting the topic sentence. The second paragraph ends with a brief commentary about the examples:

There is, as has been said, *no necessary connection between the symbol and that which is symbolized.* Just as men can wear yachting costumes without ever having been near a yacht, so they can make the noise "I'm hungry" without being hungry. Furthermore, just as social rank can be symbolized by feathers in the hair, by tattooing on the breast, by gold ornaments on the watch chain, or by a thousand different devices according to the culture we live in, so the fact of being hungry can be symbolized by a thousand different noises according to the culture we live in: *"J'ai faim,"* or *"Es hungert mich,"* or *"Ho appetito,"* or *"Hara ga hetta,"* and so on.

S. I. HAYAKAWA

Language in Thought and Action

In like manner, the memorable words of history and the proverbs of nations consist usually of a natural fact, selected as a picture or parable of a moral truth. Thus: A rolling stone gathers no moss; A bird in the hand is worth two in the bush; A cripple in the right way will beat a racer in the wrong; Make hay while the sun shines; 'Tis hard to carry a full cup even; Vinegar is the son of wine; The last ounce broke the camel's back; Long-lived trees make roots first—and the like. In their primary sense these are trivial facts, but we repeat them for the value of their analogical import. What is true of proverbs, is true of all fables, parables, and allegories.

RALPH WALDO EMERSON

"A Thread Runs Through All Things"

The settlement of the continent, once the Eastern coast ranges were crossed, proceeded with unparalleled speed, and so the naming of the new rivers, lakes, peaks and valleys, and of the new towns and districts, strained the inventiveness of the pioneers. The result is the vast duplication of names that shows itself in the Postal Guide. No less than eighteen imitative *Bostons* and *New Bostons* still appear, and there are nineteen *Bristols,* twenty-eight *Newports,* and twenty-two *Londons* and *New Londons.* Argonauts starting out from an older settlement on the coast would take its name with them, and so we find *Philadelphias* in Illinois, Mississippi, Missouri, and Tennessee; *Richmonds* in Iowa, Kansas, and nine other Western States, and *Princetons* in fifteen. Even when a new name was hit upon, it seems to have been hit upon simultaneously by scores of scattered bands of settlers; thus we find the whole land bespattered with *Washingtons, Lafayettes, Jeffersons,* and *Jacksons,* and with names suggested by common and obvious natural objects, e.g., *Bear Creek, Bald Knob,* and *Buffalo.* The Geographic Board, in its fourth report, made a belated protest against this excessive duplication. "The names *Elk, Beaver, Cottonwood,* and *Bald,*" it said, "are altogether too numerous." Of post offices alone there are fully a hundred embodying *Elk;* counting in rivers, lakes, creeks, mountains, and valleys, the map of the United States probably shows at least twice as many such names.

H. L. MENCKEN

The American Language

1. Write the topic sentence of the preceding paragraph.

_____

_____

2. List the examples Mencken gives to support the topic sentence.

_____

_____

_____

_____

_____

_____

_____

_____

_____

_____

_____

_____

_____

_____

PRACTICE ANSWERS 1. The result is the vast duplication of names that shows itself in the Postal Guide.
2. a. eighteen Bostons and New Bostons
   b. nineteen Bristols
   c. twenty-eight Newports
   d. twenty-two Londons and New Londons
   e. Philadelphias in Illinois, Mississippi, Missouri, and Tennessee
   f. Richmonds in Iowa, Kansas, and nine other Western States
   g. Princetons in fifteen states
   h. the whole land bespattered with Washingtons, Lafayettes, Jeffersons, and Jacksons
   i. names suggested by common and obvious natural objects, e.g., Bear Creek, Bald Knob, and Buffalo
   j. one hundred post offices with "Elk" in the name
   k. over two hundred Elk rivers, lakes, creeks, mountains, and valleys

WRITING ASSIGNMENT   Select one of the following topics or one provided by your instructor and develop it by giving examples. Study the examples of paragraphs by professional writers.

1. Many words are used comfortably only by women (for example, "lovely," "beautiful").
2. A knowledge of history makes us realize that our times and our problems are not really unique.
3. A knowledge of literature makes us realize that our times and problems are not really unique.
4. Modern fiction frequently portrays the unheroic hero.

5. My life is adorned with needless gadgets/people/tasks. (Pick one.)
6. Good literature is seldom happy or funny.

Illustration

An illustration is much like an example. It is specific in time, place, and action. The significant difference is that the action in an illustration is expanded; we might even say that it has plot.

Another way of looking at an illustration is that it is a story or an incident—true or fictional—that supports or develops a point. A narrative sequence with the point of the narration explicitly articulated is an expository paragraph developed by illustration.

The following paragraph is an example of one developed by illustration. Notice how the narrative sequence illustrates the idea expressed in the topic sentence:

Russians have an appealing aptitude for adding two and two and getting three or five. Hamilton Fish Armstrong, of the Council on Foreign Relations in New York, was astounded some years ago when a Russian acquaintance told him quietly that the distinguished quarterly he edits, *Foreign Affairs,* was subsidized by the House of Morgan. Mr. Armstrong, the most unsubsidized author imaginable, could not believe his ears. Blandly, triumphantly, the Russian pointed out that Russell C. Leffingwell, who is indeed a Morgan partner, was a member of the editorial board of the magazine, and had his name *printed*—ah!—on the masthead. It was impossible to convince the Russian that this did not prove, beyond peradventure of a doubt, that the Morgans ran Mr. Armstrong's magazine.

JOHN GUNTHER

Inside Russia Today

Gunther uses an incident (narrative sequence) to show what he considers to be a Russian national trait.

When using an illustration to support the validity of a conclusion, make sure that the illustration is concise and to the point, so that the reader does not lose sight of the main idea of the paragraph. The chief value of illustration is its potential to be interesting, because all readers like a story.

PRACTICE

Underline the main idea that is illustrated in this paragraph:

In the Shenandoah Valley, Union soldiers were learning that southern civilians could be exactly like the folks at home and that there could be a touch of friendship now and then between the invaders and the invaded.

The 13th Massachusetts was appealed to by a valley farmer for protection against foragers, and the colonel detailed four men to guard the place. The farmer insisted that they stay in the house and make themselves comfortable; he would go about his duties and would call them if any prowlers appeared. His wife would not let them bunk down in the yard when night came, but put them in bedrooms with soft mattresses and clean white sheets, told them to sleep until they were called in the morning, served breakfast at eight-thirty—hominy and bacon, potatoes and fried chicken, hot biscuits and coffee, all they could eat. When the regiment finally had to move on and the detail was called away, the farmer went to the colonel to testify what fine young men these soldiers were, and his wife sent a huge basket of biscuits and cakes for them to take with them. All the rest of the war the 13th Massachusetts nursed this memory.

BRUCE CATTON
This Hallowed Ground

PRACTICE ANSWER   In the Shenandoah Valley, Union soldiers were learning that southern civilians could be exactly like the folks at home and that there could be a touch of friendship now and then between the invaders and the invaded.

Following are further examples of paragraphs developed by illustration:

Another reason I hate women (and I am speaking, I believe, for the American male generally) is that in almost every case, where there is a sign reading "Please have exact change ready," a woman never has anything smaller than a ten-dollar bill. She gives ten-dollar bills to bus conductors and change-men in subways and other such persons who deal in nickels and dimes and quarters. Recently, in Bermuda, I saw a woman hand the conductor on the little railway there a bill of such huge denomination that I was utterly unfamiliar with it. I was sitting too far away to see exactly what it was, but I had the feeling that it was a five-hundred-dollar bill. The conductor merely ignored it and stood there waiting—the fare was just one shilling. Eventually, scrabbling around in her handbag, the woman found a shilling. All the men on the train who witnessed the transaction tightened up inside; that's what a woman with a ten-dollar bill or a twenty or a five-hundred does to a man in such situations—she tightens him up inside. The episode gives him the feeling that some monstrous triviality is threatening the whole structure of civilization. It is difficult to analyze this feeling, but there it is.

JAMES THURBER
"The Case Against Women"

It is clear, then, that the ignoring of contexts in any act of interpretation is at best a stupid practice. At its worst, it can be a vicious practice. A common example is the sensational newspaper story in which a few words by a public personage are torn out of their context and made the basis of a completely misleading account. There is the incident of a Veterans Day speaker, a university teacher, who declared before a high-school assembly that the Gettysburg Address was "a powerful piece of propaganda." The context clearly revealed that "propaganda" was being used, not according to its popular meaning, but rather, as the speaker himself stated, to mean "explaining the moral purposes of a war." The context also revealed that the speaker was a very great admirer of Lincoln. However, the local newspaper, ignoring the context, presented the account in such a way as to suggest that the speaker had called Lincoln a liar. On this basis, the newspaper began a campaign against the instructor. The speaker remonstrated with the editor of the newspaper, who replied, in effect, "I don't care what else you said. You said the Gettysburg Address was propaganda, didn't you?" This appeared to the editor complete proof that Lincoln had been maligned and that the speaker deserved to be discharged from his position at the university.

S. I. HAYAKAWA

Language in Thought and Action.

The principle of internal logic applies not only to the outcome of a character but to each stage of his development as well. One of the finest examples of this is Nelson Algren's "A Bottle of Milk for Mother." The story opens with a character named Lefty Bicek who is being questioned by the police. They have charged him only with having trailed a drunk, but then they begin to accuse him bluntly and apparently without evidence of being a "jackroller." The attitude of the policemen and the reporter in the room is such that we immediately sympathize with Lefty. We brace ourselves for a story of police brutality. But as Lefty begins to defend himself, we are startled to learn that he really did intend to rob the old drunk. The shift could not have been predicted, but it is consistent with what we have already learned about Lefty. The next surprise comes when his story shifts again: He really did "strong-arm" the old man. By this time we have more material to work with, so again the shift in our evaluation of Lefty appears to be "logical." As the story develops, our opinion of Lefty is knocked down step by step; and when we hear him confess that he did have a gun, that he did fire it, and when we learn that he has murdered a father of five children, we see Lefty as a pathetic, brutal, insensitive thug. And our opinion of the police has become much more complex—a mixture of basic respect and some scorn. At the very end we see Lefty in his darkened cell. He appears to be praying—another reversal which we are ready to accept as possible. But he is only looking for his cap—more credible. Then, cap found, still on his knees, he ends by softly telling himself "I knew I'd never get to be twenty-one anyhow."

STEPHEN MINOT
Three Genres

This last paragraph was written by a student:

The fact that the average consumer places far too much faith in "brand names" is as obvious as it is sad. A friend of mine, for instance, was so devoted to peanut butter marked "Skippy," shirts marked "Gant," and overalls marked "Sears" that he never questioned their worth. Once he invited a friend to watch a television special on his new color portable. The two men sat before a fuzzed screen, watching people of every unlikely color: avocado, sunshine-yellow, strawberry-red. The top halves of the actors' bodies, grossly distorted, narrowed into pointed heads; the lower halves broke into bands of rippling, fuzzy flesh. The audio interference revealed a chorus of buzz-saws accompanied by a garbage disposal. The guest tolerated the spectacle as long as he could, and then asked my friend politely if his television set needed repair. "It just, uh, doesn't seem to be working right," he explained. "Not working right?!" my friend shouted. "Of course it works right! It's an Admiral!"

WRITING ASSIGNMENT

Begin a paragraph with a topic sentence containing a conclusion you have reached about human nature. Support the validity of that conclusion with an illustration that is concise and to the point. Check first with your instructor for either a different assignment or a more specific application of this one.

Analysis

Analysis is the process of separating an object or concept into its parts and then explaining how they are related to the whole. The following paragraph written by a student is an example of analysis, which separates an object (a short story) into its component parts—plot, setting, character, conflict, resolution or climax, and theme:

A student who desires to understand a short story has to determine several things. First, what is the plot? He obviously has to determine what the events are in the story before he can determine what they mean. He also must determine the setting, where and when the events happen. He also must examine the characters and determine their universality if any, their similarity to people as we know them. Then he must carefully examine what dramatic conflict, what problem, or what dilemma the protagonist is facing. Then he has to consider how the protagonist resolves the conflict or solves the problem. Then he must ask himself, "What is the author saying when he has a protagonist who is represented as having universal qualities resolve the conflict in the particular way he does?" The answer to this question should reveal the theme; that is, the general principle of life the author is trying to dramatize.

Notice that the preceding paragraph has a purpose—to explain how to understand a short story. Analysis is not an end in itself. Like any method of development, it is a way of doing something, a means to an end, and the end is *to explain.*

If you were asked to analyze your school, you might break it down into people, curriculum, and activities. If you were asked to analyze a football team, you might break it down into offense and defense. Every spring, newspapers and magazines are filled with analyses of baseball teams, each team broken down to the component positions for evaluation, first baseman, second baseman, third baseman, and so on. Every fall, newspapers and magazines are filled with articles that tell students what kind of clothes to take with them to college. These articles are analyses of wardrobes.

The following paragraphs are developed by analysis:

Good organization of things to say is foremost among the structural devices that, whatever the subject or whoever the reader, are useful in achieving coherence and, hence, clarity. This device has been already referred to in the discussion of selection and organization and of structure and style and is implicit in the structural devices just discussed. Once a writer has chosen his subject, decided upon his thesis, and selected things to say to develop his subject and support or clarify his thesis, he faces the problem of giving these things some order. For he cannot say everything at once. If his subject is Aunt Agatha, if his thesis is that she is stingy, if he intends to support his thesis by advancing the theses that she gives nothing to charities, however worthy, and that she almost starves her family, and if he intends to support these theses by examples, then he must advance these theses and give these examples in some order; and this order may be either a good organization or a bad. One good order—of several possible good ones—is this: (1) introduction, (2) the no-charity thesis, (3) examples supporting the no-charity thesis, (4) the starvation thesis, and (5) examples supporting the starvation thesis. One bad order—there are many bad ones—is this: (1) introduction, (2) the no-charity thesis, (3) *some* examples supporting the no-charity thesis, (4) the starvation thesis, (5) *some* examples supporting the starvation thesis, (6) *some other* examples supporting the no-charity thesis, and (7) *some other* examples supporting the starvation thesis. The good organization is good because it is logical—because it classifies things, because it puts like things together—and, hence, is easy for the reader to follow and to remember. The bad organization is bad because it is illogical—because it scatters like things around—and, hence, is hard for the reader to follow and to remember.

MARTIN STEINMAN, JR., and GERALD WILLEN
Literature for Writing

This paragraph breaks down the concept of *organization* into three basic parts: introduction, thesis, and support. The purpose obviously is to explain how to organize an essay.

The following paragraph was written by a student:

Over the centuries, a phrase has evolved that encompasses the realm of an individual's character, summarizes him and packs him neatly into an admirable category. That phrase is "good taste," and is developed in three component stages: parental influence, peer influence, and educational influence. Parental influence is the foundation. Should the parents delight in country and western music and scorn the classics of Beethoven and Mozart, the product is a child who adheres exclusively to Charlie Rich. Peer influence develops the individual's confidence in himself through adolescence. Should an individual, encouraged by peers, choose to cancel a date in order to weep over John-boy's dilemma in a "Walton's" episode, he is exhibiting inherent poor taste and should choose a new circle of influence. Structured education is the most important in developing an individual with good taste; a well-rounded education consists of exposure to all elements of art, music and literature; an instructor restricting or replacing his American Writers course with Science Fiction studies is scarring his students by depriving them of the worldly prose of Fitzgerald, Hemingway and colleagues. One is to be cautioned against cultural deviants who obsessively combine Leonardo's paintings, "Love Story" movies, collect Charlie Pride LP's and can quote Mickey Spillane. Such a person has no taste. The individual who can discuss Henri Matisse and Rembrandt is probably aware of Beethoven's Fifth Symphony and that Shakespeare is worth his time. The person with good taste is not limited to the perversity of knowing very little about very little; severe deviation from the "universality" rule should lead one to be wary of such an individual. If the reader has assimilated this information, agreed with it and delighted in it, he is now to be congratulated on his impeccable taste.

PRACTICE   A good restaurant is not so simple a haven to find as one might expect, and once found, must live up to its reputation on all subsequent visits. The restaurant's exterior need not be impressive or unusual, but its

[138]   PARAGRAPH DESIGN

interior decor is important: it must feel warm and welcoming without being stifling: it should be interesting without looking cluttered; it might be vast but should not feel barny. Wood panelling and comfortable furniture or a fireplace can contribute warmth, original prints and paintings might decorate its walls, and seating areas should be divided into intimate, quiet spaces. A good restaurant's menu need not be extensive, but its selections should represent a variety of tastes and textures, and the food must be fresh, hot food served hot, cold food served cold. Serving people should be cordial without being effusive and helpful but not pushy. They should respect the patrons' desire to enjoy a superb meal according to the patrons'—not the waiters'—time schedules, to linger with coffee, brandy, and companions until sufficient energy and courage has been restored to face the fast, bright world again.

1. What are the component parts of this subject?

_____

2. What is the purpose of this analysis?

_____

1. exterior decor, interior decor, menu, food, service
2. to explain the evaluation of a good restaurant

Write an analysis of one of the terms below or one given to you by your instructor. Remember to have a purpose for your analysis— to explain something.

1. pleasure
2. the good life
3. depression
4. a satisfying meal
5. a good movie
6. an enjoyable evening

Comparison/ Contrast

Comparison/contrast is another method of developing a piece of writing, but it is not simply a way of pointing out similarities or differences. It is used for exposition, that is, to explain something. There must be a *purpose* for the comparison/contrast.

One purpose of comparison/contrast is to explain an unfamiliar item or concept by comparing or contrasting it to a familiar item or concept. For example, you might explain to someone what a dobro is by comparing/contrasting it to a guitar, which is certainly more likely to be familiar, fascism to democracy, a kayak to a canoe, quadraphonic sound to stereo, open marriage to traditional marriage.

You may also occasionally explain two unfamiliar items or concepts by comparing/contrasting them to one familiar item or concept. For example, Japanese cooking and Vietnamese cooking can be compared with the more familiar Chinese cooking, communism and socialism with capitalism.

Another purpose is to explain an unfamiliar concept by comparing/contrasting two familiar items. For example, you might explain what you mean by good drama by comparing/contrasting a familiar TV show to a familiar Shakespearean play. The concept of good poetry might be explained by comparing/contrasting verse from greeting cards to the poetry of Robert Frost. Or you might explain the concept of a good meal by comparing/contrasting a meal from the college cafeteria to a meal from an expensive restaurant.

Many of the concepts you are likely to explain with comparison/contrast involve a judgmental term such as "good" or "bad."

Keep in mind that, when you compare or contrast two things, they must be basically alike. The two items for comparison/contrast must have major areas in common. Then compare the objects on particular points, showing how the two objects are the same and how they are different. Examine the following examples of things that can be compared:

1. Good teaching and bad teaching
2. Reading for pleasure and reading for school
3. Reading for pleasure and watching TV for pleasure
4. Books and their movie versions
5. High school and college
6. Superior student and inferior student
7. Teaching by lecture and teaching by discussion
8. Ford and Chevrolet automobiles
9. Owning a house and renting an apartment
10. Traditional sex roles and nontraditional sex roles

There are two general ways of organizing comparison/contrast. You may fully present one item and then fully present the other. Or you may present a part of one item and then a part of the other, another part of the first item and another part of the second, continuing this until all significant parts are covered.

Following are paragraphs developed by comparison or contrast:

Be that as it may, I could not help thinking, as I looked at the works of Shakespeare on the shelf, that the bishop was right at least in this; it would have been impossible, completely and entirely, for any woman to have written the plays of Shakespeare in the age of Shakespeare. Let me imagine, since facts are so hard to come by, what would have happened had Shakespeare had a wonderfully gifted sister, called Judith, let us say. Shakespeare himself went, very probably—his mother was an heiress—to the grammar school, where he may have learnt Latin—Ovid, Virgil and Horace—and the elements of grammar and logic. He was, it is well known, a wild boy who poached rabbits, perhaps shot a deer, and had, rather sooner than he should have done, to marry a woman in the neighborhood, who bore him a child rather quicker than was right. That escapade sent him to seek his fortune in London. He had, it seemed, a taste for the theatre; he began by holding horses at the stage door. Very soon he got work in the theatre, became a successful actor, and lived at the hub of the universe, meeting everybody, knowing everybody, practising his art on the boards, exercising his wits in the streets, and even getting access to the palace of the queen. Meanwhile his extraordinarily gifted sister, let us suppose, remained at home. She was as adventurous, as imaginative, as agog to see the world as he was. But she was not sent to school. She had no chance of learning grammar and logic, let alone of reading Horace and Virgil. She picked up a book now and then, one of her brother's perhaps, and read a few pages. But then her parents came in and told her to mend the stockings or mind the stew and not moon about with books and papers. They would have spoken sharply but kindly, for they were substantial people who knew the conditions of life for a woman and loved their daughter—indeed, more likely than not she was the apple of her father's eye. Perhaps she scribbled some pages up in an apple loft on the sly, but was careful to hide them or set fire to them. Soon, however, before she was out of her teens, she was to be betrothed to the son of a neighbouring wool-stapler. She cried out that marriage was hateful to her, and for that she was severely beaten by her father. Then he ceased to scold her. He begged her instead not to hurt him, not to shame him in this matter of her marriage. He would give her a chain of beads or a fine petticoat, he said; and there were tears in his eyes. How could she disobey him? How could she break his heart? The force of her own gift alone drove her to it. She made up a small parcel of her belongings, let herself down by a rope one summer's night and took the road to London. She was not seventeen. The birds that sang in the hedge were not more musical than she was. She had the quickest fancy, a gift like her brother's, for the tune of words. Like him, she had a taste for the theatre. She stood at the stage door; she wanted to act, she said. Men laughed in her face. The manager—a fat, loose-lipped man—guffawed. He bellowed something about poodles dancing and women acting—no woman, he said, could possibly be an actress. He hinted—you can imagine what.

She could get no training in her craft. Could she even seek her dinner in a tavern or roam the streets at midnight? Yet her genius was for fiction and lusted to feed abundantly upon the lives of men and women and the study of their ways. At last—for she was very young, oddly like Shakespeare the poet in her face, with the same grey eyes and rounded brows—at last Nick Greene the actor-manager took pity on her; she found herself with child by that gentleman and so—who shall measure the heat and violence of the poet's heart when caught and tangled in a woman's body?— killed herself one winter's night and lies buried at some cross-roads where the omnibuses now stop outside the Elephant and Castle.

VIRGINIA WOOLF

A Room of One's Own

The next three selections were all written by students:

Lenny Bruce, as a comedian, was a confident, spontaneous, exuberant stageman who captured the public by the overt and somewhat caustic impulsiveness which he seemed to enjoy while seeking uncomfortable topics for his monologues, and enchanted his audience with the quick wit and ease in manipulating these subjects into humor when they seemed at their most offensive points. Bill Cosby also possesses this love for comedy, and he too lacked neither spirit nor spontaneity, together with the ability to slice humor out of blackened topics in a way that could mesmerize the audience, but he was not an offensive man. His character held an element of sensitivity and paralleled his feelings toward audience-comedian relationships, a quality which Bruce sidestepped during his career.

A bar worth returning to and a bar worth forgetting are easily distinguished. Both, of course, serve alcoholic drinks, always in exchange for money, but there the similarities end. A fine bar is furnished comfortably, whether in stools perched before a foot-rail or in loungeable couches and chairs, while a poor bar is furnished in fussy, stiff seats before rocky, sticky tables. A fine bar is dimmer than daylight, lighted inconspicuously, whereas a poor bar boasts yellow and red-bulbed wrought-iron lanterns or pear-shaped glasses filled with wax and covered with sequins, flocking, or plastic mesh so that no light whatever emits. Fine bars have walls which are pleasant to look at—wood panelling, aesthetic artwork, antique mirrors, wine racks—but the solitary or wistful drinker at a poor bar is abashed by an array of furry wallpaper, remote-control ball games, more wrought iron sconces, cliches decoupaged onto knotty pine by an overeager handicrafter. A fine bar seems to attract a congenial clientele while a poor bar collects nodding derelicts, polyester-covered loud-mouths, and painted hookers. In short, a fine bar resembles the living room one has just left (or would have liked to) while the poor bar reminds one of the cheap hotel best passed by.

In the surge of sex-role consciousness, there evolve two types of women: the liberated and the non-liberated. The image of these women is often deceptive, disputed and offensive. To avoid conflict, we will take the liberty of using the normative to study their similarities (stereotyping?). We find that both women pursue personal vocational interests. The liberated woman may be located in a respectable or prestigious executive position, no longer confined to the "nurse-secretary" image. The non-liberated woman may be found in her domestic confines, acting as "keeper of the keys" (and the house and the kids and the dog). She may also think that nothing else will suffice save employment as a public servant (the "nurse-secretary" syndrome). The behavior of these women around their male counterparts is sometimes discreet, but may be exposed if examined with a discerning eye. Both will react to the gestures of men (the lighting of the cigarette, the opening of the door, etc.). The liberated woman snarls at these gestures; the man may expect an onslaught of verbal chastisements. The non-liberated woman reacts to these gestures with submissive and humble gratitude. Group interaction is usually a dead give-away as to "which witch is which." The liberated woman, preferring mixed company, discusses current political and economic issues; the non-liberated woman chooses to get ideas on interior decorating and Dr. Spock from "the girls." Such are a few examples showing that, despite the current controversies over liberated and non-liberated women, both possess common ground. "Once a woman, always a woman," is an accurate statement, but we urge the reader to disregard the liberties taken here and avoid speaking in broad generalities.

PRACTICE

A very queer, composite being thus emerges. Imaginatively she is of the highest importance; practically she is completely insignificant. She pervades poetry from cover to cover; she is all but absent from history. She dominates the lives of kings and conquerors in fiction; in fact she was the slave of any boy whose parents forced a ring upon her finger. Some of the most inspired words, some of the most profound thoughts in literature fall from her lips; in real life she could hardly read, could scarcely spell, and was the property of her husband.

VIRGINIA WOOLF
A Room of One's Own

1. What are the two items being compared in this paragraph?

_____

2. Which is the one being explained?

_____

3. Which is the one being used to explain?

_____

4. What is the purpose of the comparison?

_____

PRACTICE ANSWERS

1. woman in reality and woman as she is portrayed in literature
2. woman in reality
3. woman as she is portrayed in literature
4. to explain the real life women experienced

WRITING ASSIGNMENT

Select a topic and write a paragraph developed by comparison/contrast. Remember the paragraph must have a rhetorical purpose—you are explaining something. Choose from the following list or from a list provided by your instructor.

1. reading for pleasure and reading for school
2. a superior student and an inferior student
3. a novel and its movie version
4. something you like to do and something you do not like to do.

Analogy

An *analogy* is simply an extended comparision, used most often to explain a complex, abstract, or unfamiliar idea or process. For example, a young child does not understand electricity because electrical currents are invisible. But the child does understand the flow of water through pipes and, through the likening of electrical current to water, can envision electricity flowing through conductive wires.

To effectively explain an idea or process, we must use an analogy that is similar to the idea or process. Comparing a democratic nation to a ship is a false analogy because ships are *not* commanded democratically; crew members normally do not decide a ship's course. Neither can schools produce students as factories produce cars; students are not machines.

An analogy should be more familiar or simple than the idea or process it explains. Likening a city water system to electrical flow in order to explain the water system would be a waste of time; most people understand electricity less perfectly than water.

Analogies should be original and refreshing. To liken life's "ups and downs" to the game of football, in which you "win some and lose some," but should not worry, because, after all, "it's not whether you win or lose; it's how you play the game" is to trap an idea in a cliché, a trite, now meaningless, mode of expression.

Depending on the writer's audience and purpose, the *limits* of the analogy should be indicated. No matter how similar two ideas or processes are, they will have differences, and those differences may be significant. A child, for example, should be told that, if he or she inserts a finger in a live electrical socket, it will not get wet; it will be burned. However, the limit of the following analogy by Hoyle—namely, that a raisin cake is bounded and finite whereas the universe is boundless and infinite—does not bear significantly on the similar processes of motion within the cake and the universe and doesn't concern the average reader.

Finally, analogy should never be considered *proof* of an idea or process. It can demonstrate, illustrate, and explain, but it cannot prove anything. The motion of galaxies in space is not verified by similar motion of raisins in a baking cake. The flow of water in pipes does not prove the existence of electricity.

Read the following paragraphs carefully, noting the complex ideas and processes being explained by analogous simple, fresh comparisons, and answer the questions that follow: **PRACTICE**

Observations indicate that the different clusters of galaxies are constantly moving apart from each other. To illustrate by a homely analogy, think of a raisin cake baking in an oven. Suppose the cake swells uniformly as it cooks, but the raisins themselves remain of the same size. Let each raisin represent a cluster of galaxies, and imagine yourself inside one of them. As the cake swells, you will observe that all the other raisins move away from you. Moreover, the farther away the raisin, the faster it will seem to move. When the cake has swollen to twice its initial dimensions, the distance between all the raisins will have doubled itself—two raisins that were initially an inch apart will now be two inches apart; two raisins that were a foot apart will have moved two feet apart. Since the entire action takes place within the same time interval, obviously the more distant raisins must move apart faster than those close at hand. So it happens with the clusters of galaxies.

FRED HOYLE
"When Time Began"

1. What is the idea or object being explained?

_____

2. To what familiar idea or object is it being compared?

_____

A poem compresses much in a small space and adds music, thus heightening its meaning. The city is like poetry: it compresses all life, all races and breeds, into a small island and adds music and the accompaniment of internal engines. The island of Manhattan is without any doubt the greatest human concentrate on earth, the poem whose magic is comprehensible to millions of permanent residents but whose full meaning will always remain illusive. At the feet of the tallest and plushiest offices lie the crummiest slums. The genteel mysteries housed in the Riverside Church are only a few blocks from the voodoo charms of Harlem. The merchant princes, riding to Wall Street in their limousines down the East River Drive, pass within a few hundred yards of the gypsy kings; but the princes do not know they are passing kings, and the kings are not up yet anyway—they live a more leisurely life than the princes and get drunk more consistently.

E. B. WHITE

Here Is New York

3. What is the idea or object being explained?

_____

4. To what familiar idea or object is it being compared?

_____

The following paragraph was written by a student:

If I were to awaken one morning with the uncontrollable impulse to remove all the paintings from my walls, to strip them of pigment, and to hang the blank canvasses in their place, would I still have art? The canvass would fill the space of the wall. I would have a conversation piece as I had with the originals. By some stretch of the imagination, my open-minded guest could even see beauty in some of them. But in the aesthetic sense, would I still have art? No, by removing all color, shape, and design I would in the process dissolve any aesthetic beauty. The blank canvass would serve me mechanically but I would receive no visual or mental enjoyment. With this in mind, I wholeheartedly object to any legislative controls that would eventually dissolve our family structure. By outlawing marriage, by removing personal obligations of husband to wife and to child, by controlling education for the sole purpose of governmental service, and by limiting sexual activity to that of enjoyment, the family would be dissolved. Society would be served mechanically. Children would be produced. Relationships between men and women would go on. The general ideals of life would survive. But as in the case of the blank paintings the true purpose of the family would escape. To lower the family to a mechanical function would be only one more step toward the dehumanization of life.

5. What is the idea or object being explained?

_____

6. To what familiar idea or object is it being compared?

_____

1. the movement of the galaxies in the universe
2. the movement of raisins in a baking cake
3. the city
4. poetry
5. the family with government regulations
6. paintings stripped of pigment

Write a paragraph that explains some concept by analogy. Explain a concept of your choice or one provided by your instructor. The following are suggested topics:

1. beauty
2. teaching
3. studying
4. ugliness
5. love
6. sin
7. poetry
8. paragraph

Cause and Effect

Cause and effect is a method of thinking familiar to everyone. When you ask the question "Why?" you are asking for causes of a particular effect. For example, if you ask, "Why did I fail the algebra test?" you are asking for the causes that led to your low test grade—the effect. If you say, "If you study the examples in the text, review quizzes, and ask questions in class, you should do well on the algebra test," you are giving causes and predicting the effect.

There are two basic ways of organizing paragraphs developed by cause and effect.

With the first method, you state an effect and devote the paragraph to examining probable causes. For example, perhaps you are writing a paragraph with the following topic sentence: "The average American is overweight." This is an effect. The rest of your paragraph would treat possible causes for this effect, such as inactivity, eating out of frustration, eating as the center of much social activity, and so forth.

With the second method, you state a cause and then, in a sense, predict possible effects. For illustration, let's say you are writing a paragraph with the following topic sentence: "Today's schools are not teaching students to read effectively." In the body of the paragraph you would treat the possible effects that could result from this poor teaching of reading, such as lack of success in college or a career, culturally bankrupt leisure lives, and lack of awareness of current events.

In the first method, you are looking to the past for causes. In the second method, you are looking to the future for possible effects.

In writing of cause and effect the word "because" should be emphasized in your thinking. The following transitions occur frequently in cause-and-effect writing:

so	as a result
therefore	in order that
consequently	hence
as a consequence	thus

Like any other method of thinking, cause and effect can be logical and illogical. When you write about causes and effects, be careful not to assume that event B is caused by event A simply because A precedes B in time. For example, a baseball manager wears mismatched socks one day. His team wins the game that night. He concludes the team won (event B) because he wore mismatched socks (event A). This confusion of cause and effect is called *post hoc ergo propter hoc* ("after this, therefore because of this"). Just because one event precedes another, this does not necessarily mean that a causal relationship exists.

Another common error occurs when the writer attributes the wrong cause to an effect. For example, a person goes to several rock concerts, notices that all the good rock guitarists have long hair, and mistakenly concludes that the long hair is a cause of their guitar-playing ability.

A third common error results if a writer attributes an effect to a single cause when the effect is the result of several causes. For example, during the Civil War when Abraham Lincoln was introduced to Harriet Beecher Stowe, whose book *Uncle Tom's Cabin* was instrumental in popularizing the antislavery movement, he is reported to have said, "So you're the little lady who started this great war." Although this was undoubtedly said facetiously, the humor is based on attributing an effect to a single cause when obviously there was a multitude of causes.

See the discussion of cause and effect in Chapter 12, "Writing the Expository Essay," for additional information about fallacious cause-and-effect thinking.

The following paragraph is developed by cause and effect:

This surge of demand [for oil] will soon begin to send shock waves through the American economy and transportation system. The impact of these tremors can already be anticipated: to the consumer they signal the end of a long love affair with the car, and to Detroit they offer an early warning that its 1985 growth aims are dangerously unrealistic. Unless we exercise foresight and devise growth-limits policies for the auto industry, events will thrust us into a crisis that will lead to a substantial erosion of our domestic oil supply as well as the independence it provides us with, and a level of petroleum imports that could cost as much as $20 to $30 billion per year. (This turn would produce a staggering balance-of-payments problem for the United States, and give the Middle Eastern suppliers a dangerous leverage over our transportation system as well.) Moreover, we would still be depleting our remaining oil reserves at an unacceptable rate, and scrambling for petroleum substitutes, with enormous potential damage to the environment.

STEWART UDALL
"The Last Traffic Jam"

Read this paragraph and answer the questions that follow.　　　　PRACTICE

"I started Termpapers Unlimited," Ward Warren told me last fall, "when I had a term paper to write and ran all over Boston looking for books. Do you know how many libraries there are in Boston? I was struck by the inefficiency of the process. For six hours of reading I had to spend three days on the M.T.A. So I figured if a student could hire someone to do the research, he could save himself a lot of time."

PHILIP ROSENBERG
"Why Johnny Can't Flunk"

1. What is the cause?

_____

2. What is the effect?

_____

PRACTICE ANSWERS
1. Ward Warren's being "struck by the inefficiency of the process" of research
2. the starting of "Termpapers Unlimited"

WRITING ASSIGNMENT
1. Explain the causes and effects of your obeying or disobeying some rule, law, or policy.
2. Explain the causes and effects of group persecution of a child you know.

Definition

Definition answers the question "What is it?" It does this by first placing the object to be defined in a class of objects, technically called the *genus,* and then showing how the object differs from others in the same class. These differences are technically called the *differentiae.*

A definition, then, looks like this:

Term to be defined	Genus	Differentia
literature [is]	the written record of valuable thought	having other than merely practical purposes

This is a formal definition and would generally be used as the topic sentence of a paragraph. The body of the paragraph is developed by an explanation of terms in the definition. If you were writing a paragraph with the sentence in the example above as the topic sentence, you could develop the paragraph by explaining what is meant by "written record of valuable thought" and then what is meant by "having other than merely practical purposes."

The main purpose of the body of the paragraph is to provide understanding of the differentiae; that is, to explain them. Consequently, all the modes previously discussed can be used: example, illustration, analysis, comparison/contrast, analogy, and cause and effect. (See Chapter 12 for additional discussion of definition.)

The following paragraphs are developed by definition:

Prose: In its broadest sense, the term is applied to all forms of written or spoken expression which do not have a regular rhythmic pattern (see METER). Such a definition, however, needs some elaboration, for a collection of words thrown together, a mere setting down of haphazard conversation, for instance, is not usually considered *prose*. *Prose* is most often meant to designate a conscious, cultivated writing, not merely a bringing together of vocabularies, a listing of ideas, a catalogue of objects. And, while *prose* is like VERSE in that good *prose* has a RHYTHM, it is unlike VERSE in that this RHYTHM is not to be scanned by any of the normal metrical schemes. But a clear line between *prose* and POETRY is difficult to draw. Is bad VERSE *prose*? Is rhythmical *prose* VERSE? *Is Miss Lowell's* POLYPHONIC PROSE *a prose* form, a VERSE form, or something between the two? It is easier, perhaps, to list some of the qualities of *prose:* (1) it is without sustained rhythmic regularity; (2) it has some logical, grammatical order and its ideas are connectedly stated rather than merely listed; (3) it is characterized by the virtues of STYLE, though the STYLE will vary, naturally, from writer to writer; (4) it will secure variety of expression through DICTION and through sentence structure.

C. HUGH HOLMAN, et al.

A Handbook to Literature

This concept of being a sissy is a key concept for the understanding of American character; it has no exact parallel in any other society. It has nowadays become a term of opprobrium which can be applied to anyone, regardless of age or sex; although it is analogous to some English terms of opprobrium (e.g. milksop, cry-baby, nancy, mother's darling) it is more than any of them. Schematically, it means showing more dependence or fear or lack of initiative or passivity than is suitable for the occasion. It can be applied to a gambler hesitant about risking his money, to a mother overanxious about the pain her child may suffer at the hands of a surgeon, to a boy shy about asking a popular girl for a "date," to stage fright, to overt apprehension about a visit to the dentist, to a little girl crying because her doll is broken, just as well as to occasions which directly elicit courage or initiative or independence and which may be responded to more or less adequately. It is the overriding fear of all American parents that their child will turn into a sissy; it is the overriding fear of all Americans from the moment that they can understand language that they may be taken for a sissy; and a very great deal of American speech and activity, so often misinterpreted by non-Americans, is designed solely to avert this damning judgment. Particularly self-confident Americans may say "I guess I'm just a sissy . . ." when they feel quite sure that they are not. When applied to adult males (but only in that case) the term also implies sexual passivity.

GEOFFREY GORER

The American People: A Study in National Character

A 'gender role' is a role assigned on the basis of biological sex, which defines specific personality traits and behavioural responses as appropriate to a person of that sex. Biologically, people are male or female; culturally, they are pressured to be masculine or feminine. The definition of masculinity and femininity varies between different societies and also historically within each society. Modern industrial society has created opportunities for the equality of male and female but has retained, and even heightened, the differentiation between masculinity and feminity.

ANN OAKLEY

Woman's Work

Here the term to be defined is "gender role," the genus is a "role," and the differentia is "assigned on the basis of biological sex, which defines specific personality traits and behavioural responses as appropriate to a person of that sex."

PRACTICE

PART I

Hackneyed language is a general term which includes not only the cliché but the far more dangerous area of phrases which have simply been overused. Whereas clichés usually consist only of conventionalized similes and are easily identified, hackneyed language also includes direct description which has been seen in print too long to provide impact. A seventh-grader can compile a list of clichés as readily as he can recall names of birds; but only one who has read literature extensively can identify that which is literarily hackneyed. This is one reason why vocabulary lists which are emphasized so heavily in secondary schools are no substitute for wide and varied reading.

STEPHEN MINOT

Three Genres

1. Identify the term to be defined.

   _____

2. Identify the genus.

   _____

3. Identify the differentia.

   _____

   _____

PART II

A "liberated woman" is simply a woman who controls her own life, rather than allowing it to be controlled by other people, traditions, or expectations. A "liberated woman" can be found pursuing any line of work, including housework, or no work at all. She may or may not be married; she may or may not have borne children. She may belong to any race; she may have attained any age. She may be poor or wealthy, educated or illiterate. She need have only one trait in common with her "liberated sisters": she makes her own choices, whether they be the colors on her walls or the advanced degrees she seeks. She acts of her own volition, responsible to herself, and not out of fear of what her mother, lover, or neighbor might say.

1. Identify the term to be defined in this paragraph, written by a student.

    _____

2. Identify the genus.

    _____

3. Identify the differentia.

    _____

    _____

PART I
1. hackneyed language
2. general term
3. which includes not only the cliché but the far more dangerous area of phrases which have simply been overused

PART II
1. liberated woman
2. woman
3. who controls her own life, rather than allowing it to be controlled by other people, traditions, or expectations

Write a paragraph of definition on one of the following terms or on a term from a list provided by your instructor. Remember your topic sentence should be a *definition;* that is, in it you should state the term you are defining, assign the term to class or genus, and supply differentiae that illustrate how this item differs from other items in the same class. The body of the paragraph should basically elaborate on the differentiae.

1. pornography
2. style in dressing
3. boredom
4. ecstasy
5. fear
6. assertiveness
7. taste
8. depression
9. superior student
10. worry

The Generative Nature of the Expository Essay

You will find that the concept of the generative sentence and the generative paragraph also applies to the expository essay, which could be called the generative essay.

Objectives

After completing this chapter, you should be able

1. to identify the relationship among the generative sentence, the generative paragraph, and the generative essay
2. to write a generative sentence, expanded into a generative paragraph, expanded into a generative essay outline

---

As you may recall, Chapter 2 dealt with the generative rhetoric of the sentence, that is, the sentence containing a base clause and any number of free modifiers. The following sentence is an example:

Elmer walked into the bar, crowded with college students, all shouting, trying to be heard above the blaring band, which sounded like a train.

By notating this sentence, you can see its generative structure:

1 Elmer walked into the bar,
  2 crowded with college students,
    3 all shouting,

3 trying to be heard above the blaring band,
4 which sounded like a train.

With the addition of each free modifier, the general information contained in the base clause becomes more specific because of the addition of quality, detail, and comparison, thus allowing the writer to communicate fully the action of the sentence. In other words, beginning with the base idea, the writer has generated a rather specific sentence through the addition of modifiers.

Likewise, Chapter 4 dealt with the generative rhetoric of the paragraph, that is, the topic sentence supported by any number of related sentences, as the following generative paragraph illustrates:

<u>There are roughly three New Yorks.</u> There is, first, the New York of the man or woman who was born here, who takes the city for granted and accepts its size and its turbulence as natural and inevitable. Second, there is the New York of the commuter—the city that is devoured by locusts each day and spat out each night. Third, there is the New York of the person who was born somewhere else and came to New York in quest of something. Of these three trembling cities the greatest is the last—the city of final destination, the city that is a goal. It is this third city that accounts for New York's high-strung disposition, its poetical deportment, its dedication to the arts, and its incomparable achievements. Commuters give the city its tidal restlessness; natives give it solidity and continuity; but the settlers give it passion. And whether it is a farmer arriving from Italy to set up a small grocery store in a slum, or a young girl arriving from a small town in Mississippi to escape the indignity of being observed by her neighbors, or a boy arriving from the Corn Belt with a manuscript and a pain in his heart, it makes no difference; each embraces New York with the intense excitement of first love, each absorbs New York with the fresh eyes of an adventurer, each generates heat and light to dwarf the Consolidated Edison Company.

E. B. WHITE

Here Is New York

As you can see, the same concept of addition that works on the sentence level also works on the paragraph level, but now support sentences are added to the topic sentence (underlined) to develop the paragraph.

Now, examine this paragraph after it, too, has been notated, not on the basis of free modifiers, but on the basis of support sentences:

¹There are roughly three New Yorks.

²There is, first, the New York of the man or woman who was born here, who takes the city for granted and accepts its size and its turbulence as natural and inevitable.

²Second, there is the New York of the commuter—the city that is devoured by locusts each day and spat out each night.

²Third, there is the New York of the person who was born somewhere else and came to New York in quest of something.

³Of these three trembling cities, the greatest is the last—the city of final destination, the city that is a goal.

⁴It is this third city that accounts for New York's high-strung disposition, its political deportment its dedication to the arts, and its incomparable achievements.

From the notation, you can see how each additional sentence gives the paragraph greater development in terms of adding quality, detail, and comparison to the topic sentence. Thus, the author has written a generative paragraph by establishing a topic sentence and adding to it related support sentence . Note also that many of the support sentences are themselves generative in structure.

The final phase of generative rhetoric takes place on the largest level of writing, the complete essay, which contains a *thesis statement,* supported in various ways (to be discussed later) by paragraphs in the body of the paper. Read carefully the following essay and note how generative rhetoric is at work once again:

I became a philosopher early. I *had* to become a philosopher. I was rather badly wounded in the First World War at Soissons, France, when I was twenty-two and as a result I was flat on my back for a long time. It was either get a philosophy or crack up. *background paragraph*

2   My code of living is simple. It consists of three parts. One, never be cruel; two, always be artistic; three, never lose your sense of humor. *thesis paragraph*

3   Number one I don't believe requires much explanation. Never be cruel means, of course, always be kind. I believe that kindness is the natural human instinct, not cruelty. I have no illusions about humanity. I know its faults, its frequent blindness, its capacity for making terrible mistakes. But my work as a writer takes me among all kinds of men and women, often the very rough and the very poor. Everywhere I have found generosity and nobility; men who would have gladly given their lives for me because I had done them some slight kindness. The vast majority of human beings will do the basically good thing if they are given half a chance. *first support paragraph*

4   By the second point in my code, always be artistic, I mean that whatever I do, I try to do with as much grace as possible. If I write a *second support paragraph*

book, I want to make it as beautiful as I can. If I were a shoemaker, I would want to make shoes the same way, as perfect as possible. In our madly commercialized and mechanized world we have lost our sense of the beautiful. I believe we need beauty in our lives as much as we need food on our dining room tables. A world where beauty flourishes is a happy world—a world at peace.

third support paragraph   The third part of my code, as I said earlier, is never lose your sense 5 of humor. I don't like pomposity. I don't like stuffed shirts. I'm glad I was born in a small town. It's a wonderful antidote for smugness. I remember years ago when I had a little success in New York with one of my first novels. There was the usual round of autograph parties and literary lunches and I was feeling rather pleased with myself. About this time I happened to go back to my home town in Kentucky and I saw an old fellow I had known as a boy standing on a street corner. He looked me up and down a long time and remarked lazily, "How are you, Benny? You been away a while, ain't you? You still teaching school?" That reduced life to its proper proportions.

concluding paragraph   I was over in Germany not long ago, in the ruins of Berlin, and a 6 reporter asked me to give his paper a thought for the day. That was a bit of an order for me, who had been in two wars against the Germans and had very definite physical souvenirs from both. I reflected on what I could tell the Germans under these circumstances. And then I wrote: "When all the peoples of the world remember to laugh, particularly at themselves, there will be no more dictators and no more wars."

BEN LUCIEN BURMAN
"Antidote for War"

Note how paragraphs three through five expand on, support, and give additional related information to the thesis statement. The result of this expansion is a generative essay, as notated in the right- or left-hand margin.

Examine now the following examples of a generative sentence, expanded into a generative paragraph, and finally expanded into a generative essay outline:

Fly-fishing has three elements: equipment, knowledge of stream life, and presentation.

Fly-fishing has three elements: equipment, knowledge of stream life, and presentation. The equipment centers on the artificial fly; the knowledge of stream life encompasses insects and trout; presentation is skill, acquired and magical, in presenting the fly to the trout. Fly-fishing argument, which is fabulous, revolves around the comparative value of these elements.

JOHN MCDONALD

Introduction to *The Complete Fly Fisherman,
The Notes and Letters of Theodore Gordon*

I. Statement of subject of the paper (thesis): Fly-fishing has three elements: equipment, knowledge of stream life, and presentation.
II. Topic sentence of first support paragraph: The equipment centers on the artificial fly.
III. Topic sentence of second support paragraph: The knowledge of stream life encompasses insects and trout.
IV. Topic sentence of third support paragraph: Presentation is skill, acquired and magical, in presenting the fly to the trout.
V. Conclusion: Fly-fishing argument, which is fabulous, revolves around the comparative value of these elements.

To further understand the relationship among the generative sentence, the generative paragraph, and the generative essay, study the following array, which illustrates how all levels of writing are actually expansions of general ideas made more specific through the addition of supporting information:

Level		General point to be made		Specific support
sentence	=	base clause	+	free modifiers
paragraph	=	topic sentence	+	supporting sentences
essay	=	thesis statement	+	supporting paragraphs

Self-Evaluation

PART I

Indicate your understanding of generative writing by supplying the missing terms.

1. Generative sentence = _____ _____ + _____ _____

2. _____ _____ = _____ _____ + support sentences

3. Generative essay = _____ _____ + _____ _____

On a separate piece of paper, further demonstrate your understanding of generative writing by expanding a topic (college registration, for instance, or a topic of your choice) into a generative sentence, then a generative paragraph, and finally a generative essay outline.

Answers

PART I

1. Generative sentence = base clause + free modifiers
2. Generative paragraph = topic sentence + support sentences
3. Generative essay = thesis statement + support paragraphs

PART II

Check answers with your instructor.

(Proceed to the next chapter *only* if you have answered all of the questions and if you fully understand the material in this chapter. If not, review the material or see your instructor.)

ᵐᴵ 10 Iᵉ
Formulating the Expository Essay

Before you begin the actual writing of a paper, you must narrow the scope of your general topic and convert it into a *limited subject*. The degree to which you accomplish this process of limitation will have a great bearing on the success of your writing.

Once you have your limited subject, the introductory paragraph in general, and the thesis statement in particular, will control the body of your paper. Therefore, you should formulate this part of your essay carefully.

Objectives

After completing this chapter, you should be able

1. to convert general topics into limited subjects by applying the steps outlined in the following pages
2. to write thesis statements containing limited subject and predicate areas
3. to write an Aristotelian thesis statement
4. to expand an Aristotelian thesis statement into a sentence outline
5. to list appropriate and inappropriate ways to begin an introductory paragraph
6. to give guidelines for an introductory paragraph
7. to write an introductory paragraph

Limited Subjects

After you have been assigned a topic, you are faced with the most important step in successfully writing a paper—converting a general topic into a limited subject. The choice of topic will depend on your instructor and the nature of the assignment; however, topics can be classified in the following two ways:

1. *The imposed topic* (*assigned by instructor*): Such a topic is sometimes difficult to deal with because it is given to you by someone else (the instructor); however, it will usually be based on readings done for the class, class discussion, or both, or it will be of such a general nature that you will have at least an opinion, even though you may lack specific knowledge about it.

2. *The nonimposed topic* (*free choice*): Such a topic gives you complete freedom in the selection process, allowing you to draw on your personal experience, reading background, specific knowledge about the topic, and personal interest in it. Yet, total freedom of choice can also cause problems, since, without some direction, you may waste time trying to decide what you want to write about. Such a delay can be damaging, especially if you are writing an in-class paper.

Whether your topic is imposed or nonimposed, you still have to go through the process of narrowing its scope and converting it into a limited subject that is indicative of your area of interest and allows you the opportunity to develop it fully and interestingly. The degree to which you can develop a narrowed subject depends on the length of your paper, which will often be approximately five hundred to eight hundred words. Remember that the more you restrict the scope of your topic, the more fully you will be able to support the opinion you are expressing. A sound practice is to write about a highly limited subject, which you can develop fully, rather than to write about a general topic, which you can develop only superficially.

There are numerous methods that you may use to limit the general topic and convert it into a limited subject, but you will find one method highly practical because it is simple, it saves time, and it works, whether the topic is imposed or nonimposed. This method is outlined in the following steps:

1. Begin with a general topic: <u>education</u>. A topic by itself is merely a nominal (a noun or a noun equivalent) and as such communicates nothing to the reader or to the writer, but it is a beginning.

2. Narrow the scope of the topic: <u>college education.</u> Obviously, the scope of the general topic has now been narrowed, but not narrowed enough so that it makes an assertion. It is still only a topic, not yet a subject.

3. State an opinion about the narrowed topic: <u>college education is important.</u> Now, the narrowed topic states an opinion that is

argumentative, so it is becoming a subject. But it is still far too broad, far too general, to be discussed in a five-hundred- to eight-hundred-word paper. It fails to answer such questions as:

    a. Why is an education important?

    b. To whom is an education important?

4. Make the opinion about the narrowed subject more limited yet: A college education is important to the woman who hopes to compete successfully in the male-dominated business world. Now, the scope of the subject is limited enough so that you possibly could develop a paper in support of such an assertion. At this point, you should examine the key words in the statement to see if the subject is sufficiently narrowed. If it is, you are ready to move into the next phase of writing the paper. If, however, you find there are key words that could be narrowed even further, then you need to take at least one more step in the narrowing process.

5. Having carefully examined the underlined key words in the statement to determine if any of them could be further restricted, you are ready to develop the paper or add a fifth step. In the example of a narrowed subject suggested in step four, the words "business world" are still a bit broad, so you could qualify and thus restrict them by specifying what area of the business world will be dealt with, as follows: A college education is important to the woman who hopes to compete successfully in the male-dominated business world of insurance management. At this point, the general topic has been converted into a limited subject, so that you could write a five-hundred- to eight-hundred-word essay and develop it fully.

While there is nothing magical about narrowing a general topic and converting it into a limited subject in five steps, these steps do, in fact, illustrate a process that you will find helpful. If, however, you know the topic well and know exactly what limitations you wish to place on it, you may eliminate any number of the above steps as you convert the topic into a limited subject.

PRACTICE

Select two of the following general topics and, on a separate piece of paper, convert them into limited subjects by applying the five-step procedure outlined in the preceding section. Check your answers with your instructor.

1. love
2. prejudice
3. fear
4. pets
5. books

6. education
7. hobbies
8. leisure

Use the following summary of the five-step procedure:

Step 1. general topic
Step 2. narrowed topic
Step 3. narrowed topic + opinion = subject
Step 4. more narrowed topic, answering questions of "why" or "to whom," plus opinion
Step 5. final version of topic, converted into a limited subject that could be discussed in a five-hundred- to eight-hundred-word essay

Thesis Statements

In the process of narrowing the topic to a limited subject, you were simultaneously doing another important but closely related task, formulating a *thesis statement*—the central idea, point, or purpose of the paper. Such a statement is essential because it will control the content and, in some cases, the organization of your paper. Without a thesis statement your paper will be little more than a disjointed series of paragraphs lacking focus. In short, the thesis statement serves the dual purpose of informing readers of the central point of the paper and of guiding the writer's direction and focus. A thesis statement should contain the following:

1. *a subject area* (*limited*) that announces what will be written about in the predicate area of the thesis

   EXAMPLE: <u>A college education</u>

2. *a predicate area* (*limited*) that says something specific about the subject in the following ways:

   • It is limited or restricted in its scope.
   • It makes an assertion that is meaningful about the subject.
   • It makes an assertion about the subject that is of an argumentative nature.

   EXAMPLE: A college education <u>is important to the woman who hopes to compete successfully in the male-dominated business world of insurance management.</u>

This approach to the formulation of a thesis statement reflects *only* the content (subject matter) that is to be discussed; it does not reflect the organization of the paper. What is often called the

Aristotelian thesis statement does, however, indicate not only content but also form, as the following sentence illustrates:

The movie *Cries and Whispers* gives me pleasure because it has a believable plot, interesting characters, and a subject that is relevant to my life.

The Aristotelian thesis statement has a limited subject (*Cries and Whispers*) plus a limited predicate area (gives me pleasure because it has a believable plot, interesting characters, and a subject that is relevant to my life), which also indicates the organization of the paper. The Aristotelian thesis statement could be outlined in terms of an entire paper as follows:

1. Statement of thesis (introductory paragraph): The movie *Cries and Whispers* gives me pleasure because it has a believable plot, interesting characters, and a subject that is relevant to my life.
2. Topic sentence for second paragraph: The believable plot in *Cries and Whispers* gives me pleasure because it makes it possible for me to follow the action.
3. Topic sentence for third paragraph: Another reason I find the movie pleasurable is that the characters are interesting.
4. Topic sentence for fourth paragraph: The most important reason for the pleasure I receive from *Cries and Whispers* is that I can relate the subject to my life.
5. Concluding paragraph: These three elements—a believable plot, interesting characters, and a relevant subject—cause me to enjoy *Cries and Whispers*.

You can see that the Aristotelian thesis statement serves two important functions: first, it specifies the limited subject to be discussed in the paper; second, it outlines the organizational pattern of the paper. While such an approach may not work for all writing assignments, it is often usable, especially for the five-paragraph paper.

A thesis statement, however, is usually only one sentence of an introductory paragraph. Thus, you are faced with certain questions in terms of where to locate the thesis statement and what kinds of information should accompany it. As a rule, you will find the introductory paragraph of your paper the most appropriate place for your thesis statement. In addition to informing the reader of the central purpose of the paper and possibly its organization, the thesis statement in the introductory paragraph should also engage the interest of your reader. As to the most effective location of the thesis statement in the introductory paragraph, you have two choices, namely, first or last. The following student paragraph has the thesis statement first:

I am now a college student because I didn't want to work, didn't know what else to do with myself, and didn't have the courage to do the opposite of what my friends were doing. At the tender age of eighteen, I found myself adrift, my twelve year old school security removed by graduation. Facing an uncertain future, I felt that I had two options. First, I could find a full time job, an act I found repulsive because I didn't want to become a slave to the time clock. Second, I could go to college and prepare myself to do something useful, but this option also seemed unattractive. After much deliberation, I made a decision to attend college based on, for the most part, negative reasons.

Now look at the same opening paragraph with the thesis statement located last:

At the tender age of eighteen, I found myself adrift, my twelve year old school security removed by graduation. Facing an uncertain future, I felt that I had two options. First, I could find a full time job, an act I found repulsive because I didn't want to become a slave to the time clock. Second, I could go to college and prepare myself to do something useful, but this option also seemed unattractive. After much deliberation, I made a decision to attend college based on, for the most part, negative reasons. I am now a college student because I didn't want to work, didn't know what else to do with myself, and didn't have the courage to do the opposite of what my friends were doing.

If you carefully consider these two opening paragraphs in terms of which location is more effective and why, you can see that placing the thesis statement first creates the following problems:

- The information following the thesis statement seems anticlimactic and irrelevant.
- Readers may be confused about what is the actual thesis, especially since the last sentence of the paragraph, in this case, resembles a thesis statement.
- The transition from the opening sentence of the introductory paragraph to the first support paragraph in the body of the paper is awkward, because of the number of intervening words.
- The thesis statement at the beginning of the paragraph is abrupt; it does not prepare the readers.

On the other hand, the thesis statement located at the end of the opening paragraph has distinct advantages:

- The information preceding the thesis statement introduces the readers gradually to the subject and thus prepares them.
- Readers will not be confused about the central contention of the paper if the thesis statement is the last sentence. From its very location at the end of the paragraph, which is an emphatic position, readers can assume that this is going to be the central statement of the paper.
- The transition from the thesis statement to the first support paragraph is a short one, thereby allowing the readers to see the continuity from the opening to the support part of the paper.

As a general rule, you will find that a thesis statement placed last in the introductory paragraph will be more successful than one that is the first sentence of the paragraph.

As mentioned earlier, an introductory paragraph contains more than a single sentence, the thesis statement; it also contains related information that allows the writer to move smoothly into the statement of thesis. Although the content of the additional information contained in an introductory paragraph varies, you will find that there are a number of *functional beginnings,* as illustrated in the following student paragraphs:

Introductory Paragraphs

- Begin with a brief anecdote that illustrates and leads into the thesis statement:

Running through streets, smashing windows, looting and burning stores, the mob worked itself into a mad frenzy. I was part of that mob, one of many individuals seeking to bring about a change in the system. But I failed in my objective as did the mob. I learned a lesson that day; destructive mob rule does not bring about change.

- Begin with a quotation related to the thesis:

"I never make a mistake," Will Rogers once said, "partly because I never make a decision." To characterize the first eighteen years of my life as free of mistakes would not be far from the truth, mainly because I had never made decisions of any consequence. Recently, however, I made a decision without giving it much thought. The only conclusion I have reached is that my first major decision, to buy a new car, was a mistake.

- Begin with a general overview or background summary of the subject, which will than lead into the thesis statement:

Much controversy has surrounded what is commonly labeled the women's liberation movement as to whether it is serving any useful purposes. I have read a considerable amount of literature by opponents and proponents of the movement and have also done a considerable amount of thinking. <u>I have concluded that the movement is serving a useful purpose for me because it has caused me to re-evaluate my roles as a wife and as a mother.</u>

- Begin with a rash statement, an attention getter, one that will arouse the reader's interest and also lead into the thesis:

Behind the ivy covered walls of State University, mass production of degrees is under way! The recipients of these degrees all have outstanding skills, especially in business and science related areas. Even so, they are lacking something, a discovery they make after leaving State and venturing into the real work-a-day world. <u>They are lacking speaking and writing skills.</u>

You should also be aware that there are *inappropriate beginnings* to be avoided when you are writing an introductory paragraph:

- Do not begin with an apology or an admission of your inadequacies as a writer:

I have never been a good writer because I wasn't required to write in high school. I know that I am going to have trouble with this assignment, but I'll try anyway . . .

- Do not begin with a verbatim repetition of the title of the paper (title: "We Need More Discipline in the Home"):

We need more discipline in the home, because if we don't have discipline, undisciplined children will grow up to be undisciplined adults.

- Do not begin with a vague pronoun reference to the title of the paper (title: "The Team Cannot Win"):

It is a true statement for a number of reasons . . .

- Do not begin with a formal, explicit statement of purpose:

The purpose of this essay is to prove that English classes should be abolished in the college curriculum. (*or:* I am going to prove in this paper that . . .)

- Do not begin with an overly long or rambling introduction that merely delays the statement of thesis:

You probably won't believe this because I found it hard to believe myself. In fact, it took me three years after it happened before I did believe it. Anyway, it all happened in the summer of 1971 . . .

- Do not begin with an obvious statement of common knowledge:

The electricity is what carries light to millions of people throughout the country. Power lines must go through mountains, up mountains, and over them, and wherever these wires go there are problems involved in getting them up. And then there are also resistance factors. In fact, these are sometimes the worst problems.

Regardless of the type of beginning you select, there are certain guidelines to the construction of a good introductory paragraph:

- It should merely introduce, *not* develop, the thesis of the paper.
- It should arouse the interest of the readers.
- It should be relatively short.
- It should contain a thesis statement.
- It should contain other information that relates to and leads into the thesis statement.
- It should control the focus and the content of the rest of the paper. This control is essential for both the readers and the writer (you).
- It should establish the tone (your attitude toward the subject, that is, serious, sarcastic, flippant, humorous, or whatever) for the rest of the paper.

In summary, you must remember that, after the title, the introductory paragraph is your first direct line of communication with the readers; this introduction to the subject is going to leave an impression on them, so it should be a favorable one, which will cause them to want to read the rest of the paper, at the same time informing them of the limitations of the paper and possibly even its organizational pattern. Too often the failure of a paper can be directly traced to a weak beginning. By all means, avoid the pitfalls of programming your essay to failure because of a weak introductory paragraph.

Self-Evaluation

PART I

1. On a separate piece of paper, write thesis statements for any three of the following topics. Each thesis should be limited enough that you could develop it into a five-hundred- to eight-hundred-word paper.

    a. entertainment
    b. work
    c. religion
    d. friendship
    e. honesty
    f. movies
    g. people

2. Do the same as for Question 1, but this time write Aristotelian thesis statements.
3. Expand one of your Aristotelian thesis statements into a topic sentence outline.

PART II

1. List four ways to begin an introductory paragraph.

    a. _____

    b. _____

    c. _____

    d. _____

2. List five beginnings to avoid in an introductory paragraph.

    a. _____

    b. _____

    c. _____

    d. _____

    e. _____

3. List four guidelines for writing an introductory paragraph.

    a. _____

    b. _____

c. _____

d. _____

PART III

On a separate piece of paper, demonstrate your understanding of the material in this chapter by writing an introductory paragraph. The basis for this assignment may be one of the previous topics listed in this chapter, a topic of your choice, or a topic of your instructor's choice.

Answers

PART I

Check answers with your instructor.

PART II

1. a. a brief anecdote
   b. a quotation
   c. a general overview or background
   d. a rash statement
2. (Any five)
   a. an apology
   b. verbatim repetition of title
   c. vague pronoun reference to title
   d. formal statement of purpose
   e. long, rambling introduction
   f. obvious statement of general knowledge
3. a. introduce subject
   b. gain readers' interest
   c. relatively short
   d. contain thesis statement
   e. related information
   f. focus for rest of paper
   g. establish tone

PART III

Check answers with your instructor.

(Proceed to the next chapter *only* if you have answered all of the questions correctly and if you fully understand the material in this chapter. If not, review the material and/or see your instructor.)

⋯⋟[11]⋞⋯
Unity and Coherence

If your paper is going to read well and make sense, it must have unity and coherence.

Objectives   After completing this chapter, you should be able

1. to define unity and coherence
2. to distinguish between formal and informal transition
3. to list transitional techniques
4. to indicate where transition takes place in a paper
5. to list ways of giving a paper coherence

⋯⋙⋘⋯

A problem you will face as a writer is how to make the ideas in your paper "hang together." The answer is to make sure that the paper has unity and coherence, an easy statement to make but sometimes more difficult to achieve in writing. While the terms "unity" and "coherence" are often used as though they were synonymous (there is a close relationship between the two), at the same time they do have separate meanings.

Unity refers to the singleness of purpose in an essay, as set forth in the thesis statement. In other words, it refers to the relationship of the various parts of an essay. Probably the most important step you can take to achieve unity is to do a careful job of limiting your topic. Remember that the smaller you make the focus of your paper, the more you can develop it in detail, so that you will be less inclined to include unrelated information. Thus, each paragraph following the thesis paragraph should clearly relate to and support the thesis statement; any material that fails to do so should be deleted. Likewise, all information contained in a paragraph should relate to the topic sentence. Otherwise, if the paragraphs do not relate to the thesis statement, and if the sentences within each paragraph do not relate to the topic sentences, then the paper will lack unity. Unity is not only a matter of form, but is also an indication of your ability to think in a systematic way, which you share with readers through your writing. In summary, a generative essay will have unity if the free modifiers in the sentences support the base clauses, if the sentences in the paragraphs support the topic sentences, and if the paragraphs support the thesis statement.

Coherence refers to the means by which a writer organizes the ideas of a paper so it "hangs together" and has a continuous development. There are basically two ways to give a paper coherence. First, if the paper has unity, then it will usually have coherence. In other words, the first requirement for coherence is unity. Second, the coherence sometimes needs to be indicated so the readers can easily follow the flow of thought. The flow of thought or the relationship between ideas is referred to as *transition*, which may be classified as follows:

1. *Informal transition:* The content of the paper is organized in such a way that one part of the paper naturally leads to the next part because of the logic of the natural sequence of the ideas. In other words, the relationship between any two sequential parts of the paper is evident without using formal transition.

2. *Formal transition:* Often you will find that, to move from one part of the paper to another, you will need to "bridge the gap." This bridging process is accomplished in a number of ways:

- repetition of key words
- use of synonyms for key words
- numbering
- transitional phrases
- transitional words
- transitional pronouns

The mere presence of formal transitional devices alone, however, will not assure that your paper is unified; you must first make sure that all parts of the paper relate to the thesis statement. You should also be aware that formal transitional devices actually signal to the readers the relationship of the ideas being discussed. If you fail to show how the various parts relate to each other, your paper will lack coherence and it will seem to lack unity, even though it may not. Read carefully the following list of transitional devices, noting the various types of relationships they signal:

- to signal that what follows is additional or supplementary:

in addition	as if that weren't enough	furthermore
then, too	besides	moreover
again	also	and
in fact	indeed	or, nor
	first, second, etc.	

- to signal a contradiction, antithesis, or contrast:

yet	on the contrary	although
and yet	notwithstanding	though
nonetheless	surely	whereas
still	but	in spite of this
not at all	however	even so
on the other hand	nevertheless	for all that

- to signal that what follows is similar to what precedes:

likewise	in like manner	in much the same way
similarly	once again	once more

- to signal that what follows is a result of what precedes:

as a result	wherefore	so
as a consequence	for this reason	and so
consequently	and this is why	finally
therefore	thus	all in all
hence	on the whole	

- for reasons:

because
since
for

- for concessions:

to be sure	of course
granted (that)	no doubt
certainly	doubtless

- for qualifications:

specifically	frequently
especially	occasionally
usually	in particular
	in general

- to signal that what follows is an illustration or example:

for example	for instance	to illustrate	likewise
for one thing	in other words	similarly	

- for restriction:

if provided	unless
provided	lest
in case	when

- to illustrate that what follows is a repetition or intensification of what precedes:

to put it another way	in other words	as we have seen
as has already been said	in fact	to repeat
as we noted earlier	indeed	in any case

- to signal that what follows is quite expected, quite natural, or obviously true:

naturally	surely	to be sure
for that matter	it follows, then, that	of course
		as a matter of fact

- pronouns and adjectives pointing back to an original noun:

this	whom	it	few
that	who	they	many
these	he	all of them	most
those	she	several	some

- to signal relationship in time (often used in narration):

in the meantime	beforehand	presently
thereupon	with that out of the way	the next day
thereafter	following this	when I returned
at length	from then on	meanwhile
by that time	at that very moment	soon
at last	afterwards	soon afterward
earlier	immediately	shortly
before	within an hour	later

- to signal relationship in space (often used in description):

at that altitude	about a foot to the left	a little farther on
between those cities	at the center of the circle	in the next room
across the way	on the edge of the clearing	beyond this point

- to signal that what follows is a summary:

to summarize	therefore	all in all
in brief	in short	what all this adds up to
in a word	in summary	what we have, then,

in sum	to sum up	on the whole
in conclusion	to conclude	

There are certainly other words and phrases that can be used to express these relationships, but this list will give you some idea of the kinds of relationships that statements normally have to each other, even in very simple prose, as well as some idea of the functions of transitions in making these relationships clear.

Transition, both formal and informal, takes place on all levels of writing:

- between paragraphs
- within paragraphs
- within sentences

How you arrange or order the sequence of paragraphs to give them coherence in an expository essay will largely be dictated by the nature of the subject. Generally speaking, order may be classified in the following ways:

1. *Chronological:* The arrangement is from first event to last. This order is often used in a narrative illustration, but can be used with any subject that lends itself to a natural time sequence.

2. *Logical:* One part logically leads to the next part, and so on. Although related to chronological order, logical order is actually dictated by sequence rather than time. For instance, if you were explaining how to change a tire, you would do so in terms of the logical sequence (jack up the car, remove the hub cap, and so on), which has little to do with time measurements.

3. *Arbitrary:* Sometimes neither of the preceding two orders is appropriate for a given subject, in which case you are left to select an order. Four of the options available are:
   a. Complexity: Usually start with the simplest facet of the subject and proceed to the most complex.
   b. Importance: Start with the least important facet and move to the most important, an order that adds a sense of suspense to writing.
   c. Deductive (general to specific): Start with a general idea and support it with specific details.
   d. Inductive (specific to general): Start with specific details and end with a general conclusion.

Chapter 12, "Writing the Expository Essay," will further clarify ways of organizing an essay, depending on your subject and purpose.

Read the following two paragraphs and note how the writers

give each paragraph coherence by making use of a variety of formal transitional devices:

In considering the history and development of American English we must remember that the courageous bands who ventured westward into the unknown with Captain John Smith or on board the *Mayflower,* as well as those who followed them later in the seventeenth century, were speaking and writing the English language as it was currently employed in England. Consequently, whatever linguistic processes operated to produce the differences between American and British English which exist today must either have taken place in American English after the colonists settled on this continent or have occurred in British English after the emigrants left their homeland. Or, as a third possibility, there may have been changes in both divisions of the language after the period of settlement. We cannot, however, escape the conclusion of original identity and subsequent change.

ALBERT H. MARCKWARDT
American English

There are roughly three News Yorks. There is, first, the New York of the man or woman who was born here, who takes the city for granted and accepts its size and its turbulence as natural and inevitable. Second, there is the New York of the commuter—the city that is devoured by locusts each day and spat out each night. Third, there is the New York of the person who was born somewhere else and came to New York in quest of something. Of these three trembling cities the greatest is the last—the city of final destination, the city that is a goal. It is this third city that accounts for New York's high-strung disposition, its poetical deportment, its dedication to the arts, and its incomparable achievements. Commuters give the city its tidal restlessness; natives give it solidity and continuity; but the settlers give it passion. And whether it is a farmer arriving from Italy to set up a small grocery store in a slum, or a young girl arriving from a small town in Mississippi to escape the indignity of being observed by her neighbors, or a boy arriving from the Corn Belt with a manuscript and a pain in his heart, it makes no difference: each embraces New York with the intense excitement of first love, each absorbs New York with the fresh eyes of an adventurer, each generates heat and light to dwarf the Consolidated Edison Company.

E. B. WHITE
Here Is New York

Both paragraphs demonstrate an extensive use of formal transitional devices, especially the second paragraph. Such extensive use is not always necessary, so do not overload your papers with excessive formal transition. At the same time, the transitions in the above paragraphs do cause them to hang together and make them more readable. Try omitting the transitional devices and see how this changes the sense of each paragraph. Note also that both paragraphs are highly unified. Each writer states his topic sentence, then includes only information that is related.

As a general rule, use formal transition when it is needed to show the relationship between any two parts of the paper; but, if the relationship is evident from the content, rely on informal transition.

Now read the following essay, noting how the writer has given it unity by relating everything to the thesis and coherence by making the ideas flow together with the help of transitional devices:

The English language is spoken or read by the largest number of people in the world, for historical, political, and economic reasons; but it may also be true that it owes something of its wide appeal to qualities and characteristics inherent in itself. What are these characteristic features which outstand in making the English language what it is, which give it its individuality and make it of this worldwide significance?

First and most important is its extraordinary receptive and adaptable heterogeneousness—the varied ease and readiness with which it has taken to itself material from almost everywhere in the world and has made the new elements of language its own. English, which when the Anglo-Saxons first conquered England in the fifth and sixth centuries was almost a "pure" or unmixed language—which could make new words for new ideas from its own compounded elements and had hardly any foreign words—has become the most "mixed" of languages, having received throughout its history all kinds of foreign elements with ease and assimilated them all to its own character. Though its copiousness of vocabulary is outstanding, it is its amazing variety and heterogeneousness which is even more striking: and this general receptiveness of new elements has contributed to making it a suitable and attractive vehicle in so many parts of the world.

A second outstanding characteristic of English is its simplicity of inflection—the ease with which it indicates the relationship of words in a sentence with only the minimum of change in their shapes or variation of endings. There are languages, such as Chinese, that have surpassed English in the reduction of the language in the matter of inflections to what looks like just a series of fixed monosyllabic roots: but among European languages, taken as a whole, English has gone as far as any in reducing the inflections it once had to a minimum. A natural consequence of this simplifying of inflection by reduction, however, is that since the relationship of words to each other is no longer made clear by their endings, this must be done in other ways.

A third quality of English, therefore, is its relatively fixed word order. An inflected language like Latin or Russian can afford to be fairly free in the arrangement of its words, since the inflections show clearly the proper relationship in the sentence, and ambiguity is unlikely. But in a language which does not change the forms of its words according to their relationship in the sentence-significance, the order of the words is likely to be relatively fixed; and a fixed word order in relation to meaning in the sentence takes the place of the freedom made possible by the system of inflections.

Another consequence, fourthly, of the loss or reduction to the minimum of the inflections which English once had, is the growth of the use of periphrases or roundabout ways of saying things, and of the use of prepositions to take the place of the lost inflections. The English simplified verb uses periphrases and compound tenses made with auxiliary verbs to replace the more elaborate system of tenses that once existed (though tenses had already become fairly simple before the Anglo-Saxons came to England). Similarly, English, which once had nearly as many case endings as Latin, has come to use prepositions instead of these, as easily be seen if one translates any piece of Latin into English.

A fifth quality of English—though this, like the loss of inflections and its consequences, is shared with some other languages—is the development of new varieties of intonation to express shades of meaning which were formerly indicated by varying the shapes of words. This is perhaps somewhat comparable (though only in a small way) to the vast use of intonation in Chinese as a method of expressing meaning in sentences which would otherwise seem like series of unvarying monosyllabic roots. Consider, for instance, the wonderful variety of shades of meaning we may put into the use of the word *do*, merely by varying the intonation—that is, the pitch and intensity, the tone of the voice.

Not all the above qualities are in themselves necessarily good, nor have they all contributed to the general success of English. But it seems probable that of them all it is the adaptable receptiveness and the simplicity of inflection that have done most in this regard. On the other hand, the very copiousness and heterogeneousness of English leads to vagueness or lack of clarity. Its resources are too vast for all but the well educated to use to full advantage; and such phenomena as "pidgin English," "journalese," jargon, woolliness of expression and slatternly speech and writing, are everywhere likely to be met with. It may fairly be said that English is among the easiest languages to speak badly, but the most difficult to use well.

C. L. WRENN

The English Language

Self-Evaluation

PART I

Complete these exercises on a separate piece of paper.

1. Write sentence definitions of unity and coherence.
2. Write sentence definitions of formal and informal transition.

PART II

1. List five formal transitional devices.

   a. _____

   b. _____

   c. _____

   d. _____

   e. _____

2. List the three places in a paper where transition takes place.

   a. _____

   b. _____

   c. _____

3. List two ways of giving a paper coherence.

   a. _____

   b. _____

4. List three ways of arranging the order of paragraphs in an essay.

   a. _____

   b. _____

   c. _____

Using the E. B. White paragraph about New York, make a list of each formal transition and classify it, as follows:

EXAMPLE: 1. first = numbering
2. therefore = transitional word
3. on the other hand = transitional phrase

1. _____

2. _____

3. _____

4. _____

5. _____

6. _____

7. _____

Answers

PART I

Check your answers by referring to the first part of this chapter.

PART II

1. a. words
   b. phrases
   c. numbering
   d. repetition of key words
   e. synonyms
   f. pronouns
2. a. between paragraphs
   b. within paragraphs
   c. within sentences
3. a. unity
   b. transition
4. a. chronological
   b. logical
   c. importance

d. complexity
e. inductive
f. deductive

PART III

1. first = numbering
2. second = numbering
3. third = numbering
4. cities = synonym or phrase
5. it = pronoun
6. and = transitional word
7. each = pronoun

(Proceed to the next chapter *only* if you answered all of the questions correctly and if you fully understand the material in this chapter. If not, review the material or see your instructor.)

❖[12]❖
Writing the Expository Essay

After you have converted a topic into a narrowed subject and written an opening paragraph containing a thesis statement, you are ready to support, elaborate on, and develop the thesis of the paper. In other words, you are ready to write the body of the paper; but, unlike the opening paragraph, the support paragraphs must be fully developed. Much of the following discussion of modes of development will be an expansion of Chapter 8, "The Expository Paragraph." The correlation is obvious: paragraphs are developed by modes; related paragraphs make up essays. Thus, the same approach used to develop a single paragraph is also used to develop a multiparagraph essay. Although these modes will be presented as if they existed independently of each other (which they can but seldom do), you should be aware that combinations of modes will often be used in a single paper, which we call the mixed-mode essay. For the purpose of classification, consider that a given paper has one *dominant* mode with a number of *support* modes. Notice in the various essay examples how the writers have used one dominant mode, but have also used other support modes, which are labeled in the margins of some of the essays. These modes, in the order of their presentation, are the following:

1. illustration and example
2. analysis
3. comparison/contrast
4. analogy
5. cause and effect

6. definition
7. mixed mode

You may find a brief summary of the theory of generative writing helpful at this point. In Chapter 9, the relationships of the various units of writing were shown in the following way:

Level		General point to be made		Specific support
sentence	=	base clause	+	free modifiers
paragraph	=	topic sentence	+	supporting sentences
essay	=	thesis statement	+	supporting paragraphs

Since the focus of this segment of the book is on the expository essay, you should understand how modes of development relate to generative writing. As the last part of the preceding array indicates, the essence of the generative essay is a thesis statement developed through related paragraphs. The array does not indicate, however, the various ways of developing the supporting paragraphs. Therefore, the subsequent discussion presents various modes of development as available options. Regardless of the way you develop your essay, you will build on the foundation of the thesis statement; from a general statement, you will generate detailed support paragraphs. In other words, you will be writing a generative essay.

The last section of this chapter discusses concluding paragraphs. Expository essays that have strong opening paragraphs and fully developed support paragraphs are sometimes weakened by faulty concluding paragraphs. You should, therefore, be aware of how to end your papers effectively.

Objectives

After completing this chapter, you should be able

1. to demonstrate an understanding of the following modes of essay development: illustration and example, analysis, comparison/contrast, analogy, cause and effect, definition, and mixed mode
2. to write at least two essays employing distinct, dominant modes of development
3. to write one essay employing mixed modes
4. to apply the concepts of concluding paragraphs to all of your essays

---

Illustration and Example

You are familiar with *illustration* because it is a natural part of your daily conversation. When you are talking to someone, think how often you use such expressions as "for example" or "for instance" to introduce an illustration that helps clarify a point you are making. Even if you don't actually include such transitional phrases, you still use illustration. Consider the following dialogue:

JOE: What do you think of the team this year?
MOE: Well, if they win half of their games they'll be lucky.
JOE: Do you really think they'll be that bad?
MOE: Yeah, I do.
JOE: But why?
MOE: Because the team is weak at quarterback. Dalsing is just too old and will probably get hurt the first game. The other quarterbacks are either inexperienced or simply not good enough. Payne is a rookie, so he won't help this year. Lee has been around long enough to prove that he is just an average quarterback. So, until the team comes up with an outstanding quarterback, it will be lucky to win half its games.
JOE: Yeah, you're probably right.

Simplistic as it is, the preceding dialogue does, in fact, simulate the use of verbal illustration. It also shows four possible purposes of illustration:

- to make the general more specific
- to make the abstract more concrete
- to make the complex more understandable
- to make the unfamiliar more familiar

The basic value of illustration is that it can transform feeble generalities into immediate and personally convincing writing. Read carefully the following paragraph in which a student makes effective use of illustration to support her topic sentence:

Perhaps as a result of our highly impersonal and stereotyped society, people seem to exercise great restraint and seldom display their emotions. When they don't conduct themselves in an impersonal way, but vent their emotions outwardly, they may be misunderstood by others. For instance, several years ago I met an individual who surprised me frequently with his spontaneous laughter. Not knowing him well, I was often caught off guard and even somewhat intimidated by this laughter. I wasn't sure whether it stemmed from a certain superiority, an inner self-confidence, or an actual scornful nature. Many times I felt his laughter to be at my expense; I was truly fearful of encountering him and provoking more of his perplexing laughter. Although I cannot point to an exact moment when I realized my misconceptions, I can say my reactions decidedly changed. I saw that his manner was most charming, and in a very uninhibited way, he displayed his pleasure with life through his laughter. His smile was disarming, as was his ability to throw back his head and enjoy his own laughter. These sudden outbursts were like a succession of emotional highs, and eventually quite contagious. His laugh, which I had at first found so perplexing, turned out to be one of his most endearing qualities, and a binding aspect of our relationship.

It takes little imagination to realize that this paragraph about the effects of laughter would have been ineffective as an illustration had the writer stayed on a general level, that is, had the content been filled with such generalities as "laughter can be misunderstood," or "laughter is best," or "laughter is contagious." Had she done so, she would have piled generality on top of generality, but she would not have illustrated one generality with specific details. In short, the attempt to illustrate would have been unsuccessful.

On the following pages, another student also uses illustration to support, not the topic sentence of a paragraph, but the thesis statement of an essay:

We can do whatever we choose to do, if we are willing to work at it with sincere endurance. I have spent my lifetime proving that to myself, and our brain-injured son has accomplished his aims to reinforce my confidence in that statement.

For instance, I had hoped to follow high school with college. Although I was graduated as valedictorian with four scholarships, circumstances in my family meant I had to find a job instead of a college. My senior year, I had carried seven subjects to squeeze in a year of shorthand and typing. My first job was as file clerk in the office of a trucking concern whose owner was also involved in other businesses, including insurance. When his insurance office needed a girl with shorthand, I was sent over there— a small step up. Soon I was claim agent. Then the trucking company needed a secretary for the director of transportation; I was sent back there. The war was on and my job included maintaining records on rationed products like gasoline and tires. When my boss suggested I falsify records to secure more of these things, I tossed him the files, marched into the president's office and told him if there was nothing else I could do, I would quit.

"I'm not satisfied with my new secretary," he said, "so you can be my secretary."

The traffic manager was drafted and they slid me into that slot. Later, the owner's secretary retired and I moved into her place in the insurance office. It was quickly evident that with her gone, no one else was equipped to handle underwriting. This included the rating of policies, bonds, endorsements, and miscellaneous calculations like life insurance programming. I became underwriter with eight brokers at my mercy. Field men from two dozen insurance companies lined up at my desk, asking me to swing business their way. I had my own secretary and staff. What a feeling of power! Who needed college? At twenty-four, I was doing fine!

I married and was happy to leave the pressures of the business world. But our first child was born brain-injured and new pressures presented themselves. We lived in fear of retardation. Michael seemed to progress almost normally—a little late walking, a little late talking, but he was unable to sleep more than thirty minutes at a time. This situation lasted two years and he was four before he slept through the night, but I had developed a permanent case of insomnia. I lost a baby and was told I would be unable to have more children.

As Mike grew, it became apparent his equilibrium was damaged. Handwriting was difficult; he could not copy material from the blackboard or finish tests in time. He could not play ball or engage in other sports, and he endured the cruelty of other children. He pleaded for a baby brother to keep him company. My health outlawed adoption. When Mike was nine, we were transferred to another city. There, the doctor tried a new treatment to help me. In three years, I was pregnant, and when Michael was thirteen, he had the brother he wanted for so long. We had all persisted and endured and succeeded.

Michael had not achieved enough balance to ride a two-wheel bike. Then, after crawling and creeping with his beloved baby brother, he suddenly was able to ride! About that time, people trained in the patterning advocated by the Philadelphia Institutes for the Achievement of Human Potential opened a clinic in our city. Michael was tested and assigned exercises. For two years, two hours a day, he crawled and crept and did eye exercises, at a time when most teenage boys were enjoying extracurricular activities. He was determined to improve, and he did. Reading skills zoomed, his sense of humor improved, and his driving instructor, upon putting him through the course a second time, assured us his eyes were not converging on the road. He entered college and was graduated without failing a single course. He has been working at his present job for two years and spent his vacation in Europe. It appears our years of worry for him are over.

So now I am going to college. It has taken many years of waiting. I do not begrudge them. I know I was learning all the while I waited. I am convinced we can do whatever we choose to do, if we are willing to work at it with sincere endurance. What do you want to do?

In a much more sophisticated manner, this essay, like the dialogue between Joe and Moe, also contains illustration as the dominant mode of support. Notice how all of the sentences illustrate the thesis and, in the process, make the paragraphs more specific by adding the three attributes of generative writing—quality, detail, and comparison.

Look now at the following essay, in which a professional writer uses illustration as the dominant mode to support his thesis:

The "intellectualism" of the French is found at every level of society. The café waiter, the taxicab driver, the restaurateur, the so-called "little people" of France are the most stimulating, if frequently exasperating, conversationalists in the world. Of them all, the most anarchistic and voluble is the taxicab driver. I deliberately provoke arguments with them—an easy thing to do—to see what they will say next. Of the hundreds of discussions in cabs one remains in my memory as uniquely, superbly French. It could not have occurred in any other country, except possibly in Brooklyn, where there exists a species of man akin in spirit if not in actual form to the French.

It was midnight in Paris and we were rolling along the Quai d'Orsay toward the Avenue Bosquet, where I live, on the left bank of the river Seine. As we came to the Pont Alexandre III the cab slowed down, for the traffic light was red against us, and then, without stopping, we sailed through the red light in a sudden burst of speed. The same performance was repeated at the Alma Bridge. As I paid the driver I asked him why he had driven through two red lights.

"You ought to be ashamed of yourself, a veteran like you, breaking the law and endangering your life that way," I protested.

He looked at me astonished. "Ashamed of myself? Why, I'm proud of myself. I am a law-abiding citizen and have no desire to get killed either." He cut me off before I could protest.

"No, just listen to me before you complain. What did I do? Went through a red light. Well, did you ever stop to consider what a red light is, what it means?"

"Certainly," I replied. "It's a stop signal and means that traffic is rolling in the opposite direction."

"Half-right," said the driver, "but incomplete. It is only an automatic stop signal. And it does not mean that there is cross traffic Did you see any cross traffic during our trip? Of course not. I slowed down at the light, looked carefully to the right and to the left. Not another car on the streets at this hour. Well, then! What would you have me do? Should I stop like a dumb animal because an automatic, brainless machine turns red every forty seconds? No, monsieur," he thundered, hitting the door jamb with a huge fist. "I am a man, not a machine. I have eyes and a brain and judgment, given me by God. It would be a sin against nature to surrender them to the dictates of a machine. Ashamed of myself, you say? I would only be ashamed of myself if I let those blinking lamps do my thinking for me. Good night, monsieur."

Is this bad, is this good? Frankly I no longer am sure. The intellectual originality of the French is a corrupting influence if you are subjected to it for long. I never doubted that it was wrong to drive through a red light. After more than a decade of life in Paris, however, I find my old Anglo-Saxon standards somewhat shaken. I still think it is wrong to drive through a stop signal, except possibly very late at night, after having carefully checked to make sure there is no cross traffic. After all, I am a man, not a machine.

DAVID SCHOENBRUN
The Logical Cab Driver

Schoenbrun uses an *extended illustration,* that is, a single illustration developed in great detail, to support his thesis that intellectualism is a trait of the French. Note how an extended illustration resembles narration, including dialogue, but is used for the expository purpose of explaining or clarifying the thesis. The use of dialogue depends on your subject. In this case, it helps develop the illustration and at the same time adds interest to the writing.

You may find, however, that an extended illustration does not serve your purpose, which would be better served by several illustrations. In Chapter 8, a series of illustrations was classified as development by *example*. In the following essay, the writer uses examples as the dominant mode of development:

The English language is suffering from a word shortage. This is because the world changes so fast nowadays that word makers cannot produce new words fast enough to keep up with all the new things that are happening.

For example, the Volkswagen has been with us for twenty years, but we still do not have a good word to describe the peculiar state of mind which the Volkswagen induces in its driver. Without such a word, other drivers have no effective way of dealing with the Volkswagen driver as he weaves in and out of heavy traffic, feeling dangerously like a broken-field runner on an asphalt gridiron.

All you can do when you catch one of these people at a red light is lean out the window and say, "You're suffering from lethal delusions of mobility," or something equally cumbersome. The word we need here is obviously "miniphoria," a descriptive noun suggesting the odd euphoria that comes over people hunched in miniature machines. When you catch a Volkswagen driver at the light, you simply lean out the window and roar, "You stupid miniphoriac!" and the world becomes a satisfying place again.

Another modern condition for which there is no adequate word is the appearance of women walking along the street in tightly fitting trousers, slacks or jeans. Everyone has seen this modern spectacle, but at present dozens of imprecise words are needed to discuss it. Words like "rippling," "quivering," "bulging," "ballooning," etc.

What we need is a single noun that succinctly sums up the condition. Such a word might be "juglipidity." With "juglipidity," the spectacle will no longer leave us speechless. Seeing one of these poor creatures in public, we will only have to say, "That poor woman's juglipidity is acute," and the situation will be satisfactorily disposed of.

We also need a word for the modern crime of robbery by machine. In the typical mechanized robbery, the victim puts fifteen cents into a soda-pop vending machine. The machine seizes the money, drops it into a metal loot box, and refuses to come across with the soda pop.

The victim is baffled. If he had been robbed by a man with a gun, he would know what to do. He would go to the police, report the commission of a felony and, after the bandit had been caught, testify in court to put the wretch behind bars.

Against a felonious machine, there is no apparent recourse. What is the word for this offense that has been committed? What are the victim's rights once he has futilely punched the coin-return lever a few times? Is it permissible to kick the machine? Should it be turned over to the police?

If there were a familiar word for this all-too-familiar modern crime, the victim could act with reason. The word we need is "slottery," a noun meaning "robbery by a coin-vending machine."

Give crime its proper name and man can deal with it. When the machine grabs his fifteen cents, the victim, no longer faced with an indefinable situation, will cry, "Ah ha! So slottery's your game, eh?" He will then feel perfectly justified in attacking the thief with a jack handle, recovering his money from the loot box and stuffing the machine's slots with chewing gum.

RUSSELL BAKER
"Juglipidity"

Notice that the examples are not directly related to each other but they do all relate to the thesis (first sentence). Thus, they serve a functional purpose.

Even if you do not use either as the dominant mode, you will find that illustration and examples can always be used as support modes, sometimes for only one paragraph, or in some cases only a few sentences, of an essay.

In summary, you will find the following guidelines helpful when writing an essay using an extended illustration or a series of examples as the dominant mode of development:

- The illustration or example must obviously be related to the idea being explained.
- The illustration or example should be very specific, much more specific than the idea being discussed. In other words, it should add detail, quality, or comparison to the idea being explained.

- The illustration or example must be typical of the idea being discussed, rather than an exception.
- The illustration or example can often make extensive use of narration and description.
- The illustration or example should add interest to the paper.
- The illustration or example shows readers the point being made, but it should not be looked on as proof.

1. List the four purposes of illustration.

   a. _____

   b. _____

   c. _____

   d. _____

2. Summarize the six guidelines for the use of illustration and example.

   a. _____

   b. _____

   c. _____

   d. _____

   e. _____

   f. _____

3. Distinguish between an extended illustration and a series of examples by defining each.

   _____

   _____

   _____

   _____

1. a. to make the general more specific
   b. to make the abstract more concrete
   c. to make the complex more understandable
   d. to make the unfamiliar more familiar
2. a. must obviously be related to the point being illustrated
   b. should be specific
   c. should be typical of the subject
   d. may be narrative or descriptive
   e. should add interest to the paper
   f. supports but does not prove a point
3. An extended illustration is one fully developed idea, often of a narrative nature. A series of examples contains a number of unrelated, briefly developed examples supporting the thesis.

WRITING ASSIGNMENT

Select one of the following topics and write an essay in which you support the thesis with an illustration or a series of examples. You may use Schoenbrun's essay as a possible model, but do not try to imitate it.

1. a conclusion you have reached about people in general, a group, or an individual
2. a controversial issue (such as abortion, amnesty, required classes)
3. a life style
4. a time in your life of extreme emotion
5. Topic of your choice

(After you have written a first draft of the assignment, read pages 244–245 and revise your concluding paragraph in light of the information given there.)

Analysis

As an expository mode, analysis is simply the method of dividing a subject into its component parts. Such a division allows you to examine in great detail the parts that make up the whole of the subject. It is a useful mode because it can be applied to any subject that is thought of as having parts. In fact, as you will see later, a number of other modes of development are actually specialized forms of analysis.

To understand the nature and use of analysis, you should study the following guidelines:

1. The subject to be analyzed should first be narrowed. For example, in a five-hundred- to seven-hundred-word paper, it would be an impossible task to analyze the general topic, "dogs." Therefore, go through approximately the same process to narrow and

convert a general topic into a limited subject as discussed in Chapter 10. Such a process of limitation might be indicated in the following way: dogs→show dogs→working-class show dogs→shelties→physical traits of champion shelties→(a) compact body, (b) full coat, (c) regular markings. Thesis: Champion shelties are characterized by compact bodies, full coats, and regular markings. Notice how naturally analysis lends itself to the Aristotelian thesis statement.

2. The example of the physical traits of champion shelties points out the second requirement of analysis—parallelism or consistency of the various considerations. In other words, a compact body, a full coat, and regular markings are, in fact, all physical traits. If, however, you were to divide the parts into compact body, full coat, and even disposition, the last point would violate the concept of parallelism because disposition is classified as a personality trait rather than a physical trait.

3. Analysis may be used with any subject that is thought of as having two or more parts or divisions. In other words, almost any subject can be analyzed. Whether you discuss the parts of a car engine or the symptoms of love, you can apply the principles of analysis.

4. The ultimate purpose for using analysis as an organizational mode is to make the entire subject understandable. Thus, you must always show how the various parts of the subject relate to the whole. In other words, there would be no point in simply discussing the various traits of champion shelties as though they existed independently, because they don't; each trait is essential to the overall subject.

5. The basis for the analysis will be determined by one of the following:
    a. *The nature of the subject:* There are numerous ways that you can break down a subject so as to consider its parts—for instance, according to its attributes, functions, parts, traits, purposes, causes, reasons, ingredients, steps, processes, and so forth. Obviously, such a list could go on and on; the point is that the basis for dividing the subject into its parts depends on the subject itself. For instance, if you were writing about a war, you might analyze it in terms of causes. On the other hand, you could not discuss war in terms of its ingredients, but you could discuss a recipe in terms of either ingredients or steps to be followed. Common sense will usually dictate the basis for the analysis. The basis for the division, whether it is the subject itself or your interest in it, makes analysis a highly logical,

and thus an exacting, mode of writing. It is totally different from accidental or haphazard analysis.

b. *Personal interest:* The principle of analysis may also be dictated by your interest in the subject. For instance, if you were going to discuss an orange and you were of a scientific bent, you might discuss it as a botanical structure, breaking it down into such parts as peel, seeds, pulp, and so forth. If, on the other hand, your interest happened to be more artistically inclined, you might discuss the orange as an aesthetic structure, breaking it down into color, shape, size, texture, and so forth.

6. Once you have decided on the basis for the analysis, you must then select the order of presentation or the arrangement of these parts in one of the following ways (for further discussion, refer to Chapter 11):

    a. chronological order
    b. logical order
    c. arbitrary order
        (1) complexity
        (2) importance
        (3) deductive
        (4) inductive

Generally speaking, analysis can be classified as directional (or process) and conceptual. Defined simply, a *directional or process analysis* is a "how to" approach, as in the following essay:

A trial-and-error cook, obliged to operate within easy reach of a cookbook or two, is bound to be stunned with satisfaction when any stray formula that he has picked up on his own and not from a cookbook succeeds. It does not occur to him that most cooks have long since mastered the process that he has just learned, and few subjects can inspire the zeal with which two non-cooks will exchange even the most elementary recipes. I am aware of this—aware, too, that women who may read this page may regard my findings as merely belated; but I am too earnestly the proprietor of a sour-cream venture to be able to keep quiet about it.

It is a veal dish, to be accompanied by rice. (I am still working towards a better version of rice.) It is easy to prepare, needs no touching up enroute, and yields a powerful gravy for the rice without the least effort by the cook. The ingredients: eight or ten sliced onions, a two- or three-pound slice of veal, 1" to 1½" thick, cut from the leg, and one pint of sour cream. (Serves 4–6.)

Any old time during the afternoon will do for getting the veal dish started. The onions, peeled and sliced thin, are brought to the yellow with a lump of butter in a heavy skillet over a low flame. About ten minutes, perhaps fifteen, will do it, and the onions should not be allowed to brown.

Then pile the onions at the edge of the skillet, away from the heat, and sear the veal briskly on both sides, turning up the flame for this interval. (I am assured by an M.I.T. chemist-cook that the searing causes the veal to exude a gelatinous substance which prevents the sour cream from curdling later on; yet all I know is that several women, good cooks all, warn me it will curdle anyhow, but mine does not.)

With the onions yellowed and the veal seared, the cook can suit the rest of the process to his convenience. All that remains is to turn the flame very low, add the pint of sour cream, stir the onions into the cream, clap on a sufficient lid, and let the whole thing simmer for the hour before serving. An extra few minutes won't matter, if guests are late, but the low flame matters a great deal, and the mixture should be barely bubbling while cooking. If the rice is too much trouble, one can always pick up a quart or two from a Chinese restaurant and reheat it in a colander over boiling water, or else substitute that always dependable, no-work adjunct of the trial-and-error menu—the baked potato.

The common objection to sour-cream dishes, I find, is that sour cream is fattening. It probably is, but the novice cook, seeking as he must the maximum of appeal in return for the minimum of work, is advised to let the calories fall where they may.

CHARLES W. MORTON
A Slight Sense of Outrage

For what he intended to do—explain a process—this writer has been successful. The points of analysis have been arranged in chronological order, beginning with the first step and progressing to the last. The essay contains clear, understandable directions that readers should be able to follow. Finally, the essay adheres to the guidelines previously discussed.

Look now at the following essay, in which a student analyzes the procedures to follow when taking the College Level Examination Program (CLEP) tests:

In increasing numbers, older people with only high school educations are now appearing at the colleges of the nation to rectify whatever lack they feel. Fortunately, word is getting around that they can make up some of their lost time by testing out for credits. The College Level Examination Program (CLEP) can give such people a head start on their degrees by giving credit for acquired knowledge. Having tested through my freshman year in this fashion, there are four suggestions which I would offer to anyone thinking about taking CLEP tests.

First, consider all factors of your background before arriving at a decision. How long has it been since you were graduated from high school? For me, it was thirty-five years! Have you done a lot of reading in the interval? Have you kept up on current events? Have you taken any non-credit courses in the meantime? Is your memory good and have you retained your knowledge? In my case, the answer to these questions was a decided "yes." I allowed myself only two weeks to prepare for the battery of five test areas, including English Composition, Mathematics, Social Studies, Humanities and Natural Science. If you could not answer the above questions affirmatively, it would certainly be advisable to allow two or three months for concentrated study. Since I had had only one year of algebra and one year of geometry in high school, I had to teach myself trigonometry and calculus. I had never seen a parabola until I saw one in the study textbook. Having absorbed all I could on my own, I asked two friends with mathematics backgrounds to spend an evening with me. One friend cleared up part of my uncertainties and the other friend worked out the rest.

Second, contact your local college administering CLEP and learn all you can about the many tests given. You will want to know what percentile is required for passing, dates for testing, and if the credits transfer to other colleges since not all colleges honor CLEP credits. You will also want to invest in one of the books you will hear about which give sample tests in each category. These books are available at most bookstores for a few dollars and will help you to pinpoint your areas of weakness. The book I used had two tests in each category, so I immediately took one test in each category. The type of wrong answers indicates what you need to study particularly, and the second test can be taken later to see if you have progressed. At this point, your library is your best friend.

My third hint is that you should plan a systematic approach to your study and be consistent about it. Don't make excuses for skipping days. Put as many hours a day into study as you can, and if your mind seems to tire of one subject, switch to another. The change will be a refresher. Part of your study may even include a tutor. You should also study all subject areas, especially science and math. In my case, while the sample book seemed to show the science test concentrating on biology, the actual test accented chemistry, but I hadn't cracked a chemistry book. So do spend some time studying chemistry.

Last, approach the tests with confidence and with some awareness of what to expect. To be intimidated is to be lost. Remember that one-quarter is deducted for each wrong answer. Therefore, it is generally unwise to make wild guesses. It is unnecessary to answer all the questions on the test paper; time does not allow for it in most cases and the grading seems to take that into account. So unless you have left too many unanswered questions (they are all multiple choice), it is usually better not to guess. The tests are not easy, but they are not impossible to pass. The average passing rate is about 75%, so your chances of passing are good.

Many of us have acquired valuable information in the years spent in jobs, volunteer work, or even at home in the process of living. CLEP allows recognition for the experience and knowledge that come with maturity, and adds encouragement to those of us who want to do some catching up in life. You will, as I did, find it an uplifting experience when your grades arrive in the mail five or six weeks later and you find you have passed.

This writer has systematically analyzed the steps to be followed when taking the CLEP tests, starting with the first step and proceeding to the final one. Depending, however, on the nature of your assignment, you may find that the process analysis is inappropriate for your subject. If so, you will want to employ a more complex form, which may be classified as a *conceptual analysis*. For the purposes of definition, consider any form of analysis that does not involve a "how to" sequence as conceptual. Read the following essay by Bertrand Russell, paying special attention to the order in which he presents his three points:

Three passions, simple but overwhelmingly strong, have governed my life: the longing for love, the search for knowledge, and unbearable pity for the suffering of mankind. These passions, like great winds, have blown me hither and thither, in a wayward course, over a deep ocean of anguish, reaching to the very verge of despair.

I have sought love, first, because it brings ecstasy—ecstasy so great that I would often have sacrificed all the rest of life for a few hours of this joy. I have sought it, next, because it relieves loneliness—that terrible loneliness in which one shivering consciousness looks over the rim of the world into the cold unfathomable lifeless abyss. I have sought it, finally, because in the union of love I have seen, in a mystic miniature, the prefiguring vision of the heaven that saints and poets have imagined. This is what I sought, and though it might seem too good for human life, this is what—at last—I have found.

With equal passion I have sought knowledge. I have wished to understand the hearts of men. I have wished to know why the stars shine. And I have tried to apprehend the Pythagorean power by which number holds sway above the flux. A little of this, but not much, I have achieved.

Love and knowledge, so far as they were possible, led upward toward the heavens. But always pity brought me back to earth. Echoes of cries of pain reverberate in my heart. Children in famine, victims tortured by oppressors, helpless old people a hated burden to their sons, and the whole world of loneliness, poverty, and pain make a mockery of what human life should be. I long to alleviate the evil, but I cannot, and I too suffer.

This has been my life. I have found it worth living, and would gladly live it again if the chance were offered me.

BERTRAND RUSSELL

"What I Have Lived For"

As you can see, the very subject of Russell's essay is more conceptual than Morton's or the student's. It is different also because the subject does not lend itself to a "how to" approach. In short, Russell's essay is a good example of a conceptual analysis, and the arrangement of the details is based on an order of importance sequence. Even though the first two points do not necessarily have to appear before the last one, Russell suggests that the final point is, in fact, an outgrowth of the first two. Logically, therefore, the discussion of pity must take place last, for it is his most important point.

When writing a paper of analysis that is organized according to the importance of the various points, you will determine their importance, based on your knowledge of the subject. As a general rule, the last and most important consideration is usually developed the most fully. For a final example of a conceptual analysis, read the following essay, paying particular attention to the marginal notes indicating the development of each paragraph:

introduction A question often asked is: "What are the marks of an educated man?" It is plain that one may gain no inconsiderable body of learning in some special field of knowledge without at the same time acquiring those habits and traits which are the marks of an educated gentleman. A reasonable amount of learning must of course accompany an education, but, after all, that amount need not be so very great in any one field. An education will make its mark and find its evidences in certain traits, characteristics, and capacities which have to be acquired by patient endeavor, by following good example, and by receiving wise discipline and sound instruction.

thesis paragraph These traits or characteristics may be variously described and classified, but among them there are five that should always stand out clearly enough to be seen of all men.

first point: The first of these is correctness and precision in the use of the mother tongue. The quite shocking slovenliness and vulgarity of much of the spoken English, as well as not a little of the written English, which one hears and sees proves beyond peradventure that years of attendance upon schools and colleges that are thought to be respectable have pro-
contrast duced no impression. When one hears English well spoken, with pure diction, correct pronunciation, and an almost unconscious choice of the right word, he recognizes it at once. How much easier he finds it to imitate English of the other sort!

second point A second and indispensable trait of the educated man is refined and gentle manners, which are themselves the expression of fixed habits of
examples thought and action. "Manners makyth the man," wrote William of Wykeham over his gates at Winchester and at Oxford. He pointed to a great truth. When manners are superficial, artificial, and forced, no matter what

their form, they are bad manners. When, however, they are the natural expression of fixed habits of thought and action, and when they reveal a refined and cultivated nature, they are good manners. There are certain things that gentlemen do not do, and they do not do them simply because they are bad manners. The gentleman instinctively knows the difference between those things which he may and should do and those things which he may not and should not do.

A third trait of the educated man is the power and habit of reflection. Human beings for the most part live wholly on the surface of life. They do not look beneath that surface or far beyond the present moment and that part of the future which is quickly to follow it. They do not read those works of prose and poetry which have become classic because they reveal power and habit of reflection and induce that power and habit in others. When one reflects long enough to ask the question *how?,* he is on the way to knowing something about science. When he reflects long enough to ask the question *why?,* he may, if he persists, even become a philosopher.

third point

cause and effect

A fourth trait of the educated man is the power of growth. He continues to grow and develop from birth to his dying day. His interests expand, his contacts multiply, his knowledge increases, and his reflection becomes deeper and wider. It would appear to be true that not many human beings, even those who have had a school and college education, continue to grow after they are twenty-four or twenty-five years of age. By that time it is usual to settle down to life on a level of more or less contented intellectual interest and activity. The whole present-day movement for adult education is a systematic and definite attempt to keep human beings growing long after they have left school and college, and, therefore, to help educate them.

fourth point

examples

A fifth trait of the educated man is his possession of efficiency, or the power to do. The mere visionary dreamer, however charming or however wise, lacks something which an education requires. The power to do may be exercised in any one of a thousand ways, but when it clearly shows itself, that is evidence that the period of discipline of study and of companionship with parents and teachers has not been in vain.

fifth point

contrast

Given these five characteristics, one has the outline of an educated man. That outline may be filled in by scholarship, by literary power, by mechanical skills, by professional zeal and capacity, by business competence, or by social and political leadership. So long as the framework or outline is there, the content may be pretty much what you will, assuming, of course, that the fundamental elements of the great tradition which is civilization, and its outstanding records and achievements in human personality, in letters, in science, in the fine arts, and in human institutions, are all present.

conclusion

NICHOLAS MURRAY BUTLER
"The Marks of an Educated Man"

In Russell's essay, the points of analysis were organized according to importance, with the most important point last. Butler, on the other hand, makes no distinction in terms of importance, nor is a time element involved, so he arranges his points in a random but coherent order.

A number of other modes such as comparison/contrast and cause/effect are actually special forms of analysis; therefore, you will find that an understanding of this mode of development will help you more readily grasp other related modes.

PRACTICE

PART I

1. Summarize the six guidelines for analysis.

    a. _____

    b. _____

    c. _____

    d. _____

    e. _____

    f. _____

2. List the three organizational patterns of analysis.

    a. _____

    b. _____

    c. _____

PART II
Distinguish between process and conceptual analysis by writing definitions for each, on a separate piece of paper.

PRACTICE ANSWERS

PART I
1. a. narrowed subject
   b. parallel points
   c. subject having two or more parts
   d. clear relationship of parts to whole
   e. some controlling basis for breaking the subject down into parts
   f. order of presentation

2. a. chronological
    b. importance
    c. random

PART II
Check answers with your instructor.

WRITING ASSIGNMENT

Write an essay using analysis as the dominant mode of development. Select one of the following topics.

1. a "how to" paper (process), the exact subject to be determined by you
2. the traits or characteristics of a topic (a bore, a good teacher, a friend)
3. steps by which you made a decision
4. your code of living
5. topic of your choice

   (Review pages 244–245 before you complete this writing assignment.)

Comparison/ Contrast

One of the special forms of written analysis, comparison/contrast is also a natural way of thinking and speaking. For instance, if a child asked you what a zebra is, you might give such responses as "A zebra is an animal that looks something like a mule, but it is not as large" or "A zebra has black and white stripes, but a mule is usually a solid, dark brown color. A zebra has small ears, but a mule has large ones." The above example could be outlined in the following manner:

POINTS OF COMPARISON/CONTRAST

Zebra		*Mule*
similar	general appearance	similar
smaller	size	larger
black and white stripes	color	dark brown and solid
small ears	ears	large ears

   Or, how often have you been assigned to write an essay examination in which you were asked to compare and contrast two subjects? If you found yourself at a loss as to how to deal with such an assignment, it was probably because you did not realize that organizing a systematic comparison/contrast takes careful planning. Whether you are writing an essay exam, a job report, or an English theme, if the subject involves likenesses and differences, the following guidelines should be helpful.

By definition, *comparison* shows likeness; *contrast* shows difference. Even though the terms are often used as though they were synonymous, they have different meanings.

Comparison/contrast deals with at least two different subjects, but the subjects must be members of the same class. In other words, the comparison of a zebra and a mule would be valid because both are members of the animal kingdom in general, the horse family in particular. A comparison of a zebra to a chair, however, would be invalid because they are not members of the same class.

If you use comparison/contrast as the dominant mode of development, there should be a reason, a controlling purpose, which may be classified in one of the following ways:

1. *Informative:* To explain a difficult, complex, or unfamiliar subject to the reader by relating it to something less difficult, complex, and unfamiliar. For instance, if you were discussing the British system of government (subject A), which is probably unfamiliar to many Americans, you might compare and contrast it to the American system of government (subject B).

2. *Judgmental:* To discuss two subjects for the purpose of showing that one is better, more desirable, and so forth, than the other. For instance, newspapers sometimes run advertisements in which the gas mileage, cost, and appearance of two different automobiles, such as Dodge and Ford, are compared for the purpose of convincing the reader to buy one automobile instead of the other. In other words, this judgmental type of comparison/contrast seeks to show that one subject is superior to the other.

The basic difference between an informative and a judgmental comparison/contrast is illustrated by the following statements:

High school English is comparable to college English.   (informative)

High school English is less challenging than college English.   (judgmental)

In the first statement, the writer has merely made a statement, suggesting that the purpose is informative. In the second statement, the writer has added an argumentative opinion, suggesting that the purpose is judgmental. Whether your paper is informative or judgmental will be determined by the subject and your purpose in writing about it.

When comparing or contrasting, it is important that you consistently parallel the points, as in the following array:

Subject A	Subject B
Point of comparison/contrast 1	Point of comparison/contrast 1
Point of comparison/contrast 2	Point of comparison/contrast 2
Point of comparison/contrast 3	Point of comparison/contrast 3

In addition to paralleling the points of consideration, devote a proportionate amount of development to both subjects. Even if your purpose is judgmental, do not overload the paper in favor of one side; let what you say, not how much you say, reflect your preference.

Finally, the points compared and contrasted should be typical of the two subjects, not remote exceptions.

Depending on the purpose of your paper, you will find that there are a number of *organizational patterns* available. Assume that you are comparing and contrasting high school and college English and that you are using writing, reading, and grading as the points of consideration. The following patterns are three possible ways you could organize such a paper:

Pattern I

¶1: introduction
¶2: writing in high school
¶3: reading in high school
¶4: grading in high school
¶5: writing in college
¶6: reading in college
¶7: grading in college
¶8: conclusion

This pattern is appropriate if you wish to discuss overall likenesses or differences between the two subjects. It has, however, the following limitations:

- There is quite a distance between the points being compared and contrasted, which can result in accidentally omitting one or more of them in the discussion. If so, the result is a loss of parallelism.
- It is easy to give an unbalanced discussion of one point at the expense of the opposite point. The result is a loss of proportion.
- To avoid discussing the two subjects as though they existed separately, you must take care to show the relationship, usually in the second half of the paper.

¶1: introduction
¶2: writing in high school versus college
¶3: reading in high school versus college
¶4: grading in high school versus college
¶5: conclusion

Such a pattern is appropriate if you wish to discuss points of comparison and contrast in greater detail and if you want to achieve immediacy, that is, if you want the reader to see immediately how the points compare or contrast. Of course, if you wanted to develop each point so fully that the paragraphs became large and unwieldy, then you could show the relationships by doing the following:

¶1: introduction
¶2: writing in high school
¶3: writing in college
    (and so on)

In other words, the immediacy would be achieved not within each paragraph, but by the location of each paragraph. In addition, such a pattern lessens the chances of breakdowns in parallelism and proportion.

Pattern III

¶1: introduction
¶2: writing in high school versus college
¶3: reading in high school
¶4: reading in college
¶5: grading in high school
¶6: grading in college
¶7: conclusion

This pattern combines the organization of the first and second patterns. Use it if you want to emphasize details and immediacy in part of the paper and overall points of comparison and contrast in the other parts.

As long as you observe the guidelines for writing a comparison/contrast (c/c) paper, there is no special advantage of one pattern over the others. Your choice should be dictated by your intention. More importantly, you should select the pattern with which you feel comfortable.

Observe the pattern of development Edwin Torrey uses to compare his subjects in the following essay:

Witch doctors and psychiatrists perform essentially the same function in their respective cultures. They are both therapists; both treat patients, using similar techniques; and both get similar results. Recognition of this should not downgrade psychiatrists—rather it should upgrade witchdoctors.

thesis paragraph

The term "witchdoctor" is Western in origin, imposed on healers of the Third World by 18th and 19th century explorers. The world was simpler then, and the newly discovered cultures were quickly assigned their proper status in the Order of Things. We were white, they were black. We were civilized, they were primitive. We were Christian, they were pagan. We used science, they used magic. We had doctors, they had witchdoctors.

contrasts

American psychiatrists have much to learn from therapists in other cultures. My own experience observing and working with them includes two years in Ethiopia and briefer periods in Sarawak, Bali, Hong Kong, Colombia, and with Alaskan Indians, Puerto Ricans, and Mexican-Americans in this country. What I learned from these doctor-healers was that I, as a psychiatrist, was using the same mechanisms for curing my patients as they were—and, not surprisingly, I was getting about the same results. The mechanisms can be classified under four categories.

basis of c/c

The first is the naming process. A psychiatrist or witchdoctor can work magic by telling a patient what is wrong with him. It conveys to the patient that someone—usually a man of considerable status—understands. And since his problem can be understood, then, implicitly, it can be cured. A psychiatrist who tells an illiterate African that his phobia is related to a fear of failure, or a witchdoctor who tells an American tourist that his phobia is related to possession by an ancestral spirit will be met by equally blank stares. And as therapists they will be equally ineffective. This is a major reason for the failure of most attempts at cross-cultural psychotherapy. Since a shared world-view is necessary for the naming process to be effective, then it is reasonable to expect that the best therapist–patient relationships will be those where both come from the same culture or subculture.

first point of c/c

example

The second healing component used by therapists everywhere is their personality characteristics. An increasing amount of research shows that certain personal qualities of the therapist—accurate empathy, nonpossessive warmth, genuineness—are of crucial importance in producing effective psychotherapy. Clearly, more studies are needed in this area, but if they substantiate the emerging trend, then radical changes in the selection of therapists will be in order. Rather than selecting therapists because they can memorize facts and achieve high grades, we should be selecting them on the basis of their personality. Therapists in other cultures are selected more often for their personality characteristics; the fact that they have not studied biochemistry is not considered important.

second point of c/c

cause and effect

The third component of the healing process that appears to be universal is the patients' expectations. Healers all over the world use many

third point of c/c

analysis

cause and effect

examples

analysis

examples

last point of c/c

examples

comparison of results

conclusion

ways to raise the expectations of their patients. The first way is the trip it-self to the healer. It is a common observation that the farther a person goes to be healed, the greater are the chances that he will be healed. This is called the pilgrimage. Thus, sick people in Topeka go to the Leahy Clinic in Boston. The resulting therapeutic effects of the trip are ex-actly the same as have been operating for centuries at Delphi or Lourdes. The next way to raise patients' expectations is the building used for the healing. The more impressive it is, the greater will be the patients' expec-tations. This has been called the edifice complex. Therapists in different cultures use certain paraphernalia to increase patient expectations. In Western cultures nonpsychiatric healers have their stethoscope and psy-chotherapists are supposed to have their couch. Therapists in other cul-tures have their counterpart trademark, often a special drum, mask or amulet. Another aspect of patients' expectations rests upon the therapist's training. Some sort of training program is found for healers in almost all cultures. Blackfoot Indians, for instance, had to complete a seven-year period of training in order to qualify as medicine men.

Finally, the same techniques of therapy are used by healers all over the world. Let me provide a few examples: Drugs are one of the techniques of Western therapy of which we are most proud. However, drugs are used by healers in other cultures as well. Rauwulfia root, for example, which was introduced into Western psychiatry in the 1950s as reserpine, a major tranquilizer, has been used in India for centuries as a tranquilizer, and has also been in wide use in West Africa for many years. Another ex-ample is shock therapy. When electric shock therapy was introduced by Cerletti in the 1930s, he was not aware that it had been used in some cul-tures for up to 4000 years. The technique of applying electric eels to the head of the patient is referred to in the writings of Aristotle, Pliny, and Plu-tarch.

What kind of results do therapists in other cultures—witchdoctors—achieve? A Canadian psychiatrist, Dr. Raymond Prince spent 17 months studying 46 Nigerian witchdoctors, and judged that the therapeutic re-sults were about equal to those obtained in North American clinics and hospitals.

It would appear, then, that psychiatrists have much to learn from witch-doctors. We can see the components of our own therapy system in relief. We can learn why we are effective—or not effective. And we can learn to be less ethnocentric and arrogant about our own therapy and more toler-ant of others. If we can learn all this from witchdoctors, then we will have learned much.

EDWIN FULLER TORREY

"Witchdoctors and the Universality of Healing"

Clearly, this writer has employed pattern II. By using this pat-tern, he has emphasized the likenesses or differences of each point in detail.

Read the following essay, paying attention to how the author uses a different pattern:

Up to recent decades child training has been an anthropological no man's land. Even anthropologists living for years among aboriginal tribes failed to see that these tribes trained their children in some systematic way. Rather, the experts tacitly assumed with the general public that savages had no child training at all and that primitives grew up "like little animals"—an idea which in the overtrained members of our culture arouses either angry contempt or romantic elation.

The discovery of primitive child-training systems makes it clear that primitive societies are neither infantile stages of mankind nor arrested deviations from the proud progressive norms which we represent: they are a complete form of mature human living, often of a homogeneity and simple integrity which we at times might well envy. Let us rediscover the characteristics of some of these forms of living by studying specimens taken from American Indian life.

The Sioux, under traumatic conditions, has lost the reality for which the last historical form of his communal integrity was fitted. Before the white man came, he was a fighting nomad and a buffalo hunter. The buffalo disappeared, slaughtered by invaders. The Sioux then became a warrior on the defense, and was defeated. He almost cheerfully learned to round up cattle instead of encircling buffalo: his cattle were taken from him. He could become a sedentary farmer, only at the price of being a sick man, on bad land.

Thus, step for step, the Sioux has been denied the bases for a collective identity formation and with it that reservoir of collective integrity from which the individual must derive his stature as a social being.

Fear of famine has led the Sioux to surrender communal functions to the feeding conqueror. Far from remaining a transitional matter of treaty obligation, federal help has continued to be necessary, and this more and more in the form of relief. At the same time, the government has not succeeded in reconciling old and new images, nor indeed in laying the nucleus for a conscience new in both form and content. Child training, so we claim, remains the sensitive instrument of one cultural synthesis until a new one proves convincing and inescapable.

The problem of Indian education is, in reality, one of culture contact between a group of employees representative of the middle-class values of a free-enterprise system on the one hand, and on the other, the remnants of a tribe which, wherever it leaves the shadow of government sustenance, must find itself among the underprivileged of that system.

In fact, the ancient principles of child training still operating in the remnants of the tribe undermine the establishment of a white conscience. The developmental principle in this system holds that a child should be permitted to be an individualist while young. The parents do not show any hostility toward the body as such nor do they, especially in boys, decry self-will. There is no condemnation of infantile habits while the child is developing that system of communication between self and body and self and kin on which the infantile ego is based. Only when strong in body and sure in self is he asked to bow to a tradition of unrelenting shaming by public opinion which focuses on his actual social behavior rather than on his bodily functions or his fantasies. He is incorporated into an elastic tradition which in a strictly institutionalized way takes care of his social needs, diverting dangerous instinctual tendencies toward outer enemies, and always allowing him to project the source of possible guilt into the supernatural. We have seen how stubborn this conscience has remained even in the face of the glaring reality of historical change.

In contrast, the dominating classes in Western civilization, represented here in their bureaucracy, have been guided by the conviction that a systematic regulation of functions and impulses in earliest childhood is the surest safeguard for later effective functioning in society. They implant the never-silent metronome of routine into the impressionable baby and young child to regulate his first experiences with his body and with his immediate physical surroundings. Only after such mechanical socialization is he encouraged to proceed to develop into a rugged individualist. He pursues ambitious strivings, but compulsively remains within standardized careers which, as the economy becomes more and more complicated, tend to replace more general responsibilities. The specialization thus developed has led this Western civilization to the mastery of machinery, but also to an undercurrent of boundless discontent and of individual disorientation.

Naturally the rewards of one educational system mean little to members of another system, while the costs are only too obvious to them. The undisturbed Sioux cannot understand how anything except *restoration* is worth striving for, his racial as well as his individual history having provided him with the memory of abundance. The white man's conscience, on the other hand, asks for continuous *reform* of himself in the pursuit of careers leading to ever higher standards. This reform demands an increasingly internalized conscience, one that will act against temptation automatically and unconsciously, without the presence of critical observers. The Indian conscience, more preoccupied with the necessity of avoiding embarrassing situations within a system of clearly defined honors and shames, is without orientation in conflicting situations which depend for their solution on an "inner voice."

The system underlying Sioux education is a primitive one—i.e., it is based on the adaptation of a highly ethnocentric, relatively small group of people, who consider only themselves to be relevant mankind, to one segment of nature. The primitive cultural system limits itself:

In specializing the individual child for one main career, here the buffalo hunter;

In perfecting a narrow range of the tool world which extends the reach of the human body over the prey;

In the use of magic as the only means of coercing nature.

Such self-restriction makes for homogeneity. There is a strong synthesis of geographic, economic, and anatomic patterns which in Sioux life find their common denominator in *centrifugality,* as expressed in a number of items discussed, such as:

The social organization in bands, which makes for easy dispersion and migration;

The dispersion of tension in the extended family system;

Nomadic technology and the ready use of horse and gun;

The distribution of property by the give-away;

The diversion of aggression toward prey and outgroup.

Sioux child training forms a firm basis for this system of centrifugality by establishing a lasting center of trust, namely the nursing mother, and then by handling the matter of teething, of infantile rage, and of muscular aggression in such a way that the greatest possible degree of ferocity is provoked, channelized socially, and finally released against prey and enemy. We believe that we are dealing here, not with simple causality, but with a mutual assimilation of somatic, mental, and social patterns which amplify one another and make the cultural design for living economical and effective. Only such integration provides a sense of being at home in this world. Transplanted into our system, however, the very expression of what was once considered to be efficient and aristocratic behavior—such as the disregard for property and the refusal to compete—only leads to an alignment with the lowest strata of our society.

ERIK ERIKSON
"The Transplanting of the Sioux"

This writer has used pattern I, an equally effective arrangement, one that allows him to give an overview of one subject followed by an overview of the other subject. It is effective because he has avoided the pitfalls of this pattern, that is, breakdowns in parallelism and proportion.

The following essay was written by a student, who uses examples to support the dominant comparison/contrast mode:

The typical two-story house built by our parents and grandparents is less frequently constructed by contractors today, because the preference of the home-buyer lies more strongly with the split-level or ranch style house.

To begin with, there are obvious similarities between the two styles. They may have the same materials used in exterior construction such as brick, aluminum siding, and shingled roofing. Inside, they may have identical fireplaces located in the family rooms, identical bay windows in the living rooms, and their floor tile, ceramic tile, and wallpaper may match.

Each may or may not have a basement. Each may or may not have an attached garage. Their basic purpose, to shelter a family, is certainly the same.

The comparisons of similarities, however, are usually not as influential in helping people decide what kind of house to buy as are the contrasts.

Assuming that the two houses have an equal number of square feet, there are a number of points you should consider before making a decision. The split-level is built in a series of levels which may move from a basement to the next higher level consisting, for example, of a family room, study, and bath, then moves to the next higher level where perhaps the kitchen, dining room, and living room are located. On one, sometimes two, still higher levels are the bedrooms and baths. The ranch, of course, has all the rooms of the split-level, but they are constructed on the same elevation. Thus, the major difference is that the split-level has several flights of stairs; the ranch has no stairs. Older persons who cannot cope readily with stairs may object to the series of steps connecting each level of the multi-level home. Then, too, it is easier to exit from a one-story house in the event of a fire or other emergency.

Generally the ranch house is spread at length across a sizable yard. Probably the evolution of the split-level house came about because of the rising land costs, which made it necessary to reduce lot sizes. The multiple level house can be placed more compactly in less space and lends itself to hilly, sloping landscapes which would involve costly topographical changes to accommodate the ranch style. Architecturally, the split-level probably allows for a more interesting exterior appearance, especially if there is a challenge to be met in the contours of the land.

Costwise, the ranch is likely to be more expensive to construct initially. A full basement and the larger roof requires more material than a split-level with the same number of square feet inside. On the other hand, a ranch house is easier to maintain. The problem of using a tall ladder would not exist. Washing windows would be simpler and so would the installation and removal of storm windows and screens on the ranch.

Owners of split-level houses sometimes complain it costs more to heat them, because heat moves upwards and the upper rooms become too warm, while the furnace runs longer to keep the lower floors comfortable. Zoned heat might answer this objection. The ranch, on the other hand, is more easily heated because of the single level.

You may also assume that landscaping the larger base and lot of the ranch style would be more expensive, especially since the question of privacy enters into it. With the bedrooms of the split-level usually located on the upper floors, it is less difficult to achieve privacy from outside noise and passersby, and there are fewer ground-level windows whereby intruders may trespass.

Undoubtedly, there are other comparisons and contrasts to be made, but each home-owner makes a decision and buys a home according to the demands of his own life style, pocketbook, convenience to shopping, work, and schools. These other dimensions also influence the purchase of a home. Purchasing a home is an important step, so all factors should be considered before a person makes a decision.

PRACTICE

Summarize the guidelines for writing comparison/contrast.

1. _____

2. _____

3. _____

4. _____

5. _____

6. _____

7. _____

PRACTICE ANSWERS

1. comparison shows likeness
2. contrast shows difference
3. deals with at least two subjects
4. controlling purpose
5. parallelism of points
6. proportionate development
7. typical not exceptional points of c/c

WRITING ASSIGNMENT

Write an essay using comparison/contrast as the dominant mode of development. Select from the following topics.

1. a "then and now" paper, in which you compare/contrast your feelings about a subject (person, issue, concept)
2. education—formal versus life experience
3. two books or two movies
4. your attitude about a topic versus the attitude of your parents
5. topic of your choice

   (Review pages 244–245 before you complete this writing assignment.)

Analogy

A special form of comparison, analogy may be more useful as a support than as a dominant mode of expression. Nevertheless, it is important enough as a means of expression that it deserves a separate discussion. When writing an analogy, you should consider the following guidelines:

- The subjects being compared must be from different classifications. For example, comparing Winesap and Jonathan apples is simple comparison because both subjects are from the same class, fruit. However, comparing an apple to the earth is an analogy because the two subjects are from different classes, fruit and planets.

- The two subjects being compared must have more than one point in common, even though these likenesses may not be as readily apparent as in comparison. Otherwise, you run the danger of creating a false analogy. If there are differences between the two subjects, they should be shown to exist in unimportant ways or for the purpose of admitting limitations of the analogy. Since points of difference are typical between any two subjects, analogies are usually imperfect.

Analogy does not require the same proportionate development of both subjects as does comparison/contrast. In fact, assuming that you are discussing love (subject A) and comparing it to a rose (subject B), you will possibly devote a larger proportion of your paper to subject B.

The purposes of analogy are as follows:

1. to clarify
2. to illustrate
3. to simplify by
   - making an abstract idea more concrete
   - making a difficult idea more understandable
   - making a general idea more specific
   - making an unfamiliar idea more familiar

Consequently, analogy does not require the same careful detailed paralleling of points as comparison/contrast. Thus, an analogy should not be looked on as factual or as proof of a point, but rather as support for a point. It may add interest to your paper, but it is not in itself conclusive.

To serve one of its possible purposes, the analogy must be more generally understood, more familiar, and simpler in nature than the idea or subject being explained. When writing an analogy, however, avoid those that are trite and clichéd, for example, life compared to sports. Such analogies are so overworked that they have lost their freshness and fail to be functional; in addition, they lack interest.

Read the following analogy in which the writer compares God's wrath to flood waters:

The wrath of God is like great waters that are dammed for the present; they increase more and more, and rise higher and higher, till an outlet is given, and the longer the stream is stopped, the more rapid and mighty is its course, when once it is let loose. 'Tis true, that judgment against your evil works has not been executed hitherto; the floods of God's vengeance have been withheld; but your guilt in the meantime is constantly increasing, and you are every day treasuring up more wrath; the waters are continually rising and waxing more and more mighty; and there is nothing but the mere pleasure of God that holds the waters back that are unwilling to be stopped, and press hard to go forward; if God should only withdraw his hand from the flood-gate, it would immediately fly open, and the fiery floods of the fierceness and wrath of God would rush forth with inconceivable fury, and would come upon you with omnipotent power; and if your strength were ten thousand times greater than it is, yea ten thousand times greater than the strength of the stoutest, sturdiest devil in Hell, it would be nothing to withstand or endure it.

JONATHAN EDWARDS

"Sinners in the Hands of an Angry God"

The primary purpose of this analogy is to discuss a complex subject (religion) and compare it to a less complex subject (a flood). In the process, Edwards meets all the guidelines for analogy outlined earlier. Note, in particular, that he devotes more time to the discussion of flood waters than to the discussion of religion, which is natural since he is explaining the complex in terms of the less complex and more familiar.

Now read a more fully developed analogy, in which the writer compares society to a coach:

By way of attempting to give the reader some general impression of the way people lived together in those days, and especially of the relations of the rich and poor to one another, perhaps I cannot do better than to compare society as it then was to a prodigious coach which the masses of humanity were harnessed to and dragged toilsomely along a very hilly and sandy road. The driver was hunger, and permitted no lagging, though the pace was necessarily very slow. Despite the difficulty of drawing the coach at all along so hard a road, the top was covered with passengers who never got down, even at the steepest ascents. These seats on top were very breezy and comfortable. Well up out of the dust, their occupants could enjoy the scenery at their leisure, or critically discuss the merits of the straining team. Naturally such places were in great demand and the competition for them was keen, every one seeking as the first end in life to secure a seat on the coach for himself and to leave it to his child after him. By the rule of the coach a man could leave his seat to whom he wished, but on the other hand there were so many accidents by which it might at any time be wholly lost. For all that they were so easy, the seats were very insecure, and at every sudden jolt of the coach persons were slipping out of them and falling to the ground, where they were instantly compelled to take hold of the rope and help to drag the coach on which they had before ridden so pleasantly. It was naturally regarded as a terrible misfortune to lose one's seat, and the apprehension that this might happen to them or their friends was a constant cloud upon the happiness of those who rode. . . .

I am well aware that this will appear to the men and women of the twentieth century an incredible inhumanity, but there are two facts, both very curious, which partly explain it. In the first place, it was firmly and sincerely believed that there was no other way in which Society could get along, except when the many pulled at the rope and the few rode, and not only this, but that no very radical improvement even was possible, either in the harness, the coach, the roadway, or the distribution of the toil. It had always been as it was, and it always would be so. It was a pity, but it could not be helped, and philosophy forbade wasting compassion on what was beyond remedy.

The other fact is yet more curious, consisting in a singular hallucination which those on the top of the coach generally shared, that they were not exactly like their brothers and sisters who pulled at the rope, but of finer clay, in some way belonging to a higher order of beings who might justly expect to be drawn. This seems unaccountable, but, as I once rode on this very coach and shared that very hallucination, I ought to be believed. The strangest thing about the hallucination was that those who had but just climbed up from the ground, before they had outgrown the marks of the rope upon their hands, began to fall under its influence. As for those whose parents and grandparents before them had been so fortunate as to keep their seats on the top, the conviction they cherished of the essential difference between their sort of humanity and the common article was absolute. The effect of such a delusion in moderating fellow feeling for the sufferings of the mass of men into a distant and philosophical compassion is obvious. To it I refer as the only extenuation I can offer for the indifference which, at the period I write of, marked my own attitude toward the misery of my brothers.

EDWARD BELLAMY
Looking Backward

Now read a student's analogy comparing literal treasures to treasures of the heart:

My Aunt Amber married rather late in life, and she and her new husband bought an old house dating back to the Civil War era, set on about an acre of ground among large, productive walnut trees, in a small Missouri river town. There was a great deal to be done inside in the way of restoration, so it was quite some time before the couple had opportunity to turn their attention to the outside, and particularly to an old shed at the rear of the property. Like the house, it was built of slave-made brick. It was rampant with vine and weed and had been padlocked ever since they first looked at the house with the realtor. It was an insignificant part of what they considered to be the "whole," but at last they decided to open the single door and see what use might be made of the building. They were considering having the unsightly structure removed.

Once inside, they discovered an unbelievable collection of wedding gifts, obviously waiting from the Civil War period, still packed carefully in wrappings and boxes. They tried unsuccessfully to trace old records to discover who might have owned these lovely things. There were five sets of solid sterling flatware and at least as many sets of china, plus countless other beautiful pieces some unfortunate newlyweds had never been able to enjoy. When everything had been inventoried and appraised, the items stored in the shed were valued at more than the entire property they had purchased.

Every time I look at the silver and cut glass I have inherited from Aunt Amber, I am reminded that we often miss what is closest to us. Down inside each of us there are secret areas we are wary of exposing to others. "They would laugh at me!" we tell ourselves. We fail to recognize our own gifts, and from lack of confidence in ourselves, we let too many opportunities for happiness and accomplishment pass us by. Why leave our treasures lying deep inside, buried where they are useless to people we love? Accept challenges. It should be natural for us to develop our talents fully, but often we are too lazy or timid; we let our latent abilities lie fallow and uncultivated. Our talents are not necessarily artistic gifts: they can be simple extensions of ourselves to lonely neighbors. It is said the only way to have love is to give it away.

If we reach out to the ugly, sick, old woman down the street, we may learn that she, too, has something of value to share—wisdom, perhaps, and compassion of a sort we have never encountered but she may have learned it the hard way, through the experience of living, painfully and sorrowfully.

What ever happened to trust? Friendship is such a precious and fragile thing, yet in our mobile society we are faced constantly with being uprooted and thrust among new people. It takes a long time for a friendship to develop, but we could speed it up if we would only trust each other more. Each of us has special needs and special gifts. If we were to inventory these and initiate exchanges with each other, would it not add to the fulfillment we gain from life?

Let us bring the analogy a little close to home. Aunt Amber's cache was an unexpected, delightful discovery. Yet, even within our own families where the closest of ties exist, we pass up chances to explore new depths, seek answers or reassurance from those we love most. We continue to be wrapped up in the obvious, taking everything and everyone for granted on a surface level, instead of unlocking what might be waiting for us inside.

Survey your world and see where the unopened padlocks are. What you find hidden away may have more intrinsic value than the material things Aunt Amber found. Silver tarnishes and must be polished. Cut glass and china should be washed and used to gain full benefit from their beauty. Life needs to be worked at and kept bright in the same fashion, reflecting the deep, inner part of ourselves.

Aunt Amber's shed is still standing, though she is gone. The lesson I learned didn't die with her.

PRACTICE
1. Indicate whether the following are comparisons or analogies.

_____ a. a person to a mole

_____ b. a poodle to a St. Bernard

_____ c. the heart to a water pump

_____ d. a pigeon to a dove

_____ e. love to a storm

_____ f. climbing a mountain to taking a test

_____ g. Lincoln to Kennedy

_____ h. life to a string

_____ i. small town to a city

_____ j. love to hate

2. List three purposes of analogy.

a. _____

b. _____

c. _____

PRACTICE ANSWERS
1. a. analogy
   b. comparison

c. analogy
d. comparison
e. analogy
f. analogy
g. comparison
h. analogy
i. comparison
j. comparison
2. a. to clarify
   b. to illustrate
   c. to simplify

WRITING ASSIGNMENT

Write an essay using analogy as the dominant mode of development. Select from the following topics.

1. A difficult concept you have recently encountered in a class. Explain it by using an analogy.
2. Human beings compared to _____.
3. Music compared to _____.
4. Education compared to _____.
5. Topic of your choice.

(Review pages 244–245 before you complete this writing assignment.)

Cause and Effect

Much like illustration and analysis, cause and effect is also a fundamental way of thinking and speaking. For instance, how often do you find yourself thinking and speaking in such terms as "I didn't sleep well last night because our dog howled," or "I enjoyed the movie because of the excellent acting and the interesting subject." As simple as both examples are, they do point out how natural it is to think and speak in a cause-and-effect pattern. Such a pattern is also a natural way of writing. The following guidelines are considerations you should make when you write a cause-and-effect essay:

• Once it has been established in the opening paragraph, the cause-and-effect relationship should be emphasized throughout the paper.

• Avoid establishing a faulty cause-and-effect relationship as in the following (See also *post hoc ergo propter hoc,* "after this, therefore because of this," in Chapter 14.): Mrs. Green sees a black cat. She later backs her car into a fireplug. She assumes that her bad luck was caused by the black cat.

• Common sense plays a large part in the determination of cause-and-effect relationships. Don't assume that one cause will automatically produce an effect. Since the object of using a cause-and-effect pattern is to show readers the relationship, you should explore all possible causes. Causes may be classified in the following ways:

1. *Immediate causes:* Those that readily can be seen or understood as leading to an effect. For example, Elmer failed his physics exam because he didn't study his book.
2. *Underlying causes:* Those that lead to the immediate or proximate causes. For example, Elmer failed his physics exam because he didn't study. He didn't study because he can read only on the fourth-grade level.

Whether you make a distinction between immediate or underlying causes will depend on your instructor, the nature of your assignment, and the degree to which you develop the cause-and-effect relationship. Be aware, however, that underlying causes can be endless and, before deciding how fully you will explain underlying causes, consider the scope of your paper.

• The *organization* of a cause-and-effect essay must be worked out carefully. Otherwise, your paper will be incoherent, disjointed, and confusing for both you and your reader. Since you will probably be writing a five- or six-paragraph paper of approximately five hundred to eight hundred words, you may find the following patterns helpful:

Pattern I

¶1: introduction establishing cause-and-effect relationship
¶2–4: discussion of causes
¶5: discussion of effect
¶6: conclusion

Pattern II

¶1: introduction establishing cause-and-effect relationship
¶2: discussion of the effect
¶3–5: discussion of causes
¶6: conclusion

Pattern III

¶1: introduction establishing cause-and-effect relationship
¶2: discussion of first cause and its effect
¶3: discussion of second cause and its effect
¶4: discussion of third cause and its effect
¶5: conclusion

You may arrange the causes in one of the following ways:

- Begin with immediate and move to underlying causes.
- Begin with the least important and move to the most important causes.
- Begin with the first cause and proceed to the second cause, and so forth, if there is a time-sequence relationship.

The complexity of a cause-and-effect paper will vary, as suggested by the following possibilities:

- one cause—one effect, (which is possible)
- one cause—two or more effects, (which is possible)
- two or more causes—one effect, (which is probable)
- two or more causes—two or more effects, (which is possible)

• To make sure that the effect is the result of the stated causes, you can apply the following rules of negative testing:

1. If the stated cause is ever absent when the effect takes place, there is no valid cause-and-effect relationship. For instance, Mrs. Green still could have backed into the fireplug even if the black cat hadn't been seen earlier in the day.
2. If the effect is ever absent when the stated cause is present, there is no valid cause-and-effect relationship. For instance, Mrs. Green could have seen the black cat without backing into the fire plug later.

• There are two common indications of a valid cause-and-effect relationship:

1. *Association:* The cause and effect occur together. For example, a child receives a burn each time he or she touches a hot stove.
2. *Time sequence:* If the effect comes after the cause, there *may* be a cause-and-effect relationship. For example, a student who stays up all night cramming for an exam will probably be tired in class the next morning. In other words, the activities of the night before probably cause the results of the following day; that is, the student is tired. But not all such time-sequence relationships are related. For example, a bus that arrives at eight o'clock is not necessarily caused by the preceding bus that arrived at seven o'clock (*post hoc* explanation).

You will find that cause-and-effect essays can be difficult to write. Many subjects, especially those of a personal, social, political, or religious nature, require that you be careful about establishing a cause-and-effect relationship. As a general rule, any time you write a paper using cause and effect as the dominant mode, you should know your subject well.

Read the following essay, which illustrates an effective use of cause and effect as the dominant mode of development. After

Mencken establishes the conditions or effects on the writer—
loneliness and hard work—he then discusses the various causes:

introduction

If authors could work in large, well-ventilated factories, like cigar-makers or garment workers, with plenty of their mates about and a flow of lively professional gossip to entertain them, their labor would be immensely lighter. But it is essential to their craft that they perform its tedious and vexatious operations *a capella,* and so the horrors of loneliness are added to stenosis and their other professional infirmities. An author at work is continuously and inescapably in the presence of himself. There is nothing to divert and soothe him. Every time a vagrant regret or sorrow

effect

assails him, it has him instantly by the ear, and every time a wandering ache runs down his legs it shakes him like the bite of a tiger. I have yet to meet an author who was not a hypochondriac. Saving only medical men, who are always ill and in fear of death, the literati are perhaps the most lavish consumers of pills and philtres in this world, and the most assiduous customers of surgeons. I can scarcely think of one, known to me personally, who is not constantly dosing himself with medicines, or regularly resorting to the knife.

contrast
examples

It must be obvious that other men, even among the intelligentsia, are not beset so cruelly. A judge on the bench, entertaining a ringing in the ears, can do his work quite as well as if he heard only the voluptuous rhetoric of the lawyers. A clergyman, carrying on his mummery, is not appreciably crippled by a sour stomach: what he says has been said before, and only scoundrels question it. And a surgeon, plying his exhilarating art and mystery, suffers no professional damage from the wild thought that the attending nurse is more sightly than his wife. But I defy anyone to write a competent sonnet with a ringing in his ears, or to compose sound criticism with a sour stomach, or to do a plausible love scene with a head full of private amorous fancies. These things are sheer impossibilities. The poor literatus encounters them and their like every time he enters his work-room and spits on his hands. The moment the door bangs

effect

he begins a depressing, losing struggle with his body and his mind.

Why then, do rational men and women engage in so barbarous and exhausting a vocation—for there are relatively intelligent and enlightened authors, remember, just as there are relatively honest politicians, and even bishops. What keeps them from deserting it for trades that are less onerous, and, in the eyes of their fellow creatures, more respectable?

cause

One reason, I believe, is that an author, like any other so-called artist, is a man in whom the normal vanity of all men is so vastly exaggerated that he finds it a sheer impossibility to hold it in. His overpowering impulse is to gyrate before his fellow men flapping his wings and emitting defiant yells. This being forbidden by the police of all civilized coun-

cause

tries, he takes it out by putting his yells on paper. Such is the thing called self-expression.

In the confidences of the literati, of course, it is always depicted as something much more mellow and virtuous. Either they argue that they are moved by a yearning to spread the enlightenment and save the world, or they allege that what steams them and makes them leap is a passion for beauty. Both theories are quickly disposed of by an appeal to the facts. The stuff written by nine authors out of ten, it must be plain at a glance, has as little to do with spreading the enlightenment as the state papers of the late Chester A. Arthur. And there is no more beauty in it, and no more sign of a feeling of beauty, than you will find in the décor of a night-club. The impulse to create beauty, indeed, is rather rare in literary men, and almost completely absent from the younger ones. If it shows itself at all, it comes as a sort of afterthought. Far ahead of it comes the yearning to make money. And after the yearning to make money comes the yearning to make a noise. The impulse to create beauty lingers far behind. Authors, as a class, are extraordinarily insensitive to it, and the fact reveals itself in their customary (and often incredibly extensive) ignorance of the other arts. I'd have a hard job naming six American novelists who could be depended upon to recognize a fugue without prompting, or six poets who could give a rational account of the difference between a Gothic cathedral and a Standard Oil filling-station.

comparison

examples

The thing goes even further. Most novelists, in my experience, know nothing of poetry, and very few poets have any feeling for the beauties of prose. As for the dramatists, three-fourths of them are unaware that such things as prose and poetry exist at all. It pains me to set down such inconvenient and blushful facts. If they ought to be concealed, then blame my babbling upon scientific passion. That passion, today, has me by the ear.

conclusion

H. L. MENCKEN
"The Author at Work"

In this essay, the author uses the first paragraph as an introduction that also contains an effect. The second paragraph contains a series of contrasting examples and ends with a second effect. Paragraphs three and four are discussions of the cause. The last paragraph is the conclusion. In other words, Mencken has employed organizational pattern II, that is, effects followed by causes.

Notice how the next writer uses pattern I, starting with the discussion of causes and then showing the effect:

Imagine that we stand on an ordinary seaside pier, and watch the waves rolling in and striking against the iron columns of the pier. Large waves pay very little attention to the columns—they divide right and left and reunite after passing each column, much as a regiment of soldiers would if a tree stood in their road; it is almost as though the columns had not been there. But the short waves and ripples find the columns of the pier a much more formidable obstacle. When the short waves impinge on the columns, they are reflected back and spread as new ripples in all directions. To use the technical term, they are "scattered." The obstacle provided by the iron columns hardly affects the long waves at all, but scatters the short ripples.

We have been watching a sort of working model of the way in which sunlight struggles through the earth's atmosphere. Between us on earth and outer space the atmosphere interposes innumerable obstacles in the form of molecules of air, tiny droplets of water, and small particles of dust. These are represented by the columns of the pier.

The waves of the sea represent the sunlight. We know that sunlight is a blend of many colors—as we can prove for ourselves by passing it through a prism, or even through a jug of water, or as nature demonstrates to us when she passes it through the raindrops of a summer shower and produces a rainbow. We also know that light consists of waves, and that the different colors of light are produced by waves of different lengths, red light by long waves and blue light by short waves. The mixture of waves which constitutes sunlight has to struggle past the columns of the pier. And these obstacles treat the light waves much as the columns of the pier treat the sea-waves. The long waves which constitute red light are hardly affected but the short waves which constitute blue light are scattered in all directions.

Thus the different constituents of sunlight are treated in different ways as they struggle through the earth's atmosphere. A wave of blue light may be scattered by a dust particle, and turned out of its course. After a time a second dust particle again turns it out of its course, and so on, until finally it enters our eyes by a path as zigzag as that of a flash of lightning. Consequently the blue waves of the sunlight enter our eyes from all directions. And that is why the sky looks blue.

SIR JAMES JEANS

"Why the Sky Looks Blue"

In the next paper, a student discusses the causes and effect of inadequate high school preparation:

Approximately eighty per cent of the graduating seniors in the local school district each year plan to continue their education at either a two year or at a four year college. Frequently, this decision is made only because going to college is considered to be the fashionable or "in thing" to do. With little understanding and no awareness of the challenges ahead, students go blindly into college and are often unable to handle properly the situations which develop. There are a number of causes for this inability to cope with the college scene.

The first cause is improper counseling. Counselors, who are charged with the job of guiding students, do not always live up to their responsibilities and obligations. Young people, particularly during their final year of high school, need proper guidance to be aware of future problems. Such students also need sound advice to help select suitable goals and types of work for future achievement. The counseling system in the local high school tries to be popular with the students rather than pointing them in a correct but maybe less popular direction. As a result, the system fails because a large number of high school age young people feel that they must attend a college or university, but do not realize that they have chosen a difficult road, and possibly one for which they are not prepared. High school seniors hear of the parties and the good times associated with college life, but may not realize that the commitment to a higher education includes a commitment to a life where study and research are the first rule. Aware of only the social aspects of college, students arrive at an institution of higher learning prepared to have a fun filled time—a country club type of life. When it is obvious that college involves a great deal more than just social activities, these students may be disappointed that they chose to go to college, and may be unwilling to perform the work necessary. One year may be enough, so they elect not to return to college. Counselors could alleviate this problem by helping students see the whole picture and understand all of the things involved in attending college.

Another reason why students don't do well in college is that the high school does not generate nor require respect for authority; neither does it insist on discipline. The pendulum in the school district has swung from relative strictness to almost total permissiveness. Discipline has always had a very important message associated with it which says, "I care what you do." Translated, this means that students are important. In the absence of discipline, and with no rules, some students feel that no one really cares about them. For this reason, they assume they are free to choose the things which they will or will not do, and to decide how well they will do something and how much effort they will put out. In the extreme this attitude can lead to criminal acts or the drug scene. Generally it can result in lack of motivation and less than full interest in pursuing a field or profession they have chosen. Many times the lack of discipline leads students into college unaware of the importance of study disciplines, regular study times, and the amount of study time needed for each subject. High school teachers, probably without realizing it, contribute to the general lack of respect for authority. Some educators seem to have little confidence in themselves and in the importance of the subjects they teach. Such teachers simply do not demand the consideration to which they are entitled. As a result, respect for authority breaks down.

The third cause is a lack of basic survival skills of reading, writing, and arithmetic. Somehow, high schools have overlooked this emphasis. Whether students intend to seek more knowledge by attending college, or plan to enter some business field after completing high school, these basic skills are extremely important. Reading and writing are the means we have of exchanging thoughts with one another. They are necessary in our average, customary living. Reading is the means of obtaining new information and new ideas, yet once the high school level is reached, reading is practically eliminated except for special and remedial basis, and of course a great deal of writing is necessary in all forms of college work. Writing is also a basic form of communication that will be expected in college. Not enough is being done to improve writing ability, so that people still have difficulty with sentence construction, composition, vocabulary, and even with spelling. The need for arithmetic at first may sound simplistic, but even simple mathematical skills are needed in college work, particularly in the sciences and related professions. More training is needed in high school in reading, writing, and arithmetic, which would benefit all students.

Finally, an important reason for failure is that high school students lack intellectual curiosity. There is little effort to create a love for learning and a search for knowledge. Students today seem content to do as little as may be necessary to complete an assignment, and lack desire to be better informed on a particular subject. This does not seem important to students any more. There is no emphasis on being fully informed, and only minimum knowledge is required or demanded. In many cases, students lacking curiosity become bored with school and impatient to end their studies.

Thus, there are a number of causes related to failure after high school. The high school can, however, improve the training and education of their graduates. The substantial dropout of such graduates between the first and second years of college suggests that improved, more efficient counseling might be necessary. A greater respect for discipline and for authority can be an aid to students in whatever they choose to do in later years. Increased skills in reading, writing, and arithmetic are vital to daily living after high school. Stimulation of intellectual curiosity in students will result in better informed, more well-rounded graduates. Hopefully, such improvements will result in graduates better equipped for college.

Notice the resemblance of this paper to analysis. The reasons for improperly trained high school students are broken down into four points—inadequate counseling, breakdown of authority, lack of basic skills, and lack of intellectual curiosity on the part of students. Even though the student could make a more convincing case had he used more specific examples, he nevertheless makes the cause-and-effect relationship evident at all times.

The organizational pattern you use in your writing will be the one that seems most natural. All patterns can be equally effective as long as you show the correlation between cause and effect.

Indicate whether each of the following examples represents a probable, valid cause-and-effect relationship or a post hoc relationship. (Identify them as "valid" or "post hoc.")

_____ 1. Jill recovered from the illness after drinking moonshine.

_____ 2. After bumping his head on the dashboard of his truck, Elmer had a large bump.

_____ 3. As a child, Harry watched television for hours at a time. He became a professional criminal when he grew up.

_____ 4. Priscilla received a speeding ticket for driving fifty miles per hour in a thirty-five miles per hour zone.

_____ 5. Drusilla got an "F" on her history exam because she miscopied Robert's answers.

PART II
Write brief definitions of the following terms.
1. Immediate cause

_____

2. Underlying cause

_____

PART III
Summarize the guidelines of cause and effect.

1. _____

2. _____

3. _____

4. _____

5. _____

6. _____

7. _____

8. _____

PART I
1. post hoc
2. valid
3. post hoc
4. valid
5. valid

PART II
1. one that is obvious
2. one that is not evident, but may actually be the cause of the immediate cause

PART III
1. Analysis traces causes to results.
2. Cause-and-effect relationship is emphasized throughout paper.
3. Cause-and-effect relationship is valid, not post hoc.
4. All possible causes are considered.
5. Association and time sequence are two signs of a valid cause-and-effect relationship.
6. Cause is either immediate or underlying.
7. A definite organizational pattern is necessary.

WRITING ASSIGNMENT

Write a paper using cause and effect as the dominant mode of development. Select from the following list of topics.

1. The cause and effect of a prejudice you have.
2. The loss of privacy.
3. The cause and effect of some rule or policy (at home, school, work, in government)
4. The cause and effect of a belief you have.
5. Topic of your choice.

(Review pages 244–245 before you complete this writing assignment.)

Definition

A *simple definition* is usually one sentence long and limits the scope of your paper. An *extended* (or *expanded*) *definition* is a detailed discussion of the simple definition. In short, the expanded definition grows out of the simple definition. Much of the success or failure of an expanded definition depends on your choice of a simple definition. Thus, you should observe the following guidelines.

The simple definition has three parts:

- the term to be defined (species): hedonism
- class to which the term belongs (genus): a doctrine
- the trait or traits that distinguish the term from other

members of its class (differentiae): that pleasure is the sole good in life and that moral duty is best achieved by pleasure-seeking activities

EXAMPLE: Hedonism is the doctrine which maintains that pleasure is the sole good in life and that moral duty is best achieved by pleasure-seeking activities.

In short, a simple definition is much like an equation: term = genus + differentia.

The genus and differentia should be more familiar to the reader than the term being defined. For instance, to define "a kiss" as "the act of osculation" would be in violation of using familiar terms because "osculation" is probably much less familiar to most readers than the term being defined.

The term should be placed in the most limited genus possible. The steps involved in such a process of limitation resemble those you followed when narrowing the topic of your paper, for example, Cadillac = transportation → vehicle → automobile → luxury automobile.

The differentia must distinguish the term from other members of its class. For example, to define a helicopter as "an aircraft used to transport passengers" obviously fails to distinguish it from other members of the aircraft class. But, to define a helicopter as "an aircraft that is lifted and moved forward by a large propeller mounted horizontally above the fuselage" does distinguish it from other forms of aircraft.

To determine whether a simple definition is valid, you may apply the following tests:

• *Reversibility:* Switch the order of the term with the genus and differentia. If you can do so and retain the same meaning, then the definition is valid.

EXAMPLE: Defining "a helicopter" as "an aircraft that is lifted and moved forward by a large propeller mounted horizontally above the fuselage" is, in essence, the same as saying "an aircraft that is lifted and moved forward by a large propeller mounted horizontally above the fuselage is a helicopter." The rule of reversibility works, so the definition is valid.

• *Substitution:* Substitute the genus and the differentia for the term being defined:

EXAMPLE: "He traveled in a helicopter" is in meaning the same as saying that "he traveled in an aircraft that was lifted and moved forward by a large propeller mounted horizontally above the fuselage." The rule of substitution works, so the definition is valid.

Do not define a term by a mere repetition of the term being defined:

EXAMPLE: Marinated herring is herring that is marinated. Such a definition is merely repetitive.

Also, avoid using such words as "when" or "where" in a definition. For example, look at the following definitions: "A tavern is where people go to drink"; "Love is when the heart flutters." In both cases, the "when" and "where" are incorrectly used as the genus for each definition. A tavern is not a where but a place; love is not a when but a state of being.

Although the guidelines for constructing a simple definition may seem rigid and excessive, they are, nevertheless, necessary. A simple definition may be used as a support mode or it may establish the basis for an extended definition, in which the rest of the essay develops in greater detail the simple definition. You are then faced with the question of how to develop it. There are various ways, including all of the modes covered in this chapter: illustration and example, analysis, comparison/contrast, analogy, and cause and effect.

In addition to using other modes to expand a definition, you may also define it by exclusion or *negation*, that is, defining what something is by showing what it is not. For instance, if you were defining friendship, you might say that "Friendship is not seeking out and magnifying faults," or "Friendship is not taking unfair advantage of another person's generosity."

Definition by negation alone is not enough; after showing what the subject is not, you should then show what it is. Thus, the above example could end with a statement such as "Friendship is accepting another person's weaknesses."

Read the following paragraph carefully, noting in particular how the writer uses various modes of development to expand his humorous definition:

simple definition *A fair and happy milkmaid* is a country wench, that is so far from making herself beautiful by art, that one look of hers is able to put all face-physic out of countenance. She knows a fair look is but a dumb orator to commend virtue, therefore minds it not. All her excellencies stand in her so silently as if they had stolen upon her without her knowledge. The lining of her apparel (which is herself) is far better than outsides of tissue: for
analogy though she be not arrayed in the spoil of the silk-worm, she is decked
negation in innocence, a far better wearing. She doth not, with lying long abed, spoil both her complexion and conditions; nature hath taught her too

immoderate sleep is rust to the soul; she rises therefore with chanticleer, her dame's cock, and at night makes the lamb her curfew. In milking a cow, and straining the teats through her fingers, it seems that so sweet a milkpress makes the milk the whiter, or sweeter; for never came almond glove or aromatic ointment on her palm to taint it. The golden ears of corn fall and kiss her feet when she reaps them, as if they wished to be bound and led prisoners by the same hand that felled them. Her breath is her own, which scents all the year long of June, like a new-made hay-cock. She makes her hand hard with labor, and her heart soft with pity; and when winter evenings fall early (sitting at her merry wheel), she sings a defiance to the giddy wheel of fortune. She doth all things with so sweet a grace, it seems ignorance will not suffer her to do ill, being her mind is to do well. She bestows her year's wages at next fair; and in choosing her garments, counts no bravery in the world like decency. The garden and beehive are all her physic and chirurgery, and she lives the longer for it. She dares go alone, and unfold sheep in the night, and fears no manner of ill, because she means none: yet to say truth, she is never alone, for she is still accompanied with old songs, honest thoughts, and prayers, but short ones; yet they have their efficacy, in that they are not palled with ensuing idle cogitations. Lastly, her dreams are so chaste that she dare tell them; only a Friday's dream is all her superstition: that she conceals for fear of anger. Thus lives she, and all her care is she may die in the springtime, to have store of flowers stuck upon her winding-sheet.

illustration

comparison/contrast

illustration

summary

SIR THOMAS OVERBURY

"A Fair and Happy Milkmaid"

This paragraph contains numerous modes, but it is predominantly descriptive illustration.

The next essay is a more complex definition of a term in which the author uses a variety of ways to develop the definition:

What is pornography to one man is the laughter of genius to another.

The word itself, we are told, means "pertaining to harlots"—the graph of the harlot. But nowadays, what is a harlot? If she was a woman who took money from a man in return for going to bed with him—really, most wives sold themselves, in the past, and plenty of harlots gave themselves, when they felt like it, for nothing. If a woman hasn't got a tiny streak of harlot in her, she's a dry stick as a rule. And probably most harlots had somewhere a streak of womanly generosity. Why be so cut and dried? The law is a dreary thing, and its judgments have nothing to do with life. . . .

One essay on pornography, I remember, comes to the conclusion that pornography in art is that which is calculated to arouse sexual desire, or sexual excitement. And stress is laid on the fact, whether the author or

analogy
definition
examples

cause and effect

artist *intended* to arouse sexual feelings. It is the old vexed question of intention, become so dull today, when we know how strong and influential our unconscious intentions are. And why a man should be held guilty of his conscious intentions, and innocent of his unconscious intentions, I don't know, since every man is more made up of unconscious intentions than of conscious ones. I am what I am, not merely what I think I am.

cause and effect However! We take it, I assume, that *pornography* is something base, something unpleasant. In short, we don't like it. And why don't we like it? Because it arouses sexual feelings?

negation I think not. No matter how hard we may pretend otherwise, most of us rather like a moderate rousing of our sex. It warms us, stimulates us like *contrast* sunshine on a grey day. After a century or two of puritanism, this is still true of most people. Only the mob-habit of condemning any form of sex is too strong to let us admit it naturally. And there are, of course, many people who are genuinely repelled by the simplest and most natural stirrings of sexual feeling. But these people are perverts who have fallen into hatred of their fellow-men: thwarted, disappointed, unfulfilled people, of whom, alas, our civilisation contains so many. And they nearly always enjoy some unsimple and unnatural form of sex excitement, secretly.

examples Even quite advanced art critics would try to make us believe that any picture or book which had "sex appeal" was *ipso facto* a bad book or picture. This is just canting hypocrisy. Half the great poems, pictures, music, stories of the whole world are great by virtue of the beauty of their sex appeal. Titian or Renoir, the Song of Solomon or *Jane Eyre,* Mozart or "Annie Laurie," the loveliness is all interwoven with sex appeal, sex stimulus, call it what you will. Even Michelangelo, who rather hated sex, can't help filling the Cornucopia with phallic acorns. Sex is a very powerful, beneficial and necessary stimulus in human life, and we are all grateful when we feel its warm, natural flow through us, like a form of sunshine. . . .

negation Then what is pornography, after all this? It isn't sex appeal or sex stimulus in art. It isn't even a deliberate intention on the part of the artist to arouse or excite sexual feelings. There's nothing wrong with sexual feelings in themselves, so long as they are straightforward and not sneaking or sly. The right sort of sex stimulus is invaluable to human daily life. Without it the world grows grey. I would give everybody the gay Renaissance stories to read, they would help to shake off a lot of grey self-importance, which is our modern civilised disease.

analysis But even I would censor genuine pornography, rigorously. It would not be very difficult. In the first place, genuine pornography is almost always underworld, it doesn't come into the open. In the second, you can recognise it by the insult it offers, invariably, to sex, and to the human spirit.

definition Pornography is the attempt to insult sex, to do dirt on it. This is unpar-
examples donable. Take the very lowest instance, the picture postcard sold underhand, by the underworld, in most cities. What I have seen of them have been of an ugliness to make you cry. The insult to the human body,

the insult to a vital human relationship! Ugly and cheap they make the human nudity, ugly and degraded they make the sexual act, trivial and cheap and nasty.

It is the same with the books they sell in the underworld. They are either so ugly they make you ill, or so fatuous you can't imagine anybody but a cretin or a moron reading them, or writing them. *comparison*

It is the same with the dirty limericks that people tell after dinner, or the dirty stories one hears commercial travellers telling each other in a smoke-room. Occasionally there is a really funny one, that redeems a great deal. But usually they are just ugly and repellent, and the so-called "humour" is just a trick of doing dirt on sex. *comparison*

Now the human nudity of a great many modern people is just ugly and degraded, and the sexual act between modern people is just the same, merely ugly and degrading. But this is nothing to be proud of. It is the catastrophe of our civilisation. I am sure no other civilisation, not even the Roman, has showed such a vast proportion of ignominious and degraded nudity, and ugly, squalid dirty sex. Because no other civilisation has driven sex into the underworld, and nudity to the w.c. *contrast*

The intelligent young, thank heaven, seem determined to alter in these two respects. They are rescuing their young nudity from the stuffy, pornographical hole-and-corner underworld of their elders, and they refuse to sneak about the sexual relation. This is a change the elderly grey ones of course deplore, but it is in fact a very great change for the better, and a real revolution. *cause and effect*

But it is amazing how strong is the will in ordinary, vulgar people, to do dirt on sex. It was one of my fond illusions, when I was young, that the ordinary healthy-seeming sort of men in railway carriages, or the smoke-room of an hotel or a pullman, were healthy in their feelings and had a wholesome rough devil-may-care attitude towards sex. All wrong! All wrong! Experience teaches that common individuals of this sort have a disgusting attitude toward sex, a disgusting contempt of it, a disgusting desire to insult it. If such fellows have intercourse with a woman, they triumphantly feel that they have done her dirt, and now she is lower, cheaper, more contemptible than she was before. *illustration*

It is individuals of this sort that tell dirty stories, carry indecent picture postcards, and know the indecent books. This is the great pornographical class—the really common men-in-the-street and women-in-the-street. They have as great a hate and contempt of sex as the greyest Puritan, and when an appeal is made to them, they are always on the side of the angels. They insist that a film-heroine shall be a neuter, a sexless thing of washed-out purity. They insist that real sex-feeling shall only be shown by the villain or villainess, low lust. They find a Titian or a Renoir really indecent, and they don't want their wives and daughters to see it. *illustration* *comparison*

Why? Because they have the grey disease of sex-hatred, coupled with the yellow disease of dirt-lust. The sex functions and the excrementory *cause and effect* functions in the human body work so close together, yet they are, so to speak, utterly different in direction. Sex is a creative flow, the excrementory flow is towards dissolution, de-creation, if we may use such a word. In the really healthy human being the distinction between the two is instant, our profoundest instincts are perhaps our instincts of opposition between the two flows.

conclusion

But in the degraded human being the deep instincts have gone dead, and then the two flows become identical. *This* is the secret of really vulgar and of pornographical people: the sex flow and the excrement flow is the same to them. It happens when the psyche deteriorates, and the profound controlling instincts collapse. Then sex is dirt and dirt is sex, and sexual excitement becomes a playing with dirt, and any sign of sex in a woman becomes a show of her dirt. This is the condition of the common, vulgar human being whose name is legion, and who lifts his voice and it is the *Vox populi, vox Dei.* And this is the source of all pornography.

D. H. LAWRENCE

"Pornography"

Notice how Lawrence takes a standard definition of pornography, then shows how it actually isn't a valid definition.

In both essays, the authors have answered the question "What is it?" Additionally, both writers employ a variety of modes to expand their definitions. Because there are various ways in which to expand a definition, you may find that organization is a problem; however, if you use the opening paragraph as the introduction and make the simple definition function as the thesis, you will find that the expansion in the body of the essay presents little difficulty. Just make sure that everything you include does, in fact, help to clarify the simple definition.

Finally, read a student's paper, noting in particular how comparison/contrast is used to develop the definition:

Literature, like everything else, is subject to change. In these days when 20th century pith overrides 19th century control of language and 18th century "bite," some new definitions pertain, and perhaps more in the genre of poetry than elsewhere.

Laurence Perrine, in *Sound and Sense,* defines poetry as ". . . a kind of language that says *more* and says it *more intensely* than does ordinary language . . ." The *Prose and Poetry* series of the L. W. Singer Company defines it as ". . . an artistic expression of a significant idea or experience in words designated to delight the ear and appeal to the imagination and feelings . . ."

Perhaps these definitions do not effectively state all that poetry is today. Readers of poetry are subject to change, too, and the poetry of yesterday is not necessarily "poetic" in the same sense as modern poetry. An example of a modern poem some readers do not consider "poetic" is "Tribute to Henry Ford," by Richard Kostelanetz. They base their objection on the premise that this is only a lettered design on a page, appealing to the eye but not to the ear, since it cannot be read in the usual manner. Ordinarily, we think of poetry in terms of reading it aloud, or at least enjoying its aural effects silently. Assonance, alliteration and consonance are all parts of good poetry, as well as the imagery the artist portrays for us. In the "concrete" poem cited above, which can be interpreted but not read, it scarcely complies with the old definitions of poetry.

Because readers are not all alike, tastes in poetry vary as much as tastes in food, clothing and entertainment. Perhaps one reason for the disinterest many people show toward poetry is that they have had foisted off on them as "good" or "great" poetry material that does not meet their own criteria. Stimulation of an appetite for poetry lies with the teacher these days, for too few families indulge in reading for enjoyment now that television has arrived. The effect a good teacher can have is immeasurable if tolerance, understanding and latitude of opinion are demonstrated in the dissemination of poetry. Fortunately, the new anthologies are including a wide variety of styles and types which appeal to a range of students.

No longer must a poem have meter and rhyme to be a good poem. Free verse and blank verse find their place with the older readers who can think out the meanings as they outgrow the need of younger children for rhyme and rhythm. This does not mean that the older, traditional forms, like the sonnet and the ode, must be consigned to the trash heap. Their value is demonstrated in the fact that they have survived the criticism of centuries.

The subject matter of the modern poem also varies from the formerly accepted ideas of what was fit for poetic discussion. Poetry today is more personal, not always concerned with beauty of thought or expression, but expressive of stronger subjects, even ugly or distasteful ones, which formerly were considered unsuitable for poets to deal with. This has allowed a new honesty, a depth of search and find, that did not exist in former years. Poetry is, therefore, more human.

Obviously, then, a definition of poetry will be different for different people, depending on their own needs, personality and tastes. Like art in general, allowance should be made for individual translation of the artist's conception of his subject. Sometimes we hear an opinion expressed which indicates that a certain piece of prose is "poetic." This is a valid statement. The line between poetry and prose is becoming thinner with the new style of writing. We can still apply many portions of the old definitions to poetry, however. Poetry will be better off for the addition of new interpretations and the expansion of definitions to include them. If we retain the notion that poetry is the original use of words in expression of thought or feeling in ways that excite us mentally or emotionally, we will continue to enjoy the fruits of the years in imagery, style and ideas of poets both past and present.

We should not restrict ourselves to too narrow a definition of poetry. Our horizons are broader today than ever before; more people are more highly educated than ever before. It is time poetry regained its place in society, unhampered by the inadequacies of a definition that attempts to suit us all.

PRACTICE

PART I

1. Write sentence definitions of the following terms.

a. simple definition

_____

_____

b. extended definition

_____

_____

2. List the three parts of a simple definition.

a. _____

b. _____

c. _____

PART II

Indicate whether each of the following is a valid simple definition by marking yes or no in the space provided. Be prepared to explain your "no" responses to your instructor.

_____ 1. A collar is a covering a man wears around his neck.

_____ 2. A protuberance is an object that protrudes.

_____ 3. Man is a featherless biped.

_____ 4. Internment is the act or ceremony of burying a body.

_____ 5. Patriotism is a holy sentiment.

_____ 6. Folklore is a traditional custom preserved orally among a group of people.

_____ 7. A collie is a large, long-haired dog.

PART I

1. Check your answers by referring to the first part of the section.
2. a. term
   b. genus
   c. differentia

PART II

1. no
2. no
3. no
4. yes
5. no
6. yes
7. no

Write an essay of extended definition. Select one of the following topics.

1. a current definition of a slang term ("up tight," "cool," "groovy," "getting it together," "your own thing")
2. an emotion (fear, love, hate)
3. a controversial term (pornography, free love, marriage, politics)
4. yourself
5. topic of your choice

(Review pages 244–245 before you complete this writing assignment.)

Mixed Mode

You learned earlier in this chapter that, for the sake of classification, modes of exposition are defined as dominant (those around which papers are structured) and support (those used to complement the dominant mode). A number of the essays in this chapter contain marginal notations, indicating the presence of support modes. As a general rule, you will find that, depending on the subject and the purpose of your paper, you will use one dominant mode as the basic organizational pattern. It would be virtually impossible, however, to exclude support modes. For instance, if you were comparing and contrasting characters from two novels, you would, at the very least, also use illustration to support your thesis. In other words, mixing modes is a natural way of writing.

Thus, we reach the last of the expository modes—the *mixed mode*. There is no set pattern for the organization of a mixed-mode essay, since the modes can be used in any order and combination; you will get a clearer idea of how various modes of development can complement each other by reading the following essays:

cause and effect

I became a philosopher early. I *had* to become a philosopher. I was rather badly wounded in the First World War at Soissons, France, when I was twenty-two and as a result I was flat on my back for a long time. It was either get a philosophy or crack up.

analysis
definition

My code of living is simple. It consists of three parts. One, never be cruel; two, always be artistic; three, never lose your sense of humor.

analysis

comparison/contrast

examples

examples

Number One I don't believe requires much explanation. Never be cruel means, of course, always be kind. I believe that kindness is the natural human instinct, not cruelty. I have no illusions about humanity. I know its faults, its frequent blindness, its capacity for making terrible mistakes. But my work as a writer takes me among all kinds of men and women, often the very rough and the very poor. Everywhere I have found generosity and nobility; men who would have gladly given their lives for me because I had done them some slight kindness. The vast majority of human beings will do the basically good thing if they are given half a chance.

analysis

examples

By the second point in my code, always be artistic, I mean that whatever I do, I try to do with as much grace as possible. If I write a book, I want to make it as beautiful as I can. If I were a shoemaker, I would want to make shoes the same way, as perfect as possible. In our madly commercialized and mechanized world we have lost our sense of the beautiful. I believe we need beauty in our lives as much as we need food on our dining room tables. A world where beauty flourishes is a happy world—a world at peace.

analysis

illustration

dialogue

The third part of my code, as I said earlier, is never lose your sense of humor. I don't like pomposity. I don't like stuffed shirts. I'm glad I was born in a small town. It's a wonderful antidote for smugness. I remember years ago when I had a little success in New York with one of my first novels. There was the usual round of autograph parties and literary lunches and I was feeling rather pleased with myself. About this time I happened to go back to my home town in Kentucky and I saw an old fellow I had known as a boy standing on a street corner. He looked me up and down a long time and remarked lazily, "How are you, Benny? You been away a while, ain't you? You still teaching school?" That reduced life to its proper proportions.

conclusion

I was over in Germany not long ago, in the ruins of Berlin, and a reporter asked me to give his paper a thought for the day. That was a bit of an order for me, who had been in two wars against the Germans and had very definite physical souvenirs from both. I reflected on what I could tell the Germans under these circumstances. And then I wrote: "When all the peoples of the world remember to laugh, particularly at themselves, there will be no more dictators and no more wars."

BEN LUCIEN BURMAN
"Antidote for War"

The dominant mode in Burman's essay is basically analysis, but, in the process of analyzing his subject, he also uses support modes, specifically, definition, cause and effect, comparison/contrast, and illustration. In several cases, he employs a number of modes in a single paragraph.

An expository essay may include not only various expository modes but also narration and description, as illustrated in the following essay:

Until this Palm Sunday of 1865 the word Appomattox had no meaning. It was a harsh name left over from Indian days, it belonged to a river and to a country town, and it had no overtones. But after this day it would be one of the haunted possessions of the American people, a great and unique word that would echo in the national memory with infinite tragedy and infinite promise, recalling a moment in which sunset and sunrise came together in a streaked glow that was half twilight and half dawn.

The business might almost have been stage-managed for effect. No detail had been overlooked. There was even the case of Wilmer McLean, the Virginian who once owned a place by a stream named Bull Run and who found his farm overrun by soldiers in the first battle of the war. He sold out and moved to southern Virginia to get away from the war, and he bought a modest house in Appomattox Court House; and the war caught up with him finally, so that Lee and Grant chose his front parlor—of all the rooms in America—as the place where they would sit down together and bring the fighting to an end.

Lee had one staff officer with him, and in Mr. McLean's front yard a Confederate orderly stood by while the war horse Traveler nibbled at the spring grass. Grant came with half a dozen officers of his own, including the famous Sheridan, and after he and Lee had shaken hands and taken their seats, these trooped into the room to look and to listen. Grant and Lee sat at two separate tables, the central figures in one of the greatest tableaus of American history.

It was a great tableau not merely because of what these two men did but also because of what they were. No two Americans could have been in greater contrast. (Again the staging was perfect.) Lee was legend incarnate—tall, gray, one of the handsomest and most imposing men who ever lived, dressed today in his best uniform, with a sword belted at his waist. Grant was—well, he was U. S. Grant, rather scrubby and undersized, wearing his working clothes, with mud-spattered boots and trousers and a private's rumpled blue coat with his lieutenant general's stars tacked to the shoulders. He wore no sword. The men who were with them noticed the contrast and remembered it. Grant himself seems to have felt it; years afterward, when he wrote his memoirs, he mentioned it and went to some lengths to explain why he did not go to this meeting togged out in dress uniform. (In effect, his explanation was that he was just too busy.)

Yet the contrast went far beyond the matter of personal appearance. Two separate versions of America met in this room, each perfectly embodied by its chosen representative.

There was an American aristocracy, and it had had a great day. It came from the past and it looked to the past; it seemed almost deliberately archaic, with an air of knee breeches and buckled shoes and powdered wigs, with a leisured dignity and a rigid code in which privilege and duty were closely joined. It had brought the country to its birth and it had provided many of its beliefs; it had given courage and leadership, a sense of order and learning, and if there had been any way by which the eighteenth century could possibly have been carried forward into the future, this class would have provided the perfect vehicle. But from the day of its beginning, America had been fated to be a land of unending change. The country in which this leisured class had its place was in powerful ferment, and the class itself had changed. It had been diluted. In the struggle for survival it had laid hands on the curious combination of modern machinery and slave labor, the old standards had been altered, dignity had begun to look like arrogance, and pride of purse had begun to elbow out pride of breeding. The single lifetime of Robert E. Lee had seen the change, although Lee himself had not been touched by it.

Yet the old values were real, and the effort to preserve them had nobility. Of all the things that went to make up the war, none had more poignance than the desperate fight to preserve these disappearing values, eroded by change from within as much as by change from without. The fight had been made and it had been lost, and everything that had been dreamed and tried and fought for was personified in the gray man who sat at the little table in the parlor at Appomattox and waited for the other man to start writing out the terms of surrender.

The other man was wholly representative too. Behind him there was a new society, not dreamed of by the founding fathers: a society with the lid taken off, western man standing up to assert that what lay back of a person mattered nothing in comparison to what lay ahead of him. It was the land of the mudsills, the temporarily dispossessed, the people who had nothing to lose but the future; behind it were hard times, humiliation, and failure, and ahead of it was all the world and a chance to lift oneself by one's bootstraps. It had few standards beyond a basic unformulated belief in the irresponsibility and ultimate value of the human spirit, and it could tramp with heavy boots down a ravaged Shenandoah Valley or through the embers of a burned Columbia without giving more than a casual thought to the things that were being destroyed. Yet it had its own nobility and its own standards; it had, in fact, the future of the race in its keeping, with all the immeasurable potential that might reside in a people who had decided that they would no longer be bound by the limitations of the past. It was rough and uncultivated, and it came to important meetings wearing muddy boots and no sword, and it had to be listened to.

It could speak with a soft voice, and it could even be abashed by its own moment of triumph, as if that moment were not a thing to be savored and enjoyed. Grant seems to have been almost embarrassed when he and Lee came together in this parlor, yet it was definitely not the embarrassment of an underling ill at ease in a superior's presence. Rather it was the diffidence of a sensitive man who had another man in his power and wished to hurt him as little as possible. So Grant made small talk and recalled the old days in the Mexican War, when Lee had been the polished staff officer in the commanding general's tent and Grant had been an acting regimental quartermaster, slouching about like the hired man who looked after the teams. Perhaps the oddest thing about this meeting at Appomattox was that it was Grant, the nobody from nowhere, who played the gracious host, trying to put the aristocrat at his ease and, as far as might be, to soften the weight of the blow that was about to come down. In the end it was Lee who, so to speak, had to call the meeting to order, remarking (and the remark must have wrenched him almost beyond endurance) that they both knew what they were there for and that perhaps they had better get down to business. So Grant opened his orderly book and got out his pencil. He confessed afterward that when he did so he had no idea what he was going to write.

BRUCE CATTON

"A Stillness at Appomattox"

A classic example of comparison/contrast, Catton's essay is also rich in its use of description. Notice, however, that the descriptive element is used, not for the primary purpose of sensory appeal, but as a tool to illustrate his comparison/contrast of two men, each representative of a different way of life. There is even a narrative thread running throughout the essay, a sense of something happening, but this "plot line" does not exist as pure narrative; it is a means of further illustration in the comparison/contrast of the two subjects. In other words, Catton's purpose is clearly expository—to compare and contrast—but he uses description and narration to support his thesis. In short, the essay is a good example of the compatibility of exposition in its various forms, description, and narration.

The following paper was written by a student who was instructed to employ a number of modes. See how many you can detect:

One morning as I looked up and down the street in the small Michigan community where I lived, I found myself asking, "Where have all the mothers gone?" I already knew the answer. They had gone to work, and in so doing had caused problems.

Two or three of us stay-at-home mothers remained on the long block of homes. We found ourselves appointed guardians, not always by request, but subtly, or necessarily, of those children who came home to empty houses. A small boy would come with a scraped knee, or he had lost his key, or he was just plain lonely. The children gathered after school at the few homes where mothers were on hand to offer them cookies and milk, but more importantly, to offer them security. These children were often very young, in the early grades of school. At the same time, their working mothers seldom had time to bake cookies for school parties, haul car-pools, or go on field trips. Still, my quarrel was not so much with the fact of the working mother, but with those parents who failed to make safe arrangements for their school-age youngsters. Questions began to surface in my mind at that time which have not yet been answered.

That particular community was unusual because it was a one-industry town made up largely of professional people. The women were as highly educated as their husbands, capable of holding positions commanding respect and substantial salaries. They were not sales clerks, waitresses, typists; they were chemists, teachers with advanced degrees, and sociologists, so I resented being made baby-sitter for their children when they should have made provisions for child-care. Then, several years ago we moved to a different community. The same problem existed in a different way. Many of the women whose children came home to empty houses were working because they had to; they were divorcees, widows, or members of families caught up in the inflationary spiral. Granted that by then more day-care centers had become available, still too many children were without adult supervision.

Today I still ponder some of those questions that surfaced years ago. No woman is going to deny help to an injured child even if it means she must assume another's obligation. But isn't it possible that the same child might suffer another kind of injury, perhaps emotionally, from this trend? Do we know enough about this aspect of children shifting for themselves? Working mothers are naturally defensive about the situation. Certainly children have to become responsible and independent, but at what age should all this be accomplished? I don't think turning children loose is the answer, yet the child-on-the-loose syndrome is growing.

The teenagers with too much freedom and too little attention can take care of themselves in some respects, but what opportunities for dangerous experiments are open to them in empty homes? There may be a message in the fact that smaller children seek out the homes where mothers are present, but older children seek out the homes where they can be alone with their friends. What happens when parents do arrive home after a day on the job? In a one-parent home, does that tired parent have energy and patience to attend to the needs of tired little ones? Do the teenagers get the response and understanding they require? Does a family retain its unity if it is together only under strained, weary circumstances?

Probably the push for equality for women has brought about some of these changes from the old, traditional picture. Eventually these changes may work out to the advantage of children as well as women, and families as a whole. Certainly women are entitled to live fulfilling lives, just as men are, but has the movement toward equality been detrimental to their children?

Until all the adjustments are made to the new view of a woman's role, what is going to happen? Will new answers be adequate to old questions? The world has changed around the children; the needs of the children haven't changed. They still have to have love first of all, far more than they need material things. Perhaps it is only parents who need material things. Every time I see the lonely eight-year-old boy who lives across the street come home to emptiness, the old wondering stirs again.

While the student was, in fact, told to employ various modes, she made an important discovery; she naturally used these modes and didn't have to force them into the paper. In fact, she was aware of the modes she had used only after rereading the first draft.

Thus, using a combination of modes within the framework of one dominant mode is natural. What is unnatural is to force the use of various modes. Again, your subject and your purpose will dictate what is natural. The more modes you use, however, the greater your chances of having organizational problems. Illustration with its narrative and descriptive overtones, is always usable. Comparison/contrast, analogy, cause and effect, analysis, and definition are also useful, so employ them at points in your papers where they serve a functional purpose.

Reread the student essay and indicate the following.   PRACTICE

1. the dominant mode of development _____

2. the support modes (there may be more than one per paragraph)

a. _____

b. _____

c. _____

d. _____

e. _____

f. _____

g. _____

PRACTICE ANSWERS
1. illustration
2. a. thesis, illustration
   b. illustration, comparison/contrast
   c. illustration, comparison/contrast
   d. cause and effect
   e. comparison/contrast
   f. cause and effect
   g. conclusion

WRITING ASSIGNMENT

Write a mixed-mode essay on one of the following topics.

1. your code of living
2. a look at two people
3. your reaction to working mothers, children on the loose, or a related topic
4. a current issue or problem in your life
5. topic of your choice

(Review the following section on concluding paragraphs before you complete this writing assignment.)

Concluding Paragraphs

After you have completed the body of your paper, you are ready to take the final step in the actual writing process, which is to write a conclusion. Stated simply, concluding paragraphs may be classified as ineffective and effective. *Ineffective conclusions* are characterized by one or more of the following negative traits:

- making an apology, which casts doubts on the validity of the rest of the paper
- introducing new material, which weakens the unity of the paper
- changing tone, which often insults the reader, especially if the

tone has been serious throughout the paper, but suddenly becomes sarcastic in the last paragraph
- making a major concession, which could place your entire thesis in doubt
- repeating verbatim the opening paragraph
- including wordy tags, such as "In conclusion, I would just like to close by saying that . . ."

Effective concluding paragraphs, on the other hand, will contain one of the following types of information:

- a brief summary of the major points of the paper
- a repetition of the thesis statement (clincher paragraph), but in a fresh presentation of the thesis
- a logical conclusion, often a suggestion or recommendation, based on the information in the body of the paper
- a quotation related to the thesis of the paper
- a question intended to force the reader to think about the thesis of the paper

Your choice of conclusion will often be dictated by the dominant mode of development used in the paper. The one trait that all types of concluding paragraphs should have in common is brevity. Since the body of the paper is where you develop the thesis, you should make the last paragraph an emphatic, strong one, and emphasis is best achieved by conciseness. As a general rule, the concluding paragraph often resembles the opening paragraph in terms of its relative length.

Based on the suggested ways of writing conclusions, the purposes of concluding paragraphs can be classified as follows:

- to give the paper a sense of completion
- to repeat the thesis a final time
- to sum up major points
- to add interest

Remember that the concluding paragraph is important, primarily because it is your final opportunity to leave a lasting impression on your readers, so have a strong conclusion, one that clinches the thesis of your paper.

PART I   PRACTICE

1. List four ineffective ways of concluding a paper.

   a. _____

   b. _____

c. _____

d. _____

2. List five effective kinds of conclusions to a paper.

    a. _____

    b. _____

    c. _____

    d. _____

    e. _____

3. List four purposes of concluding paragraphs.

    a. _____

    b. _____

    c. _____

    d. _____

PART II

Read the five student paragraphs that follow and indicate which type of conclusion each represents: summary, restatement of thesis, logical, quotation, or question.

Keep in mind the limitation of reading isolated concluding paragraphs. Some of the examples may be a combination of various types of conclusions, so base your answers on what seems to be the *dominant* type in each paragraph:

1. Such is the state of our leadership. Chaos rather than order is currently the trend, much to the dismay of those who seek a better way of life, but too few of us are aware of the reality of the situation; the masses are either too ignorant or too indifferent to act. The result is a classic case of an old saying that has become an actuality; "ignorance is bliss."

_____

2. In summary, I believe that Sooner High School is the best in the state, a contention I make because it has the best physical facilities, the best teachers, and the best students.

   _____

3. So you see, the outlook is bleak, but not so hopeless as it appears if we are willing to give freely of our time and our money. I, for one, am willing, but I will need help. Are you willing to help me fight for a valid cause?

   _____

4. Having examined both sides of the issue carefully, we can only conclude that one candidate is superior in her qualifications. And by applying our logical, objective minds to the situation, we can state with complete confidence that Ms. Ballinger will be the next Prom Queen.

   _____

5. Surely, therefore, my original contention, that *Blazing Saddles* should be a strong contender for best picture of the year, has been validated. If it doesn't win the award, then it proves that the judges are unfair, because *Blazing Saddles* is an outstanding movie.

   _____

PART I   PRACTICE ANSWERS

1. a. making an apology
   b. introducing new material
   c. changing tone
   d. making a major concession
   e. repeating verbatim the opening paragraph
   f. including wordy tags
2. a. brief summary
   b. repetition of thesis statement
   c. logical conclusion
   d. quotation
   e. question
3. a. to give completeness
   b. to repeat thesis
   c. to summarize
   d. to add interest

PART II

1. quotation
2. summary
3. question
4. logical
5. restatement of thesis

(Proceed to the next chapter only if you fully understand the material in this chapter. If not, review the material or see your instructor.)

·❧[13]❧·
Argument

As discussed in previous chapters, exposition is writing that informs, clarifies, sets forth, or explains. *Argument,* the focus of this chapter, does the same but goes one step further; it is intended to change the readers' way of thinking and persuade them to accept the writer's point of view about the subject.

Objectives

After completing this chapter, you should be able

1. to distinguish between inductive and deductive argument
2. to write an inductive argument
3. to write a deductive argument

———— ❧ ————

Even though the process of writing an argumentative essay is much more involved, it bears some resemblance to verbal argument, a form of expression you have engaged in all your life. Think, for instance, back to your childhood and recall the numerous times you argued with a playmate about possession of a toy. After repeated rounds of "It's mine," one of you eventually won the argument, possibly because of superior strength or possibly because of superior powers of persuasion. In other words, the argument was won through the ability to present a convincing case of ownership. More recently, you may have engaged in a conversation with a salesperson who was selling a product you really didn't want but eventually ended up buying. If so, you were again engaged in a form of argument, one that resulted in your yielding to the salesperson's persuasiveness and accepting the judgment that you did, in fact, need the product.

These simple examples of verbal argument illustrate two requirements of written argument as well. First, it must *begin in conflict*. If the subject being argued is already agreed on, or if factual documentation proves one viewpoint beyond logical argument, there is no conflict and therefore no basis for argument. Second, argument must *end in resolution*. At least the opposition should admit to the credibility of your argument; at most the opposition should be so convinced by your argument that they change their viewpoint, accept yours, and admit that you are right.

In written argument, the opposition will not be a child or a salesperson, but rather skeptical readers. Consequently, before writing an argumentative essay, you need to make the following assumptions about the readers:

- They will be opposed to and resist your argument. Remember, argument must start in conflict, so be prepared.
- They will have some knowledge, and certainly opinions, about the subject.
- They will be intelligent people.

By making these assumptions prior to writing, you will force yourself to do a more careful job of developing your argument. Otherwise, you might be lulled into a sense of false security, resulting in an unconvincing argument.

Previously, you learned that an expository essay has three basic parts—introduction, body, and conclusion. These parts also make up the divisions of the argumentative essay. The following suggestions, not intended to be all-inclusive, are offered because they represent practical considerations for writing an argumentative essay.

Introduction The purpose is the same as in the expository essay, that is, to introduce readers to the subject. This introduction should be relatively brief, usually one or two paragraphs of an eight-hundred- to one-thousand-word paper. The introduction can contain any one or a combination of the following items of information about the subject of the paper:

- brief background
- summary of two opposing views
- situation or assumption generally accepted, but one that has problems
- brief anecdote related to the subject

In addition, the introduction can suggest (implicitly) or state (explicitly) the thesis, the central issue you are going to argue. The choice of a suggested or stated thesis depends on your purpose, which will be discussed later in this chapter. Finally, the introduction of an argumentative essay not only introduces the subject to the readers, but must also set up the basis for conflict, that essential ingredient of argument. Remember that the readers are going to oppose your argument, so make sure you inform them of the issue in the introduction.

Body

This part makes up the bulk of your paper and consists of specific evidence offered in support of your argument. Generally, each bit of evidence is developed in one generative paragraph unless the evidence is so extensive that it needs more than one. The middle part of the paper should also contain the objections offered by the opposition. You can discuss these objections in each paragraph in which you present evidence supporting your argument, or you can counter them in a separate section of the paper.

The type of supporting evidence you present can take various forms, including the modes of exposition discussed in Chapter 12, "Writing the Expository Essay." In other words, depending on your subject and plan of organization, you may illustrate, analyze, compare/contrast, show cause and effect, define, or use any combination of these modes. You can also use analogy, but be cognizant of its limitations in argument. Since an analogy is a highly subjective way of seeing similarities in apparently dissimilar subjects, use it to illustrate and clarify a point of argument; do not view it as concrete evidence. You must also guard against false analogies, that is, comparisons of two subjects having no similarities or having nothing to do with the actual point of argument.

Since argument involves more than just giving an opinion about a subject, you need to be able to support your contention with reliable information. The word that most accurately describes such information is *testimony*, which may be classified in the following ways:

1. *Precedent,* more commonly labeled example, is an attempt by the writer to support his or her argument by referring to an example similar to the subject being argued. This example may be factual or fictional; the important thing is that it should relate to the subject being argued. For instance, if you were arguing that capital punishment was inhumane because it kept the convicted in a state of limbo, sometimes for years, while they awaited the outcome of various legal appeals, you might give as a precedent the

case of Harvey Hicks, who was on death row for twenty years, had five last-minute stays of execution, but was finally executed.

2. You can also use *statistics* to support an argument, but you need to make sure that they are accurate, unbiased, and reliable. The only way to do so is to check the source carefully. You must also avoid drawing unwarranted inferences from them. If, for instance, you were arguing that *Forever Together* was the most widely circulated book on campus and if you supported your argument with statistics from the library, indicating that the book had been checked out five hundred more times than any other book in the last year, you would have a statistic that was reliable, accurate, unbiased, and based on a fair sampling. If, however, you inferred from the statistic that *Forever Together* was also the best book on campus, you would be drawing an unjustified inference that would not strengthen, but weaken, your argument.

3. *Authority,* that is, opinion from a respected and recognized expert on a subject, can be a convincing form of testimony. For example, if you were arguing that gun control would lessen the number of robberies and you used the local chief of police as your authority, you would no doubt add validity to your argument. When citing authority, you need to make sure that the person is unbiased, does not offer an opinion contradicted by most other authorities in the field, and is, in fact, an acknowledged authority.

Modes of exposition, precedent, statistics, and authority are some of the ways you have available to present evidence in support of your argument. Depending on your subject, which will often dictate the type of support to be included, any one or a combination of these methods will work. The important thing for you to remember is that the middle part of your essay is where you either convince the readers of the validity of your argument or lose the argument because of weakly supported evidence.

Conclusion

Earlier you learned how to write a concluding paragraph for an expository essay. Among the possible types of conclusions discussed were the brief summary, repetition of the thesis, relevant quotation, a question, or a logical conclusion. All these are appropriate to an argumentative essay as well. The conclusion may be one paragraph, probably no more than two, and may include such information as a reminder of the weaknesses of the opposing view, some implications of your conclusion, or a recommendation for a plan of action. Of course, the conclusion you select will again be dictated by the subject and the way in which it has been presented. In brief, the conclusion should clinch your argument and leave the readers with a final feeling of "You're right."

As you can see, writing an argumentative essay is much like writing an expository essay. The major difference is that in argument you are not only informing, but also trying to change the opinion of your readers. Because of this distinction, you have to be more careful in presenting the evidence on which you base your conclusion. You must present valid supporting evidence. The following are some of the tests you should apply to determine the validity of your argument:

1. Include an *abundant sampling of evidence* supporting your argument. What is abundant is, of course, relative, depending on the complexity of your subject, and even more on the length of the assignment. For instance, if you were assigned an eight-hundred-to one-thousand-word paper, and if you were arguing the merits of a particular college, you would hardly have an abundant sampling if you offered as the only evidence the fact that the college had an outstanding teaching staff. On the other hand, if you included as evidence the outstanding teaching staff, a varied curriculum that met the needs of all students, excellent facilities, and a student-oriented administration, and if you developed each of these points fully, then, within the restrictions of the assignment, you would have included an abundant sampling of evidence.

2. The evidence presented should be *typical of the subject,* not exceptional. In the preceding example, let's assume that the college has only intramural volleyball but none of the other sports. No matter how strong the volleyball program may be, you would hardly be presenting typical evidence if you said that the college had a strong intramural program because of the outstanding volleyball team. To do so would be to offer exceptional, not typical, evidence.

3. The *focus must not change* from the subject being argued to one of the points of supporting evidence. For instance, assume you were arguing for the abolition of required English classes and you were presenting such evidence as: (a) there was no documentation to prove that students who took English classes could write better than those at the neighboring college who were not required to do so; (b) English classes failed to provide essential skills for immediate job placement; (c) English classes were boring; and (d) the high standards required in English classes were not required in other classes. You should not launch into a discussion of the skills needed for job placement and in the process ignore the basic argument—that required English classes should be abolished.

4. The supporting evidence must have an *obvious relationship to the conclusion* reached. In the previous example, such evidence as physical education classes being more fun would hardly support the conclusion that required English classes should be abolished.

5. Be prepared to *deal with arguments presented by the opposition*. This can be done by showing that they are exceptional instances, irrelevant to the issue, have limited merit, or are less convincing than your point. For instance, if you were arguing that a certain movie was good entertainment because of a strong plot, interesting characterizations, and a thought-provoking theme, but an opposing argument was that it had one scene that was long and dull, you could counter by pointing out that the long scene was an exception. How you go about dealing with the opposing view, however, will vary according to the subject and the number of points of opposition you encounter. The important thing is that you are prepared to deal with them.

6. The conclusion you reach from the supporting evidence should be *consistent with other findings* on the subject. If, for instance, you were arguing the relative safety of convertibles and concluded that they were as safe as hardtops, yet all other findings concluded the opposite, then you would be reaching a wrong conclusion.

If you disregard any of these guidelines, you will greatly weaken your chances of achieving the ultimate objective of argument, convincing your readers to accept your viewpoint, a job made more difficult since you are writing for readers who resist your argument, have knowledge of the subject, and are intelligent. In addition, careful observance of these guidelines will help you avoid emotional and logical fallacies, both caused by weak reasoning. Thus, when you write an argumentative essay, look on these guidelines as important criteria against which your paper will be judged.

One final comment needs to be made at this point. As the writer of an argument, you may appeal to your readers in the following ways:

- by appealing to emotions (pathos)
- by appealing to personality or character (ethos)
- by appealing to reason (logos)

Depending on your subject, purpose, and audience, you may find all three appeals useful. The focus of this book in general, and of this chapter in particular, however, is the last—appeal to reason. Thus, the subsequent discussion will emphasize logical argument, both inductive and deductive.

Induction You previously learned that reasoning is generally classified as inductive or deductive, classifications that also apply to the organization of argumentative essays. The first of these classifications, *inductive agrument,* begins with specific evidence that relates to and supports a generalized conclusion. The point at which you move from specific supporting evidence to the generalized conclusion is known as the *inductive leap.* In other words, induction is nothing more than drawing a general conclusion from the observation of specific evidence. The conclusion reached must be more general and include a broader scope than the evidence cited. For instance, a child who stuck a hand in a burning fireplace, was burned, and concluded that the fire was hot, would be following an inductive course of logic, but not reaching an inductive conclusion; there is no inductive leap into a general conclusion, because obviously *that* fire was hot. If, on the other hand, the child concluded that all burning fireplaces were hot, then he or she would be reaching an inductive conclusion of a general nature. This example points out only *how* the process of induction works; in a written argument, you would have to cite more than one bit of evidence on which to base a general conclusion.

Read the following paragraph, which illustrates the process of written induction:

The room in which I found myself was very large and lofty. The windows were long, narrow, and pointed, and at so vast a distance from the black oaken floor as to be altogether inaccessible from within. Feeble gleams of encrimsoned light made their way through the trellissed panes, and served to render sufficiently distinct the more prominent objects around. The eye, however, struggled in vain to reach the remoter angles of the chamber, or the recesses of the vaulted and fretted ceiling. Dark draperies hung upon the walls. The general furniture was profuse, comfortless, antique, and tattered. Many books and musical instruments lay scattered about, but failed to give any vitality to the scene. I felt that I breathed an atmosphere of sorrow. An air of stern, deep, and irredeemable gloom hung over and pervaded all.

EDGAR ALLAN POE

"The Fall of the House of Usher"

Obviously this is a descriptive, not an argumentative, paragraph, so the conclusion is not generalized, but based on the immediate content only. Nevertheless, it illustrates the inductive process of moving from specifics to a generality.

In the following essay, notice how the writer argues his case inductively, using illustration as his primary evidence:

Once I had a conversation with a taxi driver in Chicago which I shall not soon forget. It upset so many fixed ideas about people, their knowledge versus their reasoning powers.

brief background

He was driving me from the lake front, near the Planetarium, to my hotel. I could not see his face, only a thick neck between cap and jacket. description He was neither young nor old, and he handled his cab the way a cowboy handles his pony.

The Lake was high—6 or 8 inches above the normal mark—and covered part of the concrete pavement where I usually walked in search of fresh air, between lectures. I spoke of this to the driver.

"Yeah," he said, "the Lake's up, I read it in the paper. I wonder why?"

beginning of illustration
"It may have something to do," I said, "with the tilting of the earth's axis. Big glaciers and ice fields in Greenland are melting. That's what a geologist told me in Marquette on Superior the other day. Superior's up too."

analogy
"Yeah? That's a funny thing now. The earth tilting. They say it's round like a ball, see, but it looks flat to me. I never saw it round like."

"Did you ever look out over the Lake and see the funnel of a boat, maybe part of the mast, and not the hull?" I asked.

"No mister, I never did."

"Try it some clear day when there's a big ore boat out there. The reason you can't see the hull is because of the earth's curve."

"Yeah? You mean the Lake is curved? That's a hell of a thing! It looks flat to me."

illustration continued
"Do you remember," I asked, "that picture taken from a camera hitched to a rocket eighty miles up over Arizona? You could see the Gulf of California, the Colorado River, the desert, the mountains around Los Angeles, and then the curve of the earth out on the Pacific Ocean, clear as could be!"

The taxi slowed down, perhaps for a red light, perhaps while my driver thought this over. "Eighty miles straight up,' he remarked skeptically, "that's quite a way, mister, farther than Gary. Where did that rocket come down? Why wasn't the camera smashed?"

"It probably was," I said, "but the negative was O.K. They found the negative in a container out in the desert somewhere."

"And you could see the curve of the world? Jeeze! It wasn't one of those faked pictures? They're always fakin' pictures, like that Earl Browder job."

"No," I said, "it wasn't faked. The army released it. It was in all the papers; and a big full page one in *Life*. Didn't you see it?"

"No," he said, "I missed it. Jeeze! You could really see the earth curving!" He turned off from Michigan Avenue in heavy traffic, and there was a pause in our talk.

analogy
"We're like ants," he said. "Here we live in a little place like Chicago, and never get out of it. Live here all our lives, like ants. And all those things going on out there: glaciers melting, oceans curving, rockets going end of illustration to God knows where. . . . It's a funny world, mister."

"Yes," I said, "it's a funny world."

implications of the conversation
This conversation (which I put down as soon as I could get to paper

and pencil) illustrates some important characteristics of the human mind which should be of interest to logicians, philosophers, and social scientists, among others. My taxi driver was woefully ignorant, but he knew how to reason. Within his limited world of facts, he was entirely logical, with a skepticism almost scientific. Furthermore, he had the power to lift himself clear of his environment, to see himself and his neighbors "like ants" in the wilderness of Chicago. He was curious about the world.

What if he had taken an extension course at the University of Chicago? What if he had read and pondered something on how to use his mind? In Russia today, says ex-Senator William Benton, no young mind escapes all the education it can absorb at State expense.

rhetorical questions

We had best be careful of looking down our noses at what H. L. Mencken in his prejudice called the "booboisie." The main lack may be factual knowledge rather than ability to reason. Man has been called the logical animal, and a powerful reasoning mechanism may be built into every one of us, but in most of us it lies there unused. If only it could be awakened, what a world we might build!

instructive generalization and conclusion

Still, I may be overgeneralizing. One swallow does not make a summer. He was only a single taxi driver, going from the Planetarium to the Loop.

limitation of conclusion

STUART CHASE
"Logic in a Taxi"

Chase's essay is a classic example of an inductive argument; that is, he begins with background information, presents specific evidence, in this case an extended narrative illustration based on a personal experience, and ends with a generalization about humanity. In the last paragraph, he defends his conclusion by admitting to the possibility of overgeneralizing, though he obviously does not believe he has. Even so, he defends himself against readers who may accuse him of overgeneralizing.

Now read the next essay, which is much longer and contains a number of modes to develop the evidence, as indicated in the margin:

To estimate the extent to which the attitudes of the New People will affect our future, we must examine, with a modest amount of cynicism, the Educational Process, for it is there, in the school as an environment, that they are gestating.

statement of problem

We tell ourselves, of course, that American Education is superior because there is so much of it, confusing, as we invariably do, quantity with quality. But is it superior? Are we, in fact, really educated at all?

questions posed

We can be justifiably proud of the fact that the number of people in the United States who cannot read or write is negligible, but no matter where we locate ourselves on the cultural spectrum, how many of us can read or write or even *talk* with a degree of competence, much less skill?

contrast

contrast With no trouble I could quote statistics to "prove" that we are even *relatively* uneducated; that we are less literate than the Japanese; that we have fewer bookstores than Sweden; that twenty percent of our citizens are officially designated as "functionally illiterate," meaning that they do not have the equivalent of an eighth-grade education, etc.

limitation of subject But that is not my premise.

premise My premise, which is not amenable to statistics, is that we are all, as a whole, as a nation, dumb. We simply don't know very much. We are educated only in the way that a chimpanzee who sits at a table and drinks from a saucer is educated compared to a baboon. Our schools have trained us in the techniques of modern living, they have turned out excellent technologists, engineers, professional people, but they have not educated us.

examples Except for the fragmentary and specialized knowledge associated with our work, we have only the most superficial information about the world. We do not read well [1] and we do not read books. Except for a few childish folk tales, we know nothing whatever about history, and being ignorant of the past, we have no realistic idea of the future. We are surrounded by, and entirely dependent on, a technology which we cannot understand. We are intellectually *passive,* watching and listening but never understanding or remembering. Our memories are so weak that the introduction of a simple zip code causes a near panic and evokes angry howls of "I don't like it." We remember only that we are Americans, so we

questions to challenge opposition must therefore be educated. But can you identify, even vaguely, Charlemagne? Can you extract a simple square root? Do you know what a square root *is*? What is the capital of Illinois? Who were, in order, the last six Presidents of the United States? How much is eight times eight? [2]

illustration Not only do we have no data,[3] but we have only the most tenuous grip on the basis of all intelligence: language. We have a recognition, or reading, vocabulary of only a few thousand words and often only a hazy idea of their exact meaning. We have no respect for language and accept common (i.e., Roob) usage as a criterion for correctness. We believe fatuously that language is merely another convenience, like the electric toaster, which is here to serve us. We don't realize that words, words

analogy arranged in the proper sequence, are what lead men to war, are what connect us with the past, are what brought the electric toaster into being. Without words we are not even barbarians, or even apes; we once again are what deep in our hearts we know we are anyway—wolves. Without words we cannot think, and to the extent that we neglect language, to that extent are we becoming Roobs, accepting ourselves as members of the mass, capable only of emotionalism. The mass, let us not forget, has its

---

[1] As we identify quality with quantity, we also equate speed with proficiency. Hence the ridiculous "speed-reading" courses.

[2] Sixty-four!

[3] The culture abounds with data, but it's all processed and stored in machines.

own identity, its own consciousness, but it is always motivated by emotion, never by intellect.

Alas, we have forgotten, as a nation and as individuals, how to Think.[4] And this mass dumbness is not, as it was in past times, counterbalanced by a small but truly educated minority, an intelligentsia, an educated upper class. We are all there is—and we are dumb.

What then is happening in the gigantic and complex school system that we are so proud of?

transitional paragraph

Well . . .

Education, like Pet Food, Sports, Sex, Pimples and Fun, has become Big Business. It is, in fact, the *biggest* business, employing more people and paying more salaries than any other specific national enterprise.

analogy

In every section of the country we see brand-new teaching "plants," their classrooms equipped with the latest pastel-colored plastic seats, each with a patented E-Z-Swing writing arm, arranged on terraces around an electronically amplified lectern. Each plant comes complete with a poured-concrete library, a student union, a science building and a parking problem. To approach any of these new, improved schools during class time, one must struggle across an ugly tundra of parked cars which stretches in all directions much farther than any eye cares to see.[5]

illustration and analogy

Many of these new facilities are junior or community colleges which are little more than extension high schools, filled with tacky students wiping their noses on their Dacron sleeves and looking upon the Learning Experience exactly as they look upon anything that takes them away from the telephone and the Box—as a drag. They go, have done with it, and rush back to the parking lot. They are passing their time. They aren't waiting. Just passing time.

illustration continued

On the other hand, the huge universities with fifteen thousand or more undergraduates have the appearance of the Ford River Rouge Plant. Their new federally funded buildings are often, due to space limitations, jammed in between the older museum-type structures, giving the campus the look of a 1939 World's Fair.

contrast

These huge factories, however, hum night and day, turning out graduates as efficiently as the Campbell Company turns out soup, except that unlike the soup company the university has no Quality Control. But they, the universities, are not really responsible for their product. Their students' conditioning began much earlier, in primary and nursery schools, where for twenty years they have been standardized by Avant

analysis

---

[4] "One of the frightening things about our time is the number of people who think it is a sign of intellectual audacity to be stupid. A whole generation seems to be taking on an easy distrust of thought . . . it is as though information and reason itself were a form of pedantry."—Renata Adler (*The New York Times,* March, 1968).

[5] For the past two years I've been making forays into the scholastic world to give lectures at various colleges, and wherever I go, I find the Big Problem is always parking. The secondary problem is the auditorium, which will hold only four percent of the student body.

Roob mysticism and a succession of scientific theories. And strangely, this standardization of the pupil is at every level justified in the name of its opposite, Individualism.

transitional paragraph

At exactly this point in this manuscript, I went into the kitchen for my 6:30 coffee break (when writing, I get up at 4:30 A.M.) and turned on the Box, and there in front of the NBC cameras was a clutch of three college teachers discussing education. I'd heard it all before, but they saved me the trouble of reconstructing it. Compressed, this is their message:

contrast

The aim of the educator is to develop the complete child so that he becomes an integrated individual in a democratic society. Old-fashioned schooling forced students to learn rote answers to uninteresting problems and to strive for grades. Grades are definitely not the answer. Bad grades discourage the student. Rote learning inhibits his creativity. Modern teaching techniques, however, structure a learning situation in which the student finds excitement in discovering the social and scholastic skills. Once the student does not feel threatened by a fear of criticism, he is able to evaluate his own progress and create his own planning situation. In this way he can express himself and realize his potential as an individual.

example

Spokesmen for the humanities, and particularly pedagogues, seem to have not only a fondness but a talent for the spectral abstraction and the cryptic theory, and to be totally uninterested in empirical results. Means, to them, are everything and lead only to more complex Means—never to an End. They are often in the position of a lecturer who, standing beside a pan of boiling water, explains his theory that water freezes when its temperature is raised. "You will notice," he says confidently, "that when I turn the heat up under this pan, the water freezes even more rapidly," and beside him the water continues to boil.

cause and effect

Their dedication to the holy cause of Education as Panacea leads many teachers to speak of it as if it were a theology, designed to save the student's soul rather than a discipline meant to improve his mind. The widespread resistance to giving the student data, to "rote learning," seems to me very strange because what really is education if not the acquiring of information and data? An example of pure Roobthink is the

example

student who says, "I can't learn because the subject is not taught in a way that interests me. It is boring." In other words, he "doesn't like it," and when he does not learn, it is the *teacher's* fault. This student often seems to feel that if he does learn anything, it is a favor to someone—his teacher, his parents, someone. How interesting can learning the multiplication table or analytical calculus be if there is no interest within the student for learning itself? Or if there is no capacity for learning? Do they want Raquel Welch to teach them the atomic numbers and weights of the 103 elements? And how can one begin to understand English history until one memorizes the cluttered sequence of the reigns of the various rulers? How can one make a decision about anything without data related to the subject? The answer obviously is that without information one can only make an emotional, or Roob, decision based on "I like it" or "I don't like it."

Or if, as has been claimed, the purpose of education is to build Character, how can one have Character without discipline? Any organism can only recognize its characteristics, discover what it is able to do, when it is challenged. If I don't challenge myself by trying to play the piano or second base, how can I know whether or not I have the ability to be a pianist or a second baseman?

counters opposing argument

Unfortunately a real challenge involves Competition either with one's peers or with an abstract criterion of excellence; and "competition" is the Number One Bad Word in the pedagogical lexicon. Increasingly, colleges today are doing away with competitive examinations [6] and many refuse to compile or release class standings. Competition is considered undemocratic, and with it the idea that anyone is smarter, quicker or more industrious than anyone else.

In place of Competition, the pedagogues have substituted Individualism. Webster defines Individualism as "the living of one's own life without regard for others," and for twenty years young people have been brought up in the shadow of this asocial idea. It is no wonder that today they are able to submerge all of their confusions into the one need for Self-Gratification.

contrast
definition

There are certainly many excellent schools in the United States, tough schools which have no time for the numbskull or the goof-off. Schools which encourage thought and respect, originality and accomplishment. But more and more these good schools are being subjected to the pressures of rising enrollemnt, undergraduate turbulence and right-wing political power, and Roobism is insidiously gaining a foothold. At Harvard, Columbia, Berkeley, Cornell, Princeton—in all of our greatest universities—mob boorishness is the order of the day. And the examples set in these institutions and widely and constantly publicized by TV are reflected in upheavals in lesser colleges and even in many high schools. Extracurricular activity has taken the form of a South American revolution. Shots are fired; buildings are stormed; "hostages" are taken; bricks, blows and invective are exchanged, and the word "confrontation" is knocked about like a badminton bird. And on almost all large campuses these days, heroin addiction (the *reductio ad absurdum* of Fun to the ultimate vulgarity) is openly discussed as a school problem.

examples

In the larger state universities the students have been aware of the Roob Power inherent in their mass for some time, and each semester sees more of them organizing and "demanding" greater control of the universities—the right to judge teachers and vote on their tenure, the right

general conclusion

---

[6] Tests are given incessantly, but tests which "evaluate" the student's personality, adjustment, sex life and attitude toward tests.

to decide what shall be taught and who shall be admitted. Although these ad hoc gangs exhibit all the characteristics of a lynch mob and seldom reflect the majority attitude of the student body, they are often supported by the Avant Faculty (who probably have visions of a Guillotine being erected on the Mall at any moment). And more often than not, school administrators bow to the "demands" made by the mob, and we find the anonymous mass student, the burgeoning Roob, arrogantly imposing his brute standards of "I like," "I don't like" upon the entire educational framework. Soon he will control the schools as completely as he controls the mass media and industry. Soon Quality Education will be confined to a few private and parochial schools. The rest will become giant Play Pens. Fun Places.

ROGER PRICE
"Education"

Price's essay is a good example of how a variety of modes can be used to support an argument. It also conforms to the shape of an inductively organized essay, which is usually a partial triangle, as shown in Figure 2. The figure represents the shape of an inductive argument, which often begins with an opening paragraph general enough to introduce the subject, followed by the specific evidence, which in turn functions as the basis for the general conclusion reached in the last paragraph.

Before making the inductive leap, be sure that the conclusion is relevant to the evidence cited and that it is consistent with other findings on the subject. The conclusion will be more convincing if

Figure 2

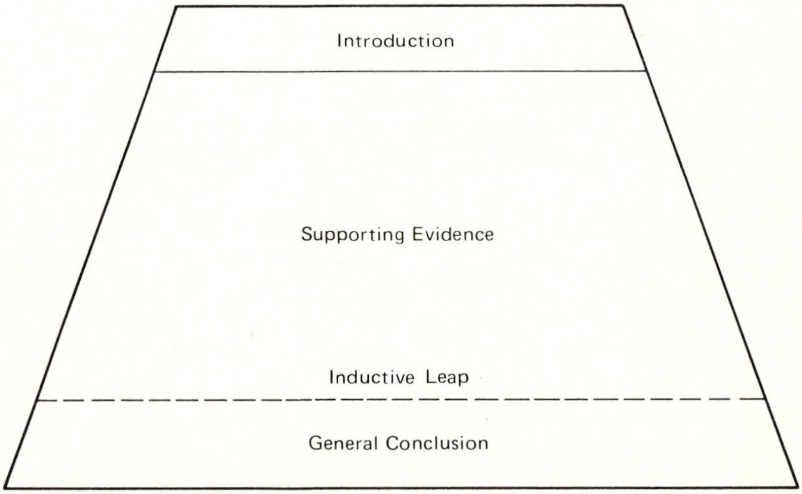

Introduction

Supporting Evidence

Inductive Leap

General Conclusion

you place a realistic limitation on its scope. A sound practice is to make the evidence specific, convincing, and fully developed, then "leap" to a conclusion of a general nature, but not necessarily all-inclusive.

While the possibilities for organizing the evidence in an inductive argument are many, the following outlines offer two practical options:

Option I

¶1: background and statement of problem
¶2: supporting evidence
¶3: supporting evidence
¶4: supporting evidence
¶5: discussion of weaknesses of opposing arguments
¶6: statement of your conclusion, implications, or recommendations

Option II

¶1: brief background
¶2: statement of problem
¶3: supporting evidence and discussion of opposing arguments
¶4: supporting evidence and discussion of opposing arguments
¶5: supporting evidence and discussion of opposing arguments
¶6: statement of your conclusion, implications, or recommendations

Possibly the main advantage of writing an inductive argument is that it forces you to think, organize, and write logically, a process that readers can follow step by step. In other words, readers are actually able to share the thought process you followed when you wrote the argument.

Deduction

Deduction, the second classification of reasoning, can also be applied to an argumentative essay. By definition, a *deductive argument* begins with an accepted general principle, which is then supported by specific evidence, and ends with a specific conclusion. In other words, deduction is a form of argument that attempts to convince readers that what is true of a general principle is also true of a particular instance. Although the term "deduction" was not used, much of the writing you did in earlier chapters was deductively organized. When writing a paragraph, you often started with a topic sentence, then supported it with specific examples, definitions, and so on; when writing expository essays, you started with an introductory paragraph containing a thesis statement, then supported it by means of paragraphs with specific points of analysis, illustration, and so forth. The general principle is usually a commonly held belief, assumption, or supposition about a given subject. It is, in fact, often a conclusion reached by inductive reasoning. This accepted principle can be stated as a proposition, that is, an assertion that can serve as the basis for an argument, that can be affirmed as true or denied as false. The term for this assertion is *premise* or *proposition*.

The most basic type of deduction is *the three-part syllogism:*

> major premise: Men are mortal.
> minor premise: I am a man.
> conclusion: I am mortal.

The *major premise* is the generalization with which the argument begins, the assertion you want the readers to accept as true. Even a superficial examination of this major premise shows how deduction begins with a conclusion reached inductively. In other words, based on a large sampling of history, we know that millions of men have died; from this extensive sampling comes the major premise—all men are mortal. Look at Figure 3. The *minor premise* is a particular situation to which the major premise is to be applied, the point you hope to prove. Notice that both premises are declarative statements asserting something about the subject. Depending on the nature of the subject, they could also deny something about it. The stated premises contain no qualifiers such as "sometimes," "maybe," or "usually." Such qualifiers would

Figure 3

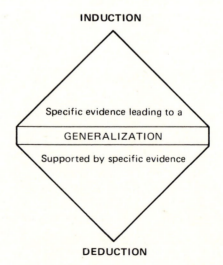

INDUCTION

Specific evidence leading to a

GENERALIZATION

Supported by specific evidence

DEDUCTION

weaken the argument by suggesting uncertainty. The *conclusion* is based on the evidence presented in the major and minor premise. In other words, major premise + minor premise = conclusion. Before a syllogism can be assumed true, it must pass three basic tests:

1. Is the major premise true; that is, has it been arrived at inductively, based on an adequate sampling of evidence? Or is it arguable, based on an assumption lacking validity?
2. Is the minor premise true and is it a specific application of the major premise? Does it ignore significant facts or data about the subject?
3. Is the conclusion valid; that is, is it actually based on the major and minor premise? Is it correct?

To restrict a discussion of deductive argument to the parts of a syllogism is an oversimplification, however, because a deductively organized argumentative essay may range from a few hundred to several thousand words. While the parts of a syllogism may actually be present in a deductive argument, what is added is the evidence supporting the premises. In other words, a syllogism is like an outline. Figure 4 indicates one way that a syllogism can be expanded into a multiparagraph argument. As you can see, the shape of a deductive argument is the opposite of an inductive

Figure 4

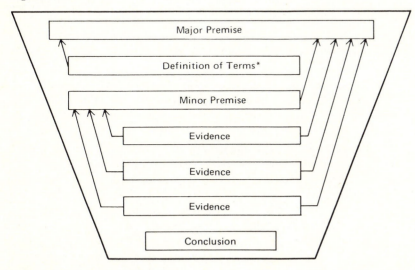

*Definition of terms is optional and may also be done with terms in the minor premise. The primary purpose is to limit the scope of the argument.

argument. The arrows indicate the systematic way deduction works. If the major premise is accurate, the supporting evidence forces acceptance of the minor premise, and both in turn reinforce the major premise and ultimately force acceptance of the conclusion.

Read the following essay and see how the syllogism can be expanded into a deductive argument:

The provost of one of our largest and most honored institutions told me not long ago that a questionnaire was distributed to his undergraduates and that 40 percent refused to acknowledge that they believed cheating on examinations to be reprehensible.

Recently a reporter for a New York newspaper stopped six people on the street and asked them if they would consent to take part in a rigged television quiz for money. He reported that five of the six said yes. Yet most of these five, like most of the college cheaters, would probably profess a strong social consciousness. They may cheat, but they vote for foreign aid and for enlightened social measures.

These two examples exhibit a paradox of our age. It is often said, and my observation leads me to believe it true, that our seemingly great growth in social morality has oddly enough taken place in a world where private morality—a sense of the supreme importance of purely personal honor, honesty, and integrity—seems to be declining. Beneficent and benevolent social institutions are administered by men who all too frequently turn out to be accepting "gifts." The world of popular entertainment is rocked by scandals. College students, put on their honor, cheat on examinations. Candidates for the Ph.D. hire ghost writers to prepare their theses.

But, one may object, haven't all these things always been true? Is there really any evidence that personal dishonesty is more prevalent than it always was?

I have no way of making a historical measurement. Perhaps these things are not actually more prevalent. What I do know is that there is an increasing tendency to accept and take for granted such personal dishonesty. The bureaucrat and disk jockey say, "Well, yes, I took presents, but I assure you that I made just decisions anyway." The college student caught cheating does not even blush. He shrugs his shoulders and comments: "Everybody does it, and besides, I can't see that it really hurts anybody."

Jonathan Swift once said: "I have never been surprised to find men wicked, but I have often been surprised to find them not ashamed." It is my conviction that though men may be no more wicked than they always have been, they seem less likely to be ashamed. If anybody does it, it must be right. Honest, moral, decent mean only what is usual. This is not really a wicked world, because morality means mores or manners and usual conduct is the only standard.

The second part of the defense, "it really doesn't hurt anybody," is equally revealing. "It doesn't hurt anybody" means it doesn't do that abstraction called society any harm. The harm it did the bribe-taker and the cheater isn't important; it is purely personal. And personal as opposed to social decency doesn't count for much. Sometimes I am inclined to blame sociology for part of this paradox. Sociology has tended to lay exclusive stress upon social morality, and tended too often to define good and evil as merely the "socially useful" or its reverse.

What social morality and social conscience leave out is the narrower but very significant concept of honor—as opposed to what is sometimes called merely "socially desirable conduct." The man of honor is not content to ask merely whether this or that will hurt society, or whether it is what most people would permit themselves to do. He asks, and he asks first of all, would it hurt him and his self-respect? Would it dishonor him personally?

It was a favorite and no doubt sound argument among early twentieth-century reformers that "playing the game" as the gentleman was supposed to play it was not enough to make a decent society. They were right: it is not enough. But the time has come to add that it is indeed inevitable that the so-called social conscience unsupported by the concept of personal honor will create a corrupt society. But suppose that it doesn't? Suppose that no one except the individual suffers from the fact that he sees nothing wrong in doing what everybody else does? Even so, I still insist that for the individual himself nothing is more important than this personal, interior sense of right and wrong and his determination to follow that rather than to be guided by what everybody does or merely the criterion of "social usefulness." It is impossible for me to imagine a good society composed of men without honor.

We hear it said frequently that what present-day men most desire is security. If that is so, then they have a wrong notion of what the real, the ultimate, security is. No one who is dependent on anything outside himself, upon money, power, fame, or whatnot, is or ever can be secure. Only he who possesses himself and is content with himself is actually secure. Too much is being said about the importance of adjustment and "participation in the group." Even cooperation, to give this thing its most favorable designation, is no more important than the ability to stand alone when the choice must be made between the sacrifice of one's own integrity and adjustment to or participation in group activity.

No matter how bad the world may become, no matter how much the mass man of the future may lose such of the virtues as he still has, one fact remains. If one person alone refuses to go along with him, if one person alone asserts his individual and inner right to believe in and be loyal to what his fellow men seem to have given up, then at least he will still retain what is perhaps the most important part of humanity.

JOSEPH WOOD KRUTCH

"The New Immorality"

Krutch's argument could be summarized in the following syllogism:

major premise: A good society has men of honor.
minor premise: Our society has too many men without honor.
conclusion: Therefore, to have a good society, each individual must be honorable.

In other words, Krutch begins with a major premise, a statement that is generally accepted as true. The minor premise, on the other hand, asserts a much more specific, arguable point, which is then supported in the body of the paper. The conclusion, then, is more limited yet, so limited that it applies to an individual application of honor.

The author of the following essay, also a deductive argument, employs a different organization pattern:

One way to go quietly insane is to think hard about the concept of eternity. Another way, for anyone living in a megalopolis * like New York, is to think hard about "progress." The eerie sensation comes over one that true progress reached the end of its cable some years ago and is now recoiling upon us, an unstoppable juggernaut ° smashing masses of human beings back toward medieval conditions of life.

The streets are littered with cigarette and cigar butts, paper wrappings, particles of food, and dog droppings. How long before they become indistinguishable from the gutters of medieval towns when slop pails were emptied from the second-story windows?

Thousands of New York women no longer attend evening services in their churches. They fear assault as they walk the few steps from bus or subway station to their apartment houses. The era of the medieval footpad † has returned, and, as in the Dark Ages, the cry for help brings no assistance, for even grown men know they would be cut down before the police could arrive.

A thousand years ago in Europe, acres of houses and shops were demolished and their inhabitants forced elsewhere so that great cathedrals could be built. For decades the building process soaked up all available skilled labor; for decades the townspeople stepped around pits in the streets, clambered over ropes and piles of timber, breathed mortar dust, and slept and woke to the crashing noise of construction.

The cathedrals, when finished, stood half-empty six days a week, but most of them had beauty.

Today, the ugly office skyscrapers go up, shops and graceful homes

---

* megalopolis: a large, crowded city.
° juggernaut: a massive force which crushes everything in its path.
† footpad: highwayman.

are obliterated, their inhabitants forced away, and year after year New Yorkers step around the pits, stumble through the wooden catwalks, breathe the fine mist of dust, absorb the hammering noise night and day, and telephone in vain for carpenter or plumber.

And the skyscrapers stand empty two days and seven nights a week. This is progress.

At the rush hour, men outrun old women for the available cab; the strong bodily crush back the weak for a place to stand in suffocating bus or subway car, no less destructive of human dignity than a cattle wagon in the time of Peter the Great. When the buses and subway cars began, they represented progress. Great parking garages are built, immediately filled with cars; the traffic remains as before, and that is progress. The renowned New York constructionist, Robert Moses, builds hundreds of miles of access highways, and they are at once crammed bumper to bumper with automobiles as long as locomotives, carrying an average of about two human beings apiece.

Parkinson's general law applies here too, for vehicles will always increase in direct proportion to the increase in spaces to hold them. So skyscrapers and boxlike apartment houses will increase as the money to build them increases. So footpads will increase as the number of possible victims increases.

But it's progress.

The secret, terrible fact is that progress, in all measurable terms of human effort, grace, and self-respect, ended some years ago in the great ant-hill cities. The juggernaut of time and effort has turned around and is now destroying the recent progressive past.

ERIC SEVAREID

"Dirt, Grime, and Cruel Crowding"

Clearly argumentative in his intent, Sevareid makes extensive use of comparison/contrast and examples to support his argument. He also uses the opening paragraph to state his thesis, which could be summarized in the following syllogism:

> major premise: True progress ended years ago.
> minor premise: Today is the same as years ago.
> conclusion: Today there is no progress.

In the body of the argument he compares/contrasts present and past and provides specific examples from each. In the final paragraph, he restates his conclusion.

In summary, writing a good argumentative essay is challenging, but you can do it if you make sure to compare your paper to the following check list:

Chect List for Argument

- Have you assumed that your readers will be opposed to your viewpoint, intelligent, and knowledgeable about the subject?
- Is the beginning of the paper functional, that is, does it contain such things as a brief summary of the background of the subject and a statement of the problem? Does the beginning introduce?
- Is the evidence in the body of the paper convincing in terms of being an adequate sampling? Are they typical samples? Do the samples clearly relate to your argument? Have you used analogy properly, that is, not for proof, but for illustration? If you cite authorities, have you made sure the information is reliable? Have you countered the opposition's arguments?
- If the argument is inductive, have you prepared the reader for the inductive leap? If the argument is deductive, have you presented an acceptable major premise? An arguable minor premise?
- Is the conclusion consistent with other findings on the subject? Is it clearly based on the evidence included in the body of the argument?

Self-Evaluation

PART I

1. Write definitions for the following.

   a. inductive argument

   _____

   _____

   b. deductive argument

   _____

   _____

2. Distinguish between the following terms by writing brief definitions of each.

   a. exposition

   _____

   b. argument

   _____

PART II

1. List three forms of support or testimony for an argument.

   a. _____

   b. _____

   c. _____

2. List any five tests you should apply to check the validity of an argument.

   a. _____

   b. _____

   c. _____

   d. _____

   e. _____

PART III

Indicate whether the following syllogisms are valid or invalid.

_____ 1. All home owners pay taxes. I am a home owner. I pay taxes.

_____ 2. All home owners pay taxes. I pay taxes. I am a home owner.

_____ 3. No cats are allowed in the shop. Minx is a cat. Therefore Minx is not allowed in the shop.

_____ 4. No cats are allowed in the shop. Minx is not a cat. Therefore Minx is allowed in the shop.

_____ 5. Freshmen are not allowed to enroll in Creative Writing. I am a freshman. Therefore I am not permitted to enroll in Creative Writing.

Answers

PART I

1. a. An inductive argument begins with specific details from which a general conclusion is reached.
   b. A deductive argument begins with a generalization that is supported by specific details.
2. a. Exposition informs or explains.
   b. Argument attempts to persuade.

PART II

1. a. precedent
   b. statistics
   c. authority
2. (Any five)
   a. abundant sampling of evidence
   b. typical evidence
   c. consistent focus
   d. evidence related to conclusion
   e. arguments by opposition countered
   f. conclusion consistent with related findings.

PART III

1. valid
2. invalid
3. valid
4. invalid
5. valid.

WRITING ASSIGNMENT

INDUCTION

Write an inductive argument, selecting your topic from the following list:

1. some facet of education
2. the need for self-esteem
3. a current issue on campus or in the community
4. a point of view about which you feel strongly
5. topic of your choice

DEDUCTION

Write a deductive argument, selecting your topic from the following list:

1. "the new immorality" (or morality) as you see it
2. an act by you or a group that results in aggression
3. your freedom to _____
4. the value of _____
5. topic of your choice

(Consult the check list for argument before you complete either assignment.)

·⊰[14]⊱·
Clear Thinking

Clear thinking is important in any form of communication, but especially in writing since you generally have little opportunity to add, "What I really meant was . . ." A writer who can think clearly and logically will have an advantage over an individual whose thinking is fuzzy and illogical.

Nothing destroys the credibility of a piece of writing as quickly and as thoroughly as an obvious error in reasoning. It is like the proverbial one bad apple spoiling the bushel; one glaring fallacy in reasoning will spoil otherwise valid reasoning in that the reader will probably pay little attention to your remaining arguments.

Consequently, a study of clear thinking is necessary in a composition course. What follows is obviously not intended to be a complete course in logic, but an introduction to some of the principles of clear thinking and some of the fallacies that can creep into compositions. It should provide an awareness that will enable you to avoid errors in logic in your own writing and to rebut others' fallacious reasoning.

Objectives

After completing this chapter, you should be able

1. to define logic
2. to distinguish between fact and opinion
3. to distinguish between sound and unsound reasoning
4. to define and identify examples of common errors in reasoning—both emotional and logical fallacies

——— ⧉ ———

Logic is a method of using evidence effectively, the system of arriving at true and/or valid conclusions from evidence. To be logical is to argue reasonably. Through logic we can determine consequences, providing we accept given premises as true. In short, logic is the process of drawing a conclusion from one or more statements or propositions (which we generally call premises).

Logic and truth, however, do not necessarily go hand in hand. It is possible to be completely logical but wrong. This occurs when you reason, or apply logic, to an incorrect premise. For example, examine the following exercise in logic:

> All college instructors are unfair.
> Jones is a college instructor.
> Therefore, Jones is unfair.

The logic is *valid* in that the conclusion reached follows from the given premises. It is not *true,* however, since the premise "All college instructors are unfair" is not true.

Reasoning is the process by which your mind moves from evidence to a conclusion. There are two types of reasoning: deductive and inductive.

Deductive reasoning moves from the general to the specific. When you use deduction, you apply a general statement or *premise* to a particular case. For example, if you say, "All freshmen at State College are required to take two semesters of history, and Linda is a freshman at State, therefore, Linda is taking history," you have made a deduction; that is, you have reasoned from the general "All freshmen at State College are required to take two semesters of history" to the specific "Linda is taking history." Remember that deduction moves from the general to the specific: a general statement or premise is applied to a particular case.

Inductive reasoning moves from the particular to the general or from the individual to the universal. For example, if you say, "I have owned five Ford automobiles, and they have all been good cars. Fords are good automobiles," you have made an induction; that is, you have reasoned from the particular five cars you have owned to the general conclusion that Ford automobiles are good. Thus, in induction you reach a general conclusion from an examination of particular or specific cases.

Whether you apply inductive or deductive logic to your writing, the key word is "logic"; you should make every effort to appeal to your readers' sense of reason. However, people are not only reasonable but also emotional beings. If your writing touches the emotions of the readers, then your chances of making your point convincingly are enhanced. However, do not intentionally play on the emotions of readers with rhetorical gimmicks; such ploys will be detected by perceptive readers who may become mistrustful and in all probability reject your whole argument. Furthermore, your recognition of emotional appeals will prepare you to attack other debaters' use of them, a use that often appears in propaganda.

Emotional appeals are often more effective in speech than in writing because speakers can give added emphasis through hand gestures, body movements, facial expressions, and voice inflections, all of which can divert the listeners' attention from what is being said to how it is being said. In writing, however, there are no gestures, movements, expressions, and inflections, but only words. Consequently, it is more difficult in writing to effectively divert the readers' attention from *what* is being said to *how* ideas are being expressed. The following are examples of *emotional appeals*, flaws in logic to be avoided:

- *selective sampling or card stacking*—presenting half-truths or suppressing relevant information in an effort to create a certain effect

  EXAMPLE: The marquee advertising a movie may lift such words as "exciting," "stimulating," and "intriguing" from a review that actually read, "While the movie is exciting at moments, it will be stimulating to only a small portion of the audience because the simplistic plot is not intriguing to a viewer familiar with earlier works of the director."

- *argumentum ad hominem, name calling, or character assassination*—deliberate attempt to discredit the character of the opposition rather than the opposition's issue

  EXAMPLES: 1. In a letter to the editor of the college newspaper, one of the candidates for student body president might write of his opponent, "Jack White is an affable fellow, but he would not make a good student body president. His sister admitted to smoking marijuana."
  2. "How can John be a decent CPA? He was dishonorably discharged from the Army."

- *plain folks*—appealing to others because of alleged common qualities or prejudices

  EXAMPLES: 1. A political candidate from New York may go to a small town in Kansas and ask people to vote for him because he's just "a little old country boy."
  2. "Like any God-fearing citizen, I maintain that America is still the greatest country in the world."
  3. "As all sophisticated people know, athletes are not very bright."

- *routing devils*—conjuring up negative connotations

  EXAMPLE: "I have never read such an idiotic statement in my life."

- *popular appeal* (*bandwagon*)—appealing to people's needs or desires to conform

  EXAMPLE: "Everyone wants a color TV; don't be the only one without it!"

- *"You're another"*—rotating a charge and leveling it at the accuser

  EXAMPLE: "You imply that I am less than honest, but I can prove that you are an outright liar."

These examples of emotional appeal have two common characteristics: they all attempt to discredit the views of the opponents; they all focus on personalities, not issues.

Given the three assumptions you should make about your readers—that they are opposed to your point of view, that they are intelligent, and that they are knowledgeable about the subject—you can see how such obvious appeals to emotion can discredit your argument and insult your readers.

All fallacies are not, however, of an emotional nature. Some are *fallacies in logic,* and can damage the argument you are making. The following are some common logical fallacies you should avoid:

1. *Confusion of fact and opinion:* One of the most common logical errors in student papers is the confusion of fact and opinion. Consequently, an extended examination of the difference between a fact and opinion is in order.

A *fact* is a statement that can be verified and is not open to debate. To illustrate, you might say, "Raquel Welch has appeared in more than five movies." This is a fact; it can be easily verified that Miss Welch has indeed appeared in more than five movies. A fact is something that is true, a statement of reality.

In contrast, an opinion is a subjective judgment incapable of being verified. If you say, "Raquel Welch is the most beautiful woman in the world," you are making a declaration of taste—not a statement of reality, but a statement of your interpretation of reality. It simply cannot be verified (objectively witnessed) that Miss Welch is the "most beautiful woman in the world."

Many times you may be unsure whether a statement is fact or opinion, but perhaps a few examples will help develop the ability to ascertain the difference:

FACT: John is five feet ten inches in height.

OPINION: John is tall.

The first sentence is fact because it can be verified with a ruler: either John is five feet ten inches in height or he is not. If there is disagreement about the validity of the statement, the conflict can be resolved. The second sentence is opinion since, if there is disagreement, the conflict cannot be resolved; it cannot be verified because "tall" is a relative term dependent on subjective judgment. For example, five feet ten inches might be tall to someone only five feet tall but not to someone who is six feet five inches tall. In other words, there is such a thing in reality as five feet plus ten inches. There is no such thing in reality as "tall." "Tall" is a conclusion one makes about what one sees—five feet and ten inches, for example.

FACT: A pack of King Edward cigars costs thirty-five cents.

OPINION: A pack of King Edward cigars is cheap.

"Cheap" is a conclusion or opinion about the economic significance of thirty-five cents.

FACT: The letter was typed without errors.

OPINION: The letter was neat.

FACT: *The Use and Misuse of Language* is used in graduate English courses at 359 universities.

OPINION: *The Use and Misuse of Language* is highly significant in the study of semantics.

FACT: The University of Kansas is located in Lawrence.

OPINION: The University of Kansas is an ugly campus.

FACT: The Model T was manufactured by the Ford Motor Company.

OPINION: The Model T was the most dependable automobile ever made.

Identify the following sentences as either fact or opinion.   PRACTICE

_____ 1. *In Memoriam* is an elegy written by Alfred, Lord Tennyson.
_____ 2. The capital of Missouri is one of the most beautiful capitals in the country.
_____ 3. Mickey Mantle was the greatest center fielder ever to play for the New York Yankees.
_____ 4. There is a ditch on each side of 111th Street.

_____ 5. He was angry.

_____ 6. *In Memoriam* is the greatest elegy.

_____ 7. Mickey Mantle hit fifty-eight home runs the same year Roger Maris hit sixty-one.

_____ 8. The book has 568 pages.

_____ 9. Baseball is the hardest sport for anyone to master.

_____ 10. Their television is an RCA Victor.

PRACTICE ANSWERS

1. fact
2. opinion
3. opinion
4. fact
5. opinion
6. opinion
7. fact
8. fact
9. opinion
10. fact

Since a fact is not open to debate, it obviously is good support for the validity of a conclusion. Remember, a given fact is not subject for debate, but whether a given statement is a fact may be questioned.

2. *Hasty generalization:* Hasty generalization results when you arrive at conclusions (inductions) after examining insufficient data. A common term for this is "jumping to conclusions":

EXAMPLES: 1. Every time I look up while driving to school, I see a new split-level house.
2. You cannot believe anyone over thirty.
3. Both Jim and Tom, who graduated from the same high school, failed their freshman English course in college; instruction in English at their high school was inferior.

Sometimes hasty generalization contains the prediction of large, usually catastrophic, conclusions from small scraps of evidence:

EXAMPLES: 1. If you do not get a degree, you will be a failure in life.
2. If automation comes, there will be fifty million unemployed.

3. If you even look at another man, then you do not love me.

3. *Confusion of cause and effect:* Confusion of cause and effect is another of the more common errors in logic found in student papers. Another name for this is *post hoc ergo propter hoc,* "after this, therefore because of this." Just because one event happens before another in time, it may be fallacious to assume that the first caused the second:

EXAMPLES: 1. A child notices that his dog barks. He then notices that the sun comes up. He concludes that his dog's barking makes the sun come up.
2. Milk is left out. Thunder is heard. The milk is found to be soured. The conclusion is reached that thunder causes the milk to sour.
3. It was noticed that people who went out at night often contracted malaria. The conclusion was reached that night air caused malaria.

4. *False analogies:* An analogy is an assertion that things resembling each other in some respects will resemble each other in some further respect. Remember, analogies do not *prove;* they only illustrate.

EXAMPLES: 1. You should not depend on the public library for access to a set of encyclopedias. You would not depend on city hall for access to a restroom.
2. Engineers do not need to know anything about literature. I intend to be an engineer. Making me take a literature course makes as much sense as teaching a polar bear how to catch an alligator.

5. *Misuse of authority:* To avoid the misuse of authority, clearly identify your authority; do not simply refer to "a leading expert" or say "experts agree." Be sure the authority is current. For example, you will not be too convincing quoting George Washington on military theory. Quote authorities only if they are expressing an opinion within their professional field of competence. You can quote a professional football player on football, but not on pantyhose.

EXAMPLES: 1. Medical experts agree that Brand X alleviates headaches more effectively than common aspirin.
2. You should try camphor shavings in kerosene for your gout because in 1879 a doctor in St. Louis said that it was an effective cure.

Two very common misuses of authority experienced by student writers are the following:

- A public figure is confused with an authority. For example, a sports figure endorses a certain dog food, or an actor sets himself up as a critic of education. Is the sports figure necessarily more knowledgeable about dog food than anyone else? What authority about education has the actor?
- Authority is attributed to a person or institution that is not intended to be authoritative. For example, Webster's dictionary states that love is "the attraction based on sexual desire," so the word is held to have no other meanings. (Dictionaries are simply describers, not prescribers of word usage.)

6. *Misuse of statistics:* Misuse of statistics occurs if irrelevant, vague, unrepresentative, biased, or inadequate data are used. Also, be especially careful in using words such as "normal" and "average," since they can be misleading.* If you compare two groups, be sure that they are similar. Can you conclude anything by comparing the attitudes of twentieth-century college students to those of nineteenth-century students without allowing for general social change?

EXAMPLES:
1. Irrelevant and inadequate data:
   a. The number of farmers has been decreasing. Americans must be eating less food.
   b. The cost of automobiles has tripled in the last ten years. Therefore, people live one-third as well as they did ten years ago.
2. Vague data:
   Ninety percent of those polled agreed to levy taxes to support a new library.
3. Biased data:
   The College of Cardinals voted not to support the practice of birth control. Therefore, birth control should not be practiced.
4. Unrepresentative data:
   Susie and Mary, both scholarship students, plan to marry rather than pursue careers. Obviously, the women's movement has therefore not changed the views of young women.
5. Misuse of "average" and "normal":
   a. The average income of Plainview families is $12,000. Obviously, the community is well-off.

---

* The word "average" can indicate (1) the arithmetical mean, (2) the simple mean, (3) the median, or (4) the mode. The word "normal" almost always has subjective connotations.

(Some families may be extremely wealthy while the majority live on welfare.)

    b. The normal American life style is to marry and raise children. Anyone who remains single is abnormal and weird. (Single people do not conform to the *norm*, but they are not therefore necessarily weird.)

7. *Self-evident truths:* These are propositions that the writer tries to pass off as so obvious that they need no proof. They are usually introduced with the following signals:

everybody knows	unquestionably
it is only too clear	it goes without saying
all intelligent people agree	

> EXAMPLES: 1. Everybody knows that college education is necessary.
> 2. It is only too clear that credit cards contribute to bankruptcy.

8. *Either-or reasoning:* The fallacy of either-or reasoning is produced by incorrectly asserting that there are only two sides to an issue.

> EXAMPLES: 1. You're either for us or against us.
> 2. We should have this medical plan for the poor or no plan at all.

9. *Black or white:* Differences in degree or severity do not count.

> EXAMPLE: Smoking a little is as dangerous as smoking a lot.

10. *Arguing in circles:* What looks like proof or a valid conclusion is really repetition of the premise.

> EXAMPLE: People who say "he don't" and "I seen" are illiterate. Literate speech is sophisticated and logical. By sophisticated and logical, I mean the avoidance of constructions like "he don't" and "I seen."

11. *Begging the question:* Begging the question occurs when one assumes to be true a premise that really needs proof or when the premise is loaded with biased language.

> EXAMPLES: 1. The unsanitary conditions in the cafeteria are detrimental to health. (You are begging the question: Are the conditions in the cafeteria unsanitary?)
> 2. The useless convention of rising when a woman enters a room should be abolished. (You are

begging the question: Is the convention of rising
when a woman enters the room useless?)

12. *Non sequitur:* The term "non sequitur" means "it does not
follow." (Consequently, any fallacy is a non sequitur.) The conclusion is not based on the stated premises.

EXAMPLES: 1. Maury Hooper doesn't drink or smoke, and so he
ought to make a good husband.
2. Harry Williams would make a good mayor because he belongs to our family's church.
3. We should know the rules of grammar because
we have inherited them from the past.

Self-Evaluation

PART I

Indicate whether each of the following is a deductive or inductive argument and whether it is
sound or unsound.

EXAMPLE: All men are mortal. Warren is a man. Therefore Warren is mortal.
Answer: deductive (sound)

_____ 1. To be a Boy Scout, a boy must be at least eleven years
old. Since Joe is a Boy Scout, he must be at least eleven
years old.
_____ 2. I am through watching television because both of the
shows I watched Sunday evening were terrible.
_____ 3. Citizens of the United States may enter Canada without a
passport. Since I am a United States citizen, I will not
need a passport when I go to Canada.
_____ 4. Those who get good grades study diligently. All students
are anxious to get good grades. All students study
diligently.
_____ 5. When the Salk vaccine against polio was given to 440,000
schoolchildren, it was reported to be 60 to 90 percent effective in preventing paralytic polio. The vaccine is an effective means of preventing polio.
_____ 6. Only members of the football team were allowed to attend last night's meeting. Since Hector attended the
meeting, he must be a member.
_____ 7. Men who like peanut butter make good husbands. Mr.
James likes peanut butter. He will make a good husband.

_____ 8. Out of three hundred students, two hundred fifty failed the last history examination. The test was not valid.

_____ 9. Students must have had Composition I before they can take Introduction to Literature. I have not had Composition I. Therefore I cannot enroll in Introduction to Literature.

_____ 10. The last three memos from the Dean's office were confusing. All administrators ought to take an English course.

PART II

Identify the following fallacies.

EXAMPLE: Do you still do a careless job with your homework?
Answer: begging the question

_____ 1. I do not like classical music because I like jazz.

_____ 2. Everybody knows that Republicans have a high degree of integrity.

_____ 3. You should not read the poetry of Byron because his private life was immoral.

_____ 4. All intelligent people agree that liking poetry is a sign of sophistication.

_____ 5. Teddy Roosevelt would have supported a responsible fiscal policy that ended deficit spending.

_____ 6. Mosca Hooper owns a new sports car. Why can't I have one, too?

_____ 7. Men are no good.

_____ 8. I may not be able to spell, but you can't work linear equations.

_____ 9. Edward's thoughts on prison reform deserve no consideration since he once was in prison.

_____ 10. Coach John Madden wears his "lucky" shirt to every game.

_____ 11. Man is the only creature capable of reason. Since Mary is not a man, she is incapable of reason.

_____ 12. When I visited the DeSimones, Mrs. DeSimone served lasagna. I know now that I do not like Italian dishes.

_____ 13. If you do not learn to type, you will not succeed in college.

_____ 14. If I use Brand X toothpaste, I will have an exciting love life.

—————————————— 15. I had acne and rubbed mud on it. A week later the acne was gone. Mud is a good cure for acne.

PART III

Define logic.

————————————————————————————————————

————————————————————————————————————

————————————————————————————————————

Answers

PART I

1. deductive (sound)
2. inductive (unsound)
3. deductive (sound)
4. deductive (unsound)
5. inductive (sound)
6. deductive (sound)
7. deductive (unsound)
8. inductive (sound)
9. deductive (sound)
10. inductive (unsound)

PART II

1. either-or reasoning
2. self-evident truth
3. non sequitur
4. bandwagon
5. misuse of authority
6. false analogy
7. hasty generalization
8. "You're another"
9. character assassination
10. confusion of cause and effect
11. faulty syllogism
12. hasty generalization
13. hasty generalization
14. hasty generalization
15. confusion of cause and effect

PART III

Logic is the method of using evidence effectively, the system of arriving at true and/or valid conclusions from evidence.

Write a well-developed paragraph on one of the following topics or on a topic supplied by your instructor.

WRITING ASSIGNMENT

1. how to lie with statistics
2. Read an editorial from your local newspaper. Analyze it for logical fallacies and write a logical critique of the piece.
3. a hasty generalization that you once made and later rejected.
4. a conclusion you reached by post hoc reasoning and later changed

Index

Instructor's Manual
Writing by Design

Klarner   Williams   Harp

Instructor's Manual

WRITING BY DESIGN

Walter E. Klarner
Johnson County Community College

James M. Williams
Johnson County Community College

Harold L. Harp
Johnson County Community College

HOUGHTON MIFFLIN COMPANY   BOSTON

Atlanta   Dallas   Geneva, Illinois
Hopewell, New Jersey   Palo Alto   London

Printed in the United States of America

ISBN: 0-395-24429-3

INTRODUCTION

Unlike most texts, <u>Writing by Design</u> does not pose questions that require answers in an instructor's manual. Indeed, the main function of <u>Writing by Design</u> is to free the instructor of some of the more mechanical demands of teaching. The text itself provides practices with answers, discussions of skills, professional and student writing samples, chapter self-evaluations, writing suggestions, and chapter rationales and objectives.

No text can teach by itself. Though self-instructional in format, <u>Writing by Design</u> cannot replace a good teacher. You undoubtedly know well how students react to the enthusiasm, support, and guidance of their teachers. The "teaching personality" is the catalyst in a most complex process. And you have certainly experienced busy, even hectic, days when the demands of preparation conflicted with your desire to work closely with students. This manual, then, offers approaches we have found useful in teaching <u>Writing by Design</u>, and suggests strategies intended to make your use of <u>Writing by Design</u> pleasant, efficient, and effective.

GENERATIVE AND TRADITIONAL RHETORIC

The utility of teaching descriptive, narrative, and expository writing need not be argued here. The traditional modes of development and such terms as "topic sentence," "support," "organization," and "unity" are also familiar enough. Even the self-instructional format of the text conforms to a widely accepted prescription. What, then, makes <u>Writing by Design</u> unusual and effective?

<u>Writing by Design</u> is a synthesis of traditional and generative rhetoric. Exposed to generative rhetoric, students quickly grasp traditional concepts that have eluded them for years. The first section of the text, "Sentence Design," introduces the concepts of quality, detail, and comparison and the scheme of levels of generality. Expect your students to create more interesting images and more concrete details. They will be able to discern <u>for themselves</u> improvements in the flow and readability of their sentences. They will begin to take pride in something they have never understood--style. The students will suddenly find themselves searching for more and better words with which to express themselves. While the early chapters do not emphasize bound modifiers, students tend to improve in this sphere of image making indirectly, often as a spin-off of their practice with free modifiers. There are, of course, many aspects of sentence style the text does not address directly. What has continued to amaze us is how much we have been able to eliminate. Mastery of parallelism and emphasis, for example, is a <u>natural</u> by-product

of the method. Let us emphasize that the generative sentence is a minority sentence--used with regularity, but not to be overdone.

The sections on "Paragraph Design" and "Essay Design" pursue the generative idea within the framework of traditional rhetoric. The types of writing and modes of exposition they deal with are familiar to you and your students. Wherever possible, traditional rhetorical ideas are explained in generative terms. This double thrust is neither a redundancy nor an attempt to force students to think only in terms of notations. In fact, the ultimate goal of this text is for students to use the method without being aware of doing so.

Students not only learn a new method of generating ideas, but also acquire a new vocabulary of functional terms. After a few weeks, students find that the criticism of their papers lets them know precisely what is right and wrong, and also that they usually sense the appropriate revision. For example, "awkward sentence" is one of the most common notations on student papers. Generative rhetoric should drastically reduce the incidence of this problem, and those awkward or choppy sentences that do crop up might receive a notation like, "Combine these sentences, forming a coordinate sequence of absolutes." In other words, paper grading can become prescriptive, and revision a productive activity.

THE TEXT AND THE METHOD

Writing by Design allows for a variety of instructional methods. Many schools offer a single mode of instruction; more and more are offering students a choice of learning styles. The most common methods of instruction are the following:

Lecture-Discussion. This is still the most common approach in colleges and universities. Most instructor-student contact occurs in the classroom, and all paper grading takes place in the absence of the student.

Discussion-Tutorial. This is the fastest-growing approach, especially in courses teaching such skills as mathematics and writing. Students have liberal opportunities for interaction with other students, but work closely with the instructor during tutorials. Most paper grading takes place in the presence of the student.

Tutorial-Individualized. This method is self-paced, involving close work with the instructor and often the "learning for mastery" system. Common in remedial programs and upper-level courses, it provides for little interaction with other students.

Writing by Design accords well with lecture-discussion because it allows the class to focus on ideas, issues, and applications of the techniques described in the text. If you employ a reader, you will be free to devote much of your class time to students' reactions to the articles and stories. Since most thematic readers include alternate tables of contents, you can synchronize the reader with the rhetoric in either of

two ways: the reader can provide additional examples of types of writing contained in Writing by Design, or Writing by Design can provide the
format for treating topics suggested by the reader. The class and group
activities described in this manual are particularly appropriate to
lecture-discussion classes. If Writing by Design is the only text used
in the course, be sure to allow time in your schedule for prewriting
discussions of topics and postwriting sharing of manuscripts.

For each section of freshman composition, the lecture-discussion
teacher usually conducts three hours of class and one or two office hours
per week. The discussion-tutorial method reverses the proportion, providing for one or two class hours and three or four hours of tutorials.
The significant difference, then, is not the total amount of contact
but the way this time is used. Discussion-tutorial teachers are free to
grade most, if not all, papers in conference. At the end of the day,
they do not face a stack of ungraded papers; they have had personal contact with twenty or more students, discussing individual writing problems and/or grading papers still fresh in the minds of the students who
wrote them. Writing by Design allows you the luxury of this style. As
you can see, the self-instructional text need not be limited to learning
labs and correspondence courses.

REVISION AND REWRITING

Revision and rewriting are crucial aspects of the process of learning to write. But if they are to be effective, they must be carefully
managed to insure that students revise and rewrite before submitting
their papers. Too often students submit substandard efforts in the
hope--too often fulfilled--that the instructor will read the paper,
point out its flaws, and make suggestions guaranteed to produce a
superior paper.

When this happens, the student is prevented from learning much
about either life or the writing process. First of all, the pressure to
do the job right the first time--a pressure the student will face
repeatedly in the real world--is removed. Second, the student who acts
like a secretary, making corrections and using ideas suggested by the
instructor in the manner suggested by the instructor, learns little
about writing. Creativity in the writing process is stifled.

With the right guidance, however, the student can turn an average
paper containing a good, sound idea roughly and ineffectively expressed
into an excellent paper by pursuing suggested improvements in rhetorical
techniques. Thus he or she can realize the truth of the bromide that
good writing is the product of rewriting.

Care must be taken if revision is to encourage good writing. Without such care, it tends to promote poor writing. One useful guideline is
to permit revision and rewriting only of papers whose content shows
promise. Rewriting to correct mechanical errors only encourages careless proofreading. Many students are happy to sit back and let their
instructors be their proofreaders.

One technique for discouraging mechanical errors is to glance over a paper quickly at the beginning of a tutorial session; if there are any errors, simply hand the paper back to the student and ask him or her to find and correct the errors while in your office, using any resources you have available. In the meantime you can hold another tutorial session.

Many good students understand only vaguely what we mean by revision. It thus makes good sense to provide students a system for revision. Without such a system, students tend to read over their papers in a haphazard fashion, catching only the most glaring mechanical errors. The following standard system works well.

Checklist for Revision

1. <u>Purpose</u>. Did you fulfill the assigned purpose of the assignment?
    a. Description. Did you tell what something looked like?
    b. Narration. Did you tell what happened?
    c. Exposition. Did you state a conclusion and then explain how you arrived at it?
        (1) Example. Did you mention several cases that support your conclusion?
        (2) Illustration. Did you relate an incident that supports your conclusion?
        (3) Definition. Did you explain what something is by assigning it to a class and then showing how it differs from other members of the same class?
        (4) Comparison/Contrast. Did you explain something unfamiliar by comparing or contrasting it with something familiar?
        (5) Analogy. Did you explain an unfamiliar item or process by comparing or contrasting it with a familiar item or process of a different class?
        (6) Cause and Effect. Did you explain the causes of a particular effect or predict an effect of a particular cause?
        (7) Analysis. Did you explain something by breaking it down into its component parts?

2. <u>Subject</u>. Did you state a conclusion about your topic?
    a. Does it fit the assignment?
    b. Is its scope appropriate to the length of the paper?
    c. Does it interest you? Will it interest a reader?
    d. Does it have particular significance for you? Or is it one half the class is likely to have chosen?
    e. Does it reflect logical and imaginative thought?

3. <u>Organization</u>. Did you comply with standard conventions of organization?
    a. Does your introduction fulfill the two requirements of an introduction?
        (1) Does it attempt to create interest in your subject?
        (2) Does it clearly state the subject?

   b. Is each paragraph characterized by a clearly stated topic sen-
       tence; logical organization; adequate development (use of
       specific, concrete details; quality; comparisons; examples;
       illustrations, and the like); and smooth transitions, internally
       and to the next paragraph?
   c. Does each paragraph have an adequate conclusion, if appropriate?

4.   <u>Style</u>. Did you choose words and structure sentences as effectively
     as possible? Did you obey the conventions of English usage--
     spelling, punctuation, tense, point of view, and the like?

SAMPLE GRADING STANDARDS

The A paper demonstrates originality of thought in stating and
developing a central idea. Its ideas are clear, logical, and thought-
provoking; it contains <u>all</u> the following characteristics of good writing:
1.   concentration on a central purpose, demonstrated by adequate develop-
     ment and valid specific support
2.   careful construction and organization of sentences and paragraphs
3.   careful choice of effective words and phrases
4.   full understanding of the concepts and ideas central to the assigned
     reading and to other material or personal experiences
5.   mechanical correctness

The B paper has a clearly stated central purpose, logically and
adequately developed. Its ideas are clear because it contains <u>some</u> of
the preceding characteristics of good writing. It is comparatively free
of errors in the use of English. Although competent, the B paper <u>lacks
the originality of thought and style that characterizes the A paper</u>.

The average paper will receive a grade of C. It has a central idea,
and is organized clearly enough to convey its purpose to the reader. It
demonstrates adequate knowledge of the concepts in question and relates
them to readings and class discussions. It avoids serious errors in the
use of English. It may, in fact, need few correction marks, but it <u>lacks
the vigor of thought and expression that would entitle it to an above-
average rating</u>.

The grade of D indicates below-average achievement in the correct
and effective expression of ideas. Most D papers contain serious errors
in the use of English and fail either to present a central idea or to
develop and support it adequately. With more careful proofreading and
fuller development, many D papers might be worth at least a C.

The grade of F usually indicates failure to state or develop a main
idea. It may also indicate serious errors in grammar, spelling, punctuation, and/or sentence structure.

The following major errors are to be avoided:
1.   comma splice
2.   sentence fragments
3.   misspelling of three or more common words

4.   lack of verb-subject agreement
5.   lack of antecedent-pronoun agreement
6.   faulty use of tense or person
7.   misplaced or dangling modifiers
8.   three or more instances of lack of parallelism
9.   three or more instances of faulty punctuation
10. run-on sentences

TUTORIAL GRADING

Paper grading probably drives more teachers out of the profession
than any other activity. The daily or weekly prospect of grading fifty
to a hundred (or more) papers can dampen the enthusiasm of the most
dedicated teacher. And there is no guarantee that critical comments
painstakingly written in the margins will be understood by the students,
if they are read at all. The controversy over paper grading has attracted considerable attention over the last few years and continues to be
debated at teacher workshops and conferences. Some instructors assign
fewer papers than they once did; others formally grade only papers submitted during the last weeks of the course. Still another approach is
to allow each student to choose, from among all the papers he or she has
written during the semester, three or four for grading; thus only the
student's best efforts are used to determine the course grade. Many
other such schemes could be described.

We have found that students must write papers and receive criticism
on a regular basis throughout the course. Students need practice to
acquire the habit of writing. They also need professional critiques of
their writing, and we have found it best to evaluate a paper with the
student present.

If you've never graded a set of papers on a tutorial basis, you're
in for a demanding but rewarding experience. To dictate how to do so
would be presumptuous of us, and we have chosen instead to share with you
our experiences, suggestions, and conclusions about tutorial grading, a
system that complements the format of Writing by Design.

To grade a set of twenty-five papers tutorially takes some planning
and endurance; to grade three or four such sets takes a lot of planning
and endurance. We have found that such planning is best done early in
the semester, so that the course outline can specify the days of the week
devoted to tutorial conferences. Such preparation will help you, and
will also make your students aware that the grading sessions are not
supplementary, but integral parts of the course.

You may have few options in choosing a place to hold tutorials. We
have found that if office space is adequate, tutorial grading is most
effectively done there because of the easy accessibility of additional
handout materials and the privacy so necessary to tutorial grading. The
only drawback of grading in the office is that you greatly increase the
student traffic, which can be annoying to colleagues. The other alternative is to hold tutorial conferences in the scheduled classroom, the
major drawback of which is a loss of intimacy. You may also find that

students who are waiting tend to wander in, which destroys the one-to-one relationship essential to tutorial grading.

There are a number of scheduling options, the most practical of which are the following:

1.   Schedule "open time"--usually regular class and/or office hours--when you are available to grade students' papers. If you are teaching multiple sections of a composition course, you will find student traffic more manageable if you restrict tutorial conferences to the scheduled class time. For instance, students enrolled in an 8:00-8:50 Monday-Wednesday-Friday class would come to you for paper grading during those periods. Additional office hours could be made available to students from all sections.

2.   Assign students "time slots" for tutorial conferences. Your assignment sheet might resemble the following:

Time	M	W	F
8:00			
8:07			
8:14			
8:21			
8:28			
8:35			
8:42			
8:49			
8:56			

Obviously, this option involves organization; you and your students know exactly when conferences are to take place. It also forces you to make efficient use of your time; in order to maintain your schedule, you must keep track of time.

Keeping in mind that you will probably have about twenty-five students per class, you must consider in advance how much time you can spend evaluating each assignment. Our experience suggests that five to ten minutes is long enough to grade a 500-800 word paper. As you gain experience with tutorial grading, you will find that you can do a thorough job in this amount of time. A former colleague who had graded papers tutorially for many years could evaluate an assignment in about three minutes, a feat that amazed students and colleagues alike. We do not, however, recommend such compression; unless you have his talent for incisiveness, you are likely to do an incomplete job of evaluation, leaving yourself open to students' reproaches that you didn't spend enough time with them. Some instructors deal with the problem of time by reading the papers prior to conferences, but we consider this a duplication of effort and a restraint on the spontaneity of tutorial grading.

Remember that one of the major purposes of tutorial grading is to give students on-the-spot feedback about their papers. As many of us have learned the hard way, our written comments on papers look impressive, especially to us, but are too often ignored by students, especially if they are satisfied with their grades. How often have you written such comments as "your paper lacks specific detail" or marked spelling errors, comma splices, fragments, poor word choices, and all the other mechanical errors students seem bent on making? Although tutorial grading will not entirely eliminate the need for such written comments and corrections, they will be noticeably less necessary if replaced by your oral critique. Instead of writing that a paper lacks specific detail, you can show its author what you mean and suggest ways to make her or his writing more specific. Instead of marking fragments, you can point out where and why fragments occur and suggest ways to correct them. We could go on, but the point is made: don't fall into the trap of feeling that you have to color each paper red. You may find it helpful to have your students take notes on the strengths and weaknesses of their papers. A few carefully written summary comments to supplement your verbal suggestions will help make tutorial grading a worthwhile experience for you and your students.

Tutorial grading is not intended to be a monologue on the part of the instructor; instead, it should be a dialogue between the instructor and the student. You should be in control of the tutorial session, and in fact dominant most of the time, but not so dominant that you discourage students' questions and comments. Some students will naturally enter into dialogue by asking questions, and possibly even by challenging you. As long as their comments are relevant to the paper at hand, encourage them--but don't forget that you are, to some degree, bound to a time schedule. Those few students who demand more time should be encouraged to see you during your office hours. But you will probably have far more "silent" students who nod at everything you say but offer no comments or questions of their own. It is these students who, if not properly channeled, can render the tutorial approach ineffective. One way to elicit responses from them is to ask direct questions about your comments until you are sure they comprehend. Another approach is to have them offer solutions to problems you have noted. After you have finished evaluating their papers, you might have them summarize the strengths and weaknesses you have pointed out. And you might, on occasion, have them read their papers aloud to you. You will be surprised how often students discover problems of syntax, semantics, logic, and the like from reading their papers. You may even reverse the process and read their papers aloud yourself. Much more could be said about the tutorial dialogue, but the point is obvious: involve your students.

If you suffer from a case of butterflies as you await the arrival of a student for your first tutorial session, you are probably typical. After all, you are about to dispel the mystique of grading by allowing your students to observe you at work. But, however nervous you may be, most of your students will be even more so. They are about to have their papers graded before their eyes, an experience most will never have had. Just remember that you each have something to learn from the other. The key to making the first grading session a success is probably to conceal your own apprehensions and help your students relax. A good way to do so is to engage them in conversation about problems they encountered writing their papers, their general impressions of college, or themselves. A little casual conversation will go a long way toward establishing rapport.

Whether it is your first or your hundredth tutorial session, you will be faced with the inevitable problem of assigning a grade. As you will discover, assigning a well-deserved C- is a bit more difficult when the student is sitting there, perhaps telling you how hard she worked on the assignment or that he must get at least a B to stay in school. In other words, tutorial grading forces the issue of personal and professional integrity. Rather than inflating grades, we have found assigning a fair grade easy if we have done a thorough job of explaining why the paper deserves that grade. In the long run, students will respect you if you assign the grades they deserve; you will also respect yourself.

Having graded papers traditionally and tutorially, and having polled students on their preferences, we have concluded that tutorial grading is far superior to the take-them-home-and-grade-them system. Students benefit from receiving on-the-spot comments about their writing, rather than waiting for the results weeks later, and we are freed from having to grade three or four sets of papers in the evening. Tutorial grading makes for better organization and better instruction. If you have graded papers tutorially, we are sure you will agree; if you haven't, you are, as we have said, in for a demanding but rewarding experience.

QUESTIONNAIRE FOR TUTORIAL GRADING

We have given the following questionnaire to our students, telling them that the results would be used to improve the program they had completed. They were encouraged to give frank and thoughtful responses, which would help identify strengths and weaknesses of tutorial instruction.

Directions: Indicate your degree of agreement or disagreement with the statements listed below. Please respond rapidly. Mark your answers on this sheet according to the following code:

    A. strongly agree
    B. agree
    C. neither agree nor disagree--neutral
    D. disagree
    E. strongly disagree

1. I feel that the conferences minimize the problem of missed classes.
2. I like the informal atmosphere of the tutorial method used in this course.
3. The instructor is available when I need help.
4. The instructor is available when I need evaluation.
5. I like to have my papers graded in conference.
6. I feel that tutorial conferences increase the fairness of grading.
7. I feel that the instructor is interested in my success in this course.
8. I feel I can work at my own pace in this class.
9. I feel challenged by this class to do my best work.

10. This method of instruction emphasizes the ideas and skills necessary to my success in this course.
11. The method of instruction used in this class makes me feel more responsible for my own learning.
12. I feel that the assignments are relevant to the major objectives of the course.
13. I like planning my own study schedule.
14. If one were offered, I would take another individualized-tutorial course.
15. If you wish to contribute additional comments, please use the back of this sheet.

SHARING WRITING

Recent congressional action has restricted the dissemination of grades, anecdotal personal information, and other data about students. Student papers may be among the kinds of materials subject to this legislation. You should inform students that their papers will be shared with fellow students and secure their permission to do so. If you have any doubts about the kind of writing that requires a release, or questions concerning the use of consent forms, consult your institution's registrar or attorney.

BIBLIOGRAPHY

Bond, C. A. "New Approach to Freshman Composition: A Trial of the
    Christensen Method," College English 33 (March 1972): 623-637.
Christensen, Francis. "A Generative Rhetoric of the Paragraph." In
    New Rhetoric, edited by Martin Steinmann, pp. 108-133. New York:
    Charles Scribner's Sons, 1967.
Christensen, Francis. Notes Toward a New Rhetoric: Six Essays for
    Teachers. New York: Harper & Row, 1967. (A brief but informa-
    tive book on generative rhetoric. Christensen clearly defines
    the terms and provides numerous examples for class discussion.
    Well worth your time.)
------. "Problem of Defining a Mature Style," English Journal 57
    (April 1968): 572-579.
Cook, P. H. "Putting Grammar to Work, The Generative Grammar in the
    Generative Rhetoric," English Journal 57 (November 1968): 1168-
    1175.
D'Angelo, Frank J. "The New Rhetoric: Implications for Secondary
    Teaching." Growing Edges of Secondary English: Essays by the
    Experienced Teacher Fellows at the University of Illinois, 1966-
    1967, edited by Charles Suhor. Champaign, Ill.: National Council
    of Teachers of English, 1968.
Emerging Outlines of a New Rhetoric. Wisconsin Council of Teachers of
    English, 1966.
Hook, J. N. "English Language Programs for the Seventies," Minnesota
    English 3 (January 1967): 1-14.
Mellon, John C. Transformational Sentence-Combining: A Method for
    Enhancing the Development of Syntactic Fluency in English Compo-
    sition. Champaign, Ill.: National Council of Teachers of
    English, 1969.
"Obituary: Francis Christensen," College English 32 (October 1970): 73.
Solkov, Arnold. "Upon First Looking into Christensen's Rhetoric,"
    English Journal 59 (September 1970): 834-836.
Tufte, Virginia. Grammar as Style. New York: Holt, Rinehart & Winston,
    1971. (The most comprehensive text on sentence style available.
    Extensive discussion and examples of generative writing. An excel-
    lent source book.)
Walshe, R. D. "Report on a Pilot Course on the Christensen Rhetoric
    Program," College English 32 (April 1971): 783-789.

Houghton
Mifflin

3-30176